The Flesh Made Text Made Flesh

PETER LANG
New York • Washington, D.C./Baltimore • Bern
Frankfurt am Main • Berlin • Brussels • Vienna • Oxford

The Flesh Made Text Made Flesh

Cultural and Theoretical Returns to the Body

EDITED BY
Zoe Detsi-Diamanti,
Katerina Kitsi-Mitakou,
and Effie Yiannopoulou

PETER LANG
New York • Washington, D.C./Baltimore • Bern
Frankfurt am Main • Berlin • Brussels • Vienna • Oxford

Library of Congress Cataloging-in-Publication Data

The flesh made text made flesh: Cultural and Theoretical
Returns to the Body/ edited by Zoe Detsi-Diamanti,
Katerina Kitsi-Mitakou, Effie Yiannopoulou.
p. cm.
Includes bibliographical references and index.
1. Body, Human, in literature. 2. Literature, Modern—History and criticism.
3. Body, Human, on television. 4. Body, Human—Social aspects.
I. Detsi-Diamanti, Zoe. II. Kitsi-Mitakou, Katerina K.
III. Yiannopoulou, Effie.
PN56.B62F54   809'.933561—dc22   2007023952
ISBN 978-0-8204-6336-0

Bibliographic information published by **Die Deutsche Bibliothek**.
Die Deutsche Bibliothek lists this publication in the "Deutsche
Nationalbibliografie"; detailed bibliographic data is available
on the Internet at http://dnb.ddb.de/.

Cover illustration by Sofia Maria Kassianidou

The paper in this book meets the guidelines for permanence and durability
of the Committee on Production Guidelines for Book Longevity
of the Council of Library Resources.

© 2007 Peter Lang Publishing, Inc., New York
29 Broadway, 18th floor, New York, NY 10006
www.peterlang.com

All rights reserved.
Reprint or reproduction, even partially, in all forms such as microfilm,
xerography, microfiche, microcard, and offset strictly prohibited.

Printed in the United States of America

To our children,
Who have made return to flesh inevitable—

Contents

Acknowledgments ix

1. The Flesh Made Text Made Flesh: An Introduction 1
   *Zoe Detsi-Diamanti, Katerina Kitsi-Mitakou,
   and Effie Yiannopoulou*

Part I: Theater/Performance

2. Body/Art and Technological Transformations: A Workshop 13
   Johannes Birringer
3. Digital Divas: Sex and Gender in Cyberspace 27
   Sue-Ellen Case
4. Millennial Artaud: Rethinking Cruelty and Representation 43
   Elizabeth Sakellaridou
5. The "Bacchanalian" Body in Theodoros Terzopoulos' Theater:
   A Case of Interculturalism 55
   Pinelopi Hatzidimitriou

Part II: Narrative(s)

6. Dissecting Bodies and Selves in the Early Modern Period 75
   Effie Botonaki
7. From Rejection to Affirmation of Their Bodies:
   The Case of Afro-German Women Writers 87
   Jennifer E. Michaels

8. Re-Mapping Nation, Body and Gender in Michael Ondaatje's
   The English Patient   99
   Lilijana Burcar
9. Classical Enfleshments of Love   111
   Leah Bradshaw

Part III: Popular Culture

10. The Racial Gaze and the Monstrous African in
    The X-files Program "The Teliko"   127
    Nigel C. Gibson
11. Speculate and Punish: British Lifestyle TV
    and the Anxious Body   139
    David Roberts and Joss West-Burnham
12. Glamour and Beauty—Imagining Glamour in the Age
    of Aesthetic Surgery   151
    Sander L. Gilman

List of Contributors   167
Index   171

Acknowledgments

This project was inspired by the thematic axis of the international conference "The Flesh Made Text: Bodies, Theories, Cultures in the Post-Millennial Era," which was hosted by Aristotle University of Thessaloniki, Greece, in May 2003. Following a number of intriguing presentations on the return to "enfleshed" materiality, we realized the need for a volume that would pull together cross-disciplinary research on the complexities of the current interest in the fleshiness of bodies. Along the way, we have been fortunate to work with many talented and ingenious scholars. Our thanks go to our contributors whose fresh vision and original research helped redefine the limits, meanings and potentialities of the return to flesh.

A slightly modified version of Sue-Ellen Case's essay "Digital Divas" has been published in a collection of essays edited by Janelle G. Reinelt and Joseph Roach under the title *Critical Theory and Performance: A Revised and Enlarged Edition*, University of Michigan Press, 2006. The essay is reprinted with permission from the publisher.

1. *The Flesh Made Text Made Flesh: An Introduction*

Zoe Detsi-Diamanti, Katerina Kitsi-Mitakou, and Effie Yiannopoulou

The Flesh "Strikes Back"

The demolition of Saddam Hussein's statue in a public square in Iraq in 2003 was an image broadcast around the globe meant to signify the end of his totalitarian regime. The arrest of the former dictator a few months later, however, and the public exposure of his wretched and abused body hinted at the beginning of his corporeal demise. On December 30, 2006 a video of Saddam Hussein's hanging in Baghdad again traveled around the world: what we saw this time was his once almighty body now turned into a powerless, distressed piece of flesh, a rope around its neck, led to extinction. This video shot by a cell phone, which sneaked into an individual's most private moment, announced a scandalous return to the public, physical desecration of the body. If penal justice went through centuries of reformation in order to achieve a novel form of "non-corporeal" penality, a "utopia of judicial reticence," in Foucault's words (11), that eliminates pain and the spectacle, what we witness in 2006 is an inarguable return to the "spectacle of the scaffold," as well as a renewed fixation with the body. The ultimate extinction of Saddam's political system materializes, as today's dominant politics reflected in the world media suggest, only with his fleshy death.

The flesh made text made flesh: It is the aim of this collection, as the cyclical pattern of the title implies, to explore, on the one hand, this contemporary fascination with flesh which we witness today not only in the media, but also in a variety of different discourses—scientific, artistic or even philosophical—and, on the other, to trace in such tendencies the recurrence of past practices related to flesh. This oscillation between text and flesh is quite characteristic in the history of the West. Even if the mind/body binarism has framed most of Western thinking on embodiment, it has never been a fixed conceptual structure and has frequently failed to sustain the logocentric mind in an uncontested position of dominance.[1] In classical antiquity, for example, Plato's philosophy, which officially established the mind/body dualism, warned against the corruptive nature of crude flesh and counseled faith on the world of ideas. Christianity later on retained this dichotomy, but perceived the body as an indispensable means to the salvation of the soul; "the Word was made flesh" in order to bring "grace and truth" to the world (John 1: 14, 17). And, in the anatomy theaters of early Modernity, the book was inscribed on the body; as the eye and the knife of the new scientist cut deep into the dark spaces and mysteries of the body in the name of "objective" truth, their aim was to control the flesh and construct economically useful and politically conservative subjects.

The struggle to pursue scientific truth in modernity is epitomized in the textualization of the body, or, in other words, the turning of the fleshy body into a body of knowledge. Postmodernity continues to write on the body, in more or less subversive ways, yet many of its practices are marked by a rather complex return to "enfleshed" materialism, which is instigated by multiple socio-economic, political and cultural factors. First and foremost, of course, are the novel technological and medical advances, which have not only posed new, perplexing ethical dilemmas, but have made redefinition of flesh a subject that needs to be a top priority on philosophical, scientific and artistic agendas. The invention of digitalized environments, for instance, has made interaction between the human and the technological inescapable and incited conflicting reactions: the belief, on the one hand, that the reshaping of flesh in relation to technology brings forth a more dynamic and empowering body, and, on the other hand, the insistence on the "organic," "essential" body—a concept not entirely unproblematic, as we shall see. In addition, the discovery of modern methods of discerning and preventing genetic "anomaly/deviance" has raised the question of whether science can or must impose reforming strategies upon individuals, while discourses of "self-improvement" and the medicalization of bodily difference proliferate (fat, ugliness, smoking are classed today as high health and social risks that must be addressed through dieting, surgery, fashion makeovers, and self-discipline).

It is exactly this profound shift in the political usefulness of the body that fuels the reinvigorated interest in flesh in our days. If the body has always been the target of controlling and reforming systems, then resistance to such tactics has to be launched by the body itself, the primal site of difference. In that sense, does return to flesh embody the potential to liberate from such hegemonies?

Flesh today, more permeable and transparent than at any other moment in history, stars in cosmetic surgery operations performed even in public, in multibillion-dollar scientific research, in the new brutalism of in-yer-face theater, or in the revival of anatomical exhibitions,[2] and defies its "textualization" in ways which may be also indicative of a form of resistance. The flesh "strikes back" in the sense that it often escapes monolithic prescriptions or its sanitation and subjection to scientific and political power, and blurs the borders of progressive and reactionary activity, as most of the essays in this collection will argue. What, for example, does the predominance of the laboring female body signify in a primarily philosophical text such as Plato's *Symposium*? How can flesh dictate methods of knowing the soul, even in discourses like Christianity, where it is equivalent to decline and corruption? Or, in which cases can the shaping of a glamorous body through cosmetic surgery alternatively be considered a revisionist performance?

The contributors to this volume take the opportunity to perform their own "returns" to present and past artistic and theoretical configurations of the body, in order to pick out the problematic implications following from this return to a visceral body, but also suggest new social and political possibilities that are opened up by the inevitable redefinition of bodily matter that is under way in this cultural shift. They both re-evaluate the meanings of embodiment dominant today and reconsider those that left their stamp on previous historical periods, especially seventeenth-century England and classical Greece. From a wide range of angles this collection highlights the complexities of the current interest in the fleshiness of bodies, reflects the dilemmas running through research in literature, theater, performance and cultural studies, and proposes a set of questions that will, we hope, open up new horizons for further explorations.

(Re)Turning (to) the Corporeal

The logic of return underpinning the essays in this volume, both as analytical target and methodological approach, is structured around two basic assumptions. First, it is understood to be variable and diverse. It is telling that none of the essays manage, or even attempt, to articulate a uniform response to the body problematic written into projects that work to restore the presence of flesh in cultural politics and aesthetic practices. As a result, the analyses and assessments of the current interest in material bodies that are given here present readers with different, often conflictual, positions and perspectives. Whether voicing endorsement or skepticism, they all testify to the difficulty of ever fully returning to and recovering the body as the origin of organic and subjective existence. In the post-Jacques Derrida and Gilles Deleuze age, it is perhaps a theoretical commonplace to posit that repetitions are destined never to reproduce the original copy they set out to simulate. It is, nonetheless, instructive to remind ourselves, drawing equally on the dynamic insights of diasporic literature and experience, that origins are hard to locate and home is fundamentally dislocated and estranged.[3] It is our contention in this collection that there is no one single or monolithic way of returning to the origin of existence that the body represents. The politics of corporeal return is fundamentally differential and power-bound and, for this reason, the essays in this volume have been especially selected to highlight the diversity of interpretations, evaluations and analyses that the contemporary re-engagement with the physicality of existence has triggered off.

To give a brief example, Sander Gilman reads the almost frantic interest in cosmetic surgery gripping the West at the start of this century through an argument that recasts aesthetic interventions into flesh as a critique against scripts of bodily authenticity. To him, aesthetic surgery foregrounds the artificiality of the body, as it produces the body as a simulacrum, a copy without an original. On a different note, David Roberts and Joss West-Burnham address the question of cosmetic bodily makeovers with suspicion, regarding the rapid extension of such discourses into the popular domain of lifestyle TV as a worrying sign of the unprecedented massification of bodily technologies that effectively promote the denial of flesh.

The second assumption shaping up our understanding of corporeal return holds that the flesh retrieved and reclaimed is not a single discursive or biological category. How Johannes Birringer's "body-as-interface," Pinelopi Hatzidimitriou's "bacchanalian body" and Sue-Ellen Case's "virtual body" configure flesh rests largely on the distinct political agendas directing the authors' projects and their diverse assessments of the body's impact on human contact, social positioning and cultural sensibilities. Where, for example, the body-as-interface celebrates the possibilities opening up by a new digitalized bodily materiality, Case's theorization of the on-line avatar assumes a body unable to shake off conventional gender, ethnic or racial markers and which, thus, continues to disseminate existing global, corporate discourses and practices in cyberspace. This very diversity in the semantic encoding of corporeality underlines the impossibility of pinning down the languages and realities within which the body comes into being. In this sense, all essays foreground the recognition that the body is plural in that it is never divorced from thought processes, cultural production, historical developments, ideological and material interests. As Sara Ahmed and Jackie Stacey have observed, drawing on the pioneering work of Jane Gallop, the "practices of thinking are not separated from the realm of the body but are implicated in the passion, emotions and materiality that are associated with lived embodiment" (3).

What the essays in this volume also share, however, is the desire to think the human body away from crude, modern and postmodern, understandings which, in textualizing the body, prioritize its standing as an organic category that is exclusively and unidirectionally written on, shaped and determined by circumstance and context. They attempt, instead, to restore to view flesh as a material unit that is in conversation with the forces and environments that help it signify, to assign it a more active role in the production of meaning, to recast it as a force that answers back and confuses social prescription, technological and biological determinism. Acting on this desire, many essays in this collection throw their weight on the "turn" that is encoded in any act of re-turning, promoting a change of direction in the thinking about material bodies that demands and activates more complex and challenging conceptualizations of what constitutes flesh and how it intervenes in the construction of new lived realities.

In this light, Elizabeth Sakellaridou's reappraisal of Antonin Artaud's theories is not just a bash on the "sensationalist," "graphic," "perverse" and "unimaginative" return to Artaud, and to flesh, enacted on the British stage in the 1990s. It is an insightful comment on the ignored somatics of the written word in contemporary theater. What is missed out in the recent brutalist stage representations of the suffering body, her argument holds, is the recognition that a corporeal theater strives both in "sweat and articulation." Logos is posited here as a necessary channel through which physical pain is spoken, yet, significantly, only on condition that the "physicality" of language is first addressed and reclaimed. Likewise, in investigating the ways in which the digitally transformed environments, within which performers move, modify bodily perceptions, Birringer calls for a recognition that digitalized technologies are, in return, "physicalized" as they inevitably respond to the motion of the performer's body. The human body living amidst the technological infrastructure, as he puts it, becomes "constitutive of the digital object" and not just transformed by it.

Still, is somatizing the word and re-materializing fleshy living always politically beneficial and ideologically stimulating? While *The Flesh Made Text Made Flesh* as a whole emphasizes the extent to which modernity and postmodernity are always already framed by the responses of the bodies that they construct as their objects, it also addresses the possibility that invocations of physicality do not always necessarily make a gesture to the text of political progressivity. One of the questions it raises calls for us to think under what circumstances the very act of reclaiming flesh ceases to be a tool of cultural critique and becomes a means of erasing the "contingency, locatedness, the irreducibility of difference [. . .] and the worldliness of being" (Ahmed 3). Theodoros Terzopoulos' directorial philosophy, as Hatzidimitriou reveals, balances dangerously on the borderline between rebellious intent and conservative practice and is perhaps a good example of the dangers involved in (re)turning (to) the human body (as)/into an origin that houses the undeniable truth of the subject or culture. His fiery polemic against the debilitating dominance of postmodern disembodied living rests on a brand of interculturalism that smacks suspiciously of ethnographic primitivism as it extols the virtues of a visceral, universal body lost to the West and in need of recuperation. Yet, how can one deploy the idea of the "universal" (body) in ways that do not privilege Europe and do not reproduce the registers and taxonomies underwriting imperialist, or globalizing, thinking? What are the conditions under which material existence can be called upon to draft the future without resurrecting the ghost of "the" body, undifferentiated, unlocalized, dehistoricized, the body as a retrievable origin? This book (re)turns to these questions at a point in history when the need to escape the insecurity ruling over the deterritorialized and unbounded cultures of the twenty-first century often finds expression in the desire to pin down a bodily essence. In asking the question of the past anew, it is at once asking the question of the future anew, heading back to the future by returning to the body—but with a difference.

The Essays

In the first part of the book, the authors investigate the politics of corporeal return in theater and performance, where the return to flesh is experienced through an essential contradiction: the emergence, on the one hand, of a new digitalized corporeality on stage; on the other hand, a return to the physicality of bodily existence through the deployment of an alternative dramatic language that resists the simulated construction of (cyber)space and bodies. More specifically, the relation of the human body and technology that has taken new and radical dimensions in the theater has led to a redefinition of corporeal reality and the conventional understanding of the human body in real-time space.

Johannes Birringer, in "Body/Art and Technological Transformations: A Workshop," introduces the concept of the "body-as-interface." He creates computer-based environments as alternative trans-theatrical spaces for action and explores how the boundaries of the performers' bodies can be subject to modification through the use of cameras, sensors, microphones, and computer softwares. In this way, the interaction of the human body with technology acts out a new politics of embodiment that leads to a "composition of fictions" around the subject, to a generative rather than representational body-space.

In a similar vein, Sue-Ellen Case focuses on the on-line female avatar in "Digital Divas: Sex and Gender in Cyberspace." Through the deployment of the concept of "inter-fetish object relations," she concludes that conventional gender and race stereotypes continue to be active in the cybersphere and serve the commercial interests of international corporations. Towards the end of her analysis, however, she contends that the use of alternative on-line body images, such as those of the poor, the weak, and the disenfranchised, could radicalize cyberspace.

Elizabeth Sakellaridou adopts a more skeptical attitude toward the return to flesh in contemporary theater. Her essay, "Millennial Artaud: Rethinking Cruelty and Representation," focuses on the "death" of dramatic theater and its displacement by technologized performance, which threatens to replace traditional verbal drama with mere sensational tricks. Through a re-reading of Artaud's theory on physical theater and cruelty, Sakellaridou criticizes the "new brutalist theater" in Britain and its practice of stage cruelty and body suffering. By contesting Derrida's "anti-text" philosophy and Elaine Scarry's pain theory, she attempts to restore faith in the performativity of the dramatic text, and the phenomenology of the written and spoken word.

In "The 'Bacchanalian' Body in Theodoros Terzopoulos' Theater: A Case of Interculturalism," Pinelopi Hatzidimitriou introduces the work of the Greek director Theodoros Terzopoulos, who has developed a theater practice and training system that promote a return to an "essential," universal, and archetypal body. The "bacchanalian" body, as he terms it, enables the performers to enter a state of manic transgression, and, through re-experiencing unconscious fears and desires, to transcend the effects of Western logos on the subject. This idea has led Terzopoulos to a study of the transcendental rituals of other cultures, a fact which has encouraged the intercultural character of his theater.

In the second part of the book, return to flesh embodies the potential not only of suggesting new and alternative corporealities, but also of exploring the self and its relation to nation, gender, race and love. The essays review theories of embodiment dominant in the present and in past historical periods, reading the material body as carrier of history, metaphor of imperial practices, indicator of difference, or even a route to the divine. Effie Botonaki's essay, "Dissecting Bodies and Selves in the Early Modern Period," offers a re-evaluation of the status of the body in seventeenth-century England. Through its emphasis on modernity's fascination with anatomic dissection, a medical practice also metaphorically performed in seventeenth-century guide books and spiritual diaries, the essay argues that the gap between the body and the soul grows narrower in this period. The body, which had been held in disrespect for centuries, acquires a new-found importance amply illustrated by the fact that it serves as the model for knowing the soul.

Jennifer E. Michaels also explores how emphasis on the body, its skin color, or its deviation from dominant beauty standards can be reflective of a reclaiming of the self and can lead to self-awareness. In her essay, "From Rejection to Affirmation of Their Bodies: The Case of Afro-German Women Writers," she studies a number of contemporary Afro-German women writers, who have achieved a reassessment of the social and psychological implications of their black female bodies. By connecting to African and African-American notions of beauty, rather than Western ones, and not seeking to conform to Western standards of beauty, Afro-German women in post-WWII Germany map in their texts their journey from self-hatred and rejection of their blackness to affirmation of and pride in their black bodies.

In a like manner, Lilijana Burcar investigates the possibility for a redefined politics of embodiment that challenges nationalist discourses and their prescribed, fixed identities in her essay "Re-Mapping Nation, Body and Gender in Michael Ondaatje's *The English Patient*." By focusing on the concept of rhizomatic corporeality, Burcar argues that Ondaatje's novel calls into question the tenacity of national boundaries and draws attention to the constantly changing materiality of the body. In this way, it proposes a new form of embodiment that resists fixity and embraces transformability and multiplicity. The weaving of corporeality as a set of operational linkages and connections is reflective of the collapse of fixed national and racial boundaries and stereotypes. This new schema of embodiment, however, is gender-specific, as women remain locked in the traditional network of their culturally ascribed materiality.

Leah Bradshaw, in her theoretical return to flesh, traces the origin of this association of woman with matter in ancient Greek thought. In "Classical Enfleshments of Love," she attempts to illuminate the paradox in Plato's *Symposium*, where Socrates appropriates the generative image of childbirth through the voice of the priestess Diotima in order to describe philosophy and exalt divine love—love, that is, unsoiled by any form of materiality. Bradshaw concludes by showing how this ideal model of love is also undermined in Plato's dialogue by the presence of Alcibiades, the very image of carnality and fleshy desire. Moreover, Bradshaw argues that a number of postmodern feminists, by amplifying Diotima's voice, and drawing upon her metaphors of birth and the mother-child relationship, have tried to pull the notion of divine love back to the flesh and have raised interesting questions about the fundamental pathology of love in its most primal incarnation.

The last part of the book examines how the return to enfleshed materiality is addressed in popular cultural practices and texts, and follows the responses it elicits in its engagement with racial discourses, contemporary consumption capitalism, and the production of social and cultural categories. Nigel Gibson's essay, "The Racial Gaze and the Monstrous African in *The X-files* Program 'The Teliko'," investigates how recourse to enfleshment works to stave off anxieties and recuperate certainties in contemporary multi-racial American society. Gibson contends that anxiety over immigration and the difficulty of controlling fluid national and racial borders in contemporary America result in the fear of black bodies. *The X-files*'s episode discussed in the essay is read in light of the above as seeking to combat the consequences of racial hybridity and cultural mobility on the national fabric by pathologizing black flesh. Gibson strongly suggests that returning the black, African body to the register of the monstrous, the diseased and the primitive effectively extends the unequal racial hierarchies of modernity into postmodernity.

The need to constrain and control the "pathological" or "abnormal" body through disciplinary processes of transformation is also discussed in David Roberts and Joss West-Burnham's "Speculate and Punish: British Lifestyle TV and the Anxious Body." The authors invite us to think how British television lifestyle programs, concerned with fashion and plastic surgery, mould the participants' and the viewers' expectations regarding body shape along the lines suggested by dominant ideologies of beauty and gender. A discourse of anxiety regarding bodily limits is, thus, encouraged in order to justify the interventionist action promised by plastic surgery or slimming, and to preserve the power of normative definitions of beauty and femininity. Furthermore, bodily transformation in these programs is shown to be inextricably linked to discourses of consumption and capitalism, which ally "fleshiness" with an ideological position of conformity and constraint.

In the volume's final essay, "Glamour and Beauty—Imagining Glamour in the Age of Aesthetic Surgery," Sander L. Gilman offers a different perspective on the bodily transformations encouraged by the glamour industry. Following closely Cindy Jackson's literal metamorphosis into a live Barbie and the work of the French performance artist Orlan, he concludes that, in producing the body as a copy of copies, aesthetic surgery draws attention to the body's artificiality and thus challenges discourses of bodily authenticity. For Gilman, (re)producing flesh with the help of the surgeon does not necessarily signify simple subjection to dominant aesthetic norms but is a guarantee of the very modern nature of our bodies.

Notes

1. The instability encoded into the mind/body dualism explains the fact that the hegemony of the mind is encountered only in a fraction of recorded history, and is perhaps one more reason why there has been a consistent preoccupation with the body throughout Western history. Thinking subjects have always inhabited organic bodies and have always been attracted by their material aspects, a fact which makes this binary a self-defying concept. Caroline Bynam has argued convincingly that to claim that from Plato to Descartes Western thought was dualist is an implausible generalization: "Hundreds of years of controversy, in which person was seen as a unity [. . .], a particular individual [. . .], and a yearning stuff [. . .] have profoundly shaped Western tradition" (33). The late Middle Ages considered the flesh to be the instrument of salvation, as God offered redemption by becoming flesh. And, of course, Cartesian dualism was also subverted by nineteenth-century philosophers, such as Hegel, Marx, Nietzsche, and mainly by twentieth-century phenomenology,

with Husserl, Heidegger, Sartre, Marleau-Ponty and psychoanalysis later, with Lacan and Kristeva.
2. Such is the case of Gunther von Hagens' Body Worlds exhibitions, the first public anatomical exhibitions of real human plastinates, targeted mainly at a lay audience, which offer a detailed picture of the inner workings of the body by replacing the body's fluids with liquid plastic. These educational exhibitions have had unparalleled success, as they have been on display worldwide since 1995 and so far, more than 20 million visitors have viewed the exhibits at venues in cities across Asia, Europe, the United States and Canada. For more details on the nature, mission and reception of this project, visit <http://www.bodyworlds.com/en.html >.
3. For a useful discussion of the meanings of home in diasporic experience, see Avtar Brah's *Cartographies of Diaspora*.

Works Cited

Ahmed, Sara and Jackie Stacey. "Introduction: Dermographies." *Thinking Through the Skin*. Ed. Sara Ahmed and Jackie Stacey. London and New York: Routledge, 2001.

Brah, Avtar. *Cartographies of Diaspora: Contesting Identities*. London and New York: Routledge, 1996.

Bynum, Caroline. "Why All the Fuss about the Body? A Medievalist Perspective." *Critical Inquiry* 22 (1995): 1–33.

Carroll, Robert and Stephen Prickett, eds. *The Bible, Authorized King James Version*. Oxford UP, 1997.

Foucault, Michel. *Discipline and Punish: The Birth of the Prison*. Trans. Alan Sheridan. Penguin: Harmondsworth, 1987.

von Hagens, Gunther. 26 Feb. 2007 <http://www.bodyworlds.com/en.html>.

Part I
Theater/Performance

2. Body/Art and Technological Transformations: A Workshop

JOHANNES BIRRINGER

In the context of an international conference, which deals so extensively with theories, texts, and a vast archive of literatures and cultural representations of the human body, the occurrence of a short performance workshop constitutes a modest proposal: a group of people meets in a studio for a few hours and works together physically. Nothing more and nothing less. The results of this rehearsal process are shown at an evening presentation to which a public audience is invited.

Under normal circumstances, for example, an acting or dance workshop conducted by a master teacher, one would not show the results to a public audience, since the training environment would be constructed for the experience of the participants only. Furthermore, it would be counterproductive to "exhibit" the in-body training or methodology, as professional actors and dancers—or students and beginners, for that matter—generally avoid confusing their technique classes with rehearsed performances which are presented to the public at the end of a long compositional process.

In this case, however, the premise of the workshop was different. "The Flesh Made Text"[1] inspired me to conduct a media laboratory with a specific aim, namely the public installation—open to anyone interested in joining—of a media structure or architecture, an interactive environment for the transformation of physical phenomena that would be investigated in the interface between bodies and technologies. The workshop was intended to set up a sensing environment for the processing of information ("the flesh made data") generated by actions of human bodies, and in such a sensing environment, each body—highly trained or un-prepared—affects the system of the media structure (video cameras, sensors, microphones, computers, etc.) which detects movement or other physical action and transforms it into digital objects.

The laboratory was designed to introduce digital media and real-time synthesis as a performance processing of physical information within an interactive computer-based environment of sound and video, which allows the live transformation of images of a human agent in real time. I would first like to thank all the volunteer participants (dancers, writers, journalists, students of literature, architecture, and design) who took part in the workshop and who shared with me the experiential process I describe here. I particularly want to thank Marija Stamenkovic Herranz (Barcelona) and Rân Ymân (from the group Afotek, Vancouver), two independent choreographers/dancers, who saw the announcement of the workshop and traveled to Thessaloniki to join me as volunteer assistants in the workshop. The creative work of the group forms an important part of my theoretical reflections.

The Environment

One of the main premises of my work is a deliberate emphasis on the environment, the physical space and constructed architecture in which we work as performers who interact with intelligent systems. Performance processes, as I understand them today, are indebted to the traditions of live art, body art, and installation art and their concern is with site-specificity and intermedial temporal process, not with the representational apparatus and visual perspective of the theatrical stage. At the turn of the new century, many interests in related fields (film, digital arts, science and technology, design, engineering, robotics, communications, etc.) enhance our understanding of the complementary thinking processes that drive new interdisciplinary research and conceptual models influenced by the computer's information-processing capabilities and the Internet's global reach. Paradoxically, "live art" or performance art today is often considered live in the sense of "real-time" processing, involving immediate capture, translation, generation, feedback, manipulation, and rendering procedures which incorporate an array of instruments—such as cameras, microphones, sensors, video-projectors, mixers, synthesizers, loudspeakers, and computer hardware and software—into the physical setting. In fact, performance under such conditions takes place both in a physical environment, which can be any site that is transformed into an interactive environment, and a programming environment, which includes the software and the controllers determining the capabilities and limitations of the interactions between the various signals and media inputs/outputs.

If we had had more time, I would have liked to instruct the participants how to set up the infrastructure for such a space. But by the time the volunteers arrived, we had hung the lights, turned on the computers, and installed the software. A computer-enhanced environment was waiting, ready for action and improvisation, in which the volunteers were able to experience and produce other kinds of perceptions of reality, beyond subjectivity or the conventional understanding/identification of body (as flesh or figure or character) in real time space. The interaction with real-time, digital processes has different premises; "real time" is a technical term referring to instant communications between two systems in an interface where input and output of computer signals are processed. Real time actually indicates the nearly imperceptible delay that happens in these communications. For our discussion here, I will limit myself to three dimensions in which meaning is created in such interaction. The first relates to the definition of the "environment" itself as digital space; the second relates to the effects of interaction on the sensory perception of the body and the transformability of images of bodies and "roles" (e.g., the role of the body as interface); the third relates to an acoustic and kinesthetic dimension of rhythm which became one of the most fascinating aspects of our workshop, since it was both unexpected and particularly challenging to the general preponderance of the visual in contemporary experimentations with new media.

The Digital Space of Interactivity

Performance which integrates technologies and interactive designs needs a different environment for its evolution and the particular kind of mediated presence it constitutes. Digital media imply a methodology which I have described elsewhere as "navigations and interfaces."[2] The relationship between navigation and interactivity becomes obvious once we recognize that performance, or any kind of action that could be carried out by a visitor or audience member, is here understood not primarily as subjectivity or expression, but as interaction with an environment that responds directly—there is a feedback between input and output, action and reaction. A sensory environment, which we could also think of as a digital space or, in the broadest sense, a virtual reality, thus contains certain potential behaviors. It is a space of virtualities. It needs to be navigated since these behaviors are based on a complex system of communicative acts and interfaces.

The technology which controls the digital space and makes it intelligible challenges bodily boundaries and spatial realities, profoundly affecting the relations between humans, materiality, and machines.[3] In the workshop, I introduced the subject of real time synthesis with some examples from contemporary arts practice, drawing attention to the work of choreographers, composers, sound artists, and programmers as well as to Stelarc's even more radical projects of redesigning the body through prosthetic engineering and remote control/telematic technologies which wire the body to the Internet and, in *Ping Body* (1996) and *Parasite: Event for Invaded and Involuntary Body* (1997), to a muscle stimulation system that drives the body in response to images gathered from the World Wide Web and mapped onto the body (Grzinic 18–19). While most choreographers (such as Merce Cunningham, William Forsythe, Wayne McGregor, Hellen Sky, Pablo Ventura, and others) work with an invisible mapping of space and remove the machines from sight, Australian performance artist Stelarc has become known for his direct and explicit modifications of the body and his wiring of the body to heavy machinery and robotic prostheses. I also hinted at some connections between real-time synthesis and current research in arts and science (transgenic art, virtual reality systems, motion capture/animated human figure creation, synthetic embodiment/avatars, distributed systems, and networks), suggesting that we could only accomplish a very limited hands-on experiment in the framework of the workshop, namely addressing the relations between computer sciences and biotechnologies from an artistic/cultural viewpoint—the practice of image rendering.

In my own work, I approach the relations between humans and machines from a sculptural point of view. The environments for my performances are constructed; they have a plasticity and materiality, textures, colors, tactilities, and forms that become part of the total sensuality of the space. I often choose organic materials in my installations to heighten the ambiguities between analogue and digital media, between the concrete and immaterial aspects in the design of a given space. Even if we use few solid objects and masses, and rely on projective space (film, video, light), image projections have their own materiality and need surfaces. To create an interesting projective space is an architectural dilemma, since we must first work through the limitations of a given physical space and organize the fields of action and the perceptional space. If the workshop is site-specific, and audiences are expected to arrive at some point, we must determine how to adapt our activities to the environment, for example an abandoned building or industrial plant, or how to transform it into an installation. In almost all cases of an interactive performance design not prepared for the conventional theater stage, the space is turned into an installation that "houses" the media infrastructure needed for the digital organization of the space.

In Thessaloniki, we were given the large and beautiful University Ceremony Hall, which is generally used as a concert or assembly stage, its huge auditorium and balcony facing a large, blue-tiled mosaic depicting scenes from the legendary history of the city and its patron saint. The large mosaic, created in the style of Byzantine art as a two-dimensional representation, a flattened image without depth, was fascinating in its own right. We tried to read it and noted its particular "gestural" language, the angular postures of arms and hands which also resembled some of the urban architectures in the iconostasis. We then discovered that it could be partially occluded by a huge film screen that was lowered in front of it. We had two other screens which were movable and could be placed in any location we wanted in the space. Since we did not have time to build any other sculptural objects, we relied mostly on the flexible screens and our interactive tools (cameras, microphones linked to the laptops, projectors, and sound processing machines).

We opened the physical workshop with a rhythmic warm-up led by Marija and Rân, paying attention to our breathing and the space between inhaling and exhaling, to the time of acceleration and deceleration. We began the subsequent rehearsals by exploring basic relations in space, structured around dialogs between a single performer and a single camera person.

The tasks were simple: short improvisations, no longer than three minutes, allowing the "couples" to grasp an understanding of the "physical camera" interface. As in film production on a set, such work makes no pretense of being created in a whole, linear dramaturgy that unfolds over time and gains the kind of emotional logic we expect in the theater or the circus. Rather, we worked in a modular way with short "takes," each of which involved a study of how the body is capturable by the camera and responds to the presence of the camera. Interactivity as a choreographic phenomenon, in this sense, became a study of the reciprocal relations between mover and camera lens, the lens here functioning both as an image-framing and a motion-tracking device.

The video camera is one of the important input devices for interactive systems, since it can see space and track motion and color, and it is easily set up and connected to the computer software. Other types of sensing devices commonly used for interactive design are haptic sensors (pressure, touch, flex, and proximity) and non-haptic sensors (distance sensors such as ultrasound), microphones, and electrodes attached to the muscles, heart or pulse (e.g., Bioradio). Magnetic and optical motion capture technologies, which are not as easily accessible, are now also used in some laboratories and studios to record human movement in three dimensions to control real-time, computer graphics animation.

Sensory Experience in Intermedial Performance

Our "short takes" were a basic exercise in visual perception and physical awareness as well as synchronization of movement and sight to examine the relation between the body, the human eye, and the camera. I wanted to draw attention to both the body and the camera as sensory systems. All the participants, movers and camera operators, exchanged roles, moving in front of and behind the camera. I tried to encourage an intuitive camera work in which the camera does not watch the movement from the outside as much as dances itself and becomes a bodily extension. I wanted to invoke a synaesthetic experience rather than that of a mere "controller" function of the camera, encouraging a more improvised shooting/tracking of movement, rather than precisely constructed shots of choreographed movement. I suggested that we would aim at three-minute duets, some of which might also be shared with our audience if they were interested in the process.

Performing the duet and observing the camera choreography (video) were separate stages in our exploration. In the first hour of "short takes," we paid less attention to the projection of the images, since the emphasis was on physical interaction and proprioception. We also paid no attention to perspective and sight lines, or the kind of orientations we use in the theater (upstage/downstage). Our navigation of the space was random and chaotic. The emphasis was on the emerging relationships in space. In the second hour, we connected the cameras to the video projectors (closed circuit) and placed the screen to the sides of the space, allowing the performers and camera operators to glance at the projected images or even "control" their camera movement, not by looking at the viewfinder but at the image-screens. The screens also became a kind of framework for the space, just as the overwhelming Byzantine mosaic formed a backdrop for our activity.

The incorporation of projective space alters the feedback process, since the physical (internal) experience of self and movement now becomes complicated. The performer can observe her image while moving, manipulate and generate the image-movement, to a certain extent, as well as seek to integrate her (inverted) mirror image into her self-image and her intuitive understanding or deep consciousness of her own kinesthetic experience. At the same time, the interactive environment acts differently from the conventional space: it can substitute body space through the retransmission of body input movements that are computer processed. Video and sound projections are amplified. The scale of video images can be so large (in immersive environments that surround the performer) that there is an imbalance between projection and live action. We sought to avoid this by using relatively small screens and reducing the size of the images to maintain a more intimate relationship between action and projected images.

But interactivity always reflects back on the question of the body and its physical-sensory relationship to the surrounding space and the world. I want to suggest that video need not be a dominating, non-tactile, visual medium, but that it can connect to our sense of touch. Interactive environments allow a different "programming" of physical motion and motion sensing. For example, the "Very Nervous System" (VNS) design, developed by sound artist David Rokeby, is a system combining video cameras and software to create a space in which body movements are translated into sound, music, or video projection. The entire environment becomes resonant, and the performer's gesture and touch reach beyond the immediate physical location: "sensing" gains a dimension reaching beyond the physical and organic understanding of bodily anatomy, musculature, and proprioceptive spatial awareness of moving-within-the-kinesphere.

The imaginative repertoire for movement is extended. In more than one sense, it involves the entire sphere of movement as interaction, encompassing perceptive and receptive processes. If movement is a "continuous current," as Rudolf Laban taught us, a new understanding of interconnected spaces emerges, for example in telematic performance which follows the same principles of the physical camera interface we explored in the workshop, with the exception that the camera-generated image is broadcast to a remote site via the Internet. The performer is sensually connected with (the image of) the remote body of a partner who can respond to the same feedback loop of sensory and perceptual data which propel the articulation on this site.

We explored this double-sitedness when we had two teams perform simultaneously, side by side. There were some beautiful moments when a symbiotic relationship seemed to emerge, one performer working with voice, her camera person focusing on facial expression, while the other responded or led with her movement, her camera person framing, enlarging or distending the limbs of a body whose nervous system extended into the whole space, controlling things (sounds, images), without any material contact with them. For a few moments, it appeared as if these performers knew each other intimately or allowed their sensual connection to happen in the moment, their images touching each other and influencing each other's expression. I decided that we would show this scene again in the evening, but this time only as video projections, placing the two screens between the audience and the performers so that the physical performers would no longer be seen, but only the images they generated.

My intention was to focus the audience experience on the body-as-interface and on the mediating role of the camera, with the projected video creating a flat kinetic iconostasis on a human scale in front of the enormous, Byzantine mosaic. I was also interested in the content of the interface and the relationship that had emerged between the women performing the scene. We were fortunate that we did not have to spend an excessive amount of time on getting the technical infrastructure to work or programming new interfaces and testing their functionalities. We stayed with a few settings and parameters that I had prepared, and concentrated mostly on the physical and creative work, with the whole group responding extremely well to the tasks and the collaborative sensibility that evolved during the afternoon.

The most significant technological intervention into the physical experience of movement is the dis-location, and subsequent re-distribution, of movement as captured and processed image, sampled ghost. The computer has a memory and can store the samples we create with the software, and these samples can be called up at any moment and mixed into the live input, the present thus merging with the past in real-time. Marina Grzinic argues that interactivity generates virtually-processed body images in a two-dimensional film space, and that "it is possible in the virtual to conjoin ideological fantasmatic constructs, similarly to what we have in film" (100). Grzinic tends to think of cameras as (computer-controlled) machines for seeing, however, and not as physical tools and extensions of the body, on the one hand, nor as sensing devices which detect changes in the image plane without knowing what they mean, on the other. The computer's processing of data is an algorithmic process, it does not "understand" what happens in the way a body's sensing system processes information. But in my experience, the dance of the camera tends to be much more interconnected with muscles and pulse and breath, whereas the computer's processing of movement data follows a different logic, which makes it interesting for us to design different generative parameters. We will need to investigate the complex functions of sensors more thoroughly to reach a theory on these systems of seeing and sensing, taking into account that they might see more than our bodies or eyes see, and that their gaze can also be delayed, occluded, limited, or confused, as in the case of an optical motion capture system that mistakes a leg for an arm or loses sight of the sternum when it is occluded by the head. In any case, the processed image or the mapping of a figure animation is no longer a "real reflection" of our selves or our images of our selves, but a synthesized image produced in a transductive process.[4] It is always constructed with the help of the computer, and, in the strictest sense, it forms a digital object (data). It does not "displace the body," as critics of technology or technocentric discourse argue, but is just one example of the complexity of human-technical involvement which marks the entire history of technologies in our collective cultures. It is, therefore, also quite nonsensical to speak of the "posthuman body" in this context, since the human performers in our media structure are constitutive of the digital objects. The body lives amidst the technical infrastructure.

The generated image of movement, as it is used in interactive and networked performance-installations, is not a continuous current with space itself but continuously crosses between real space, projected space (video/animation) and software code. Space is dematerialized, movement is captured, commuted, transferred and reconfigured/rematerialized elsewhere; we interact with sensory information such as video, which projects different three-dimensional kinesthetic perceptions of movement energy, position, and velocity (cf. slow motion, close-ups, different scale, etc.). To program interfaces between dancers and the computer implies the creation of an unstable system. The intensities of the event develop a kind of autopoiesis. Video images emerge that may not bear any relation to the physical phenomena we know, and thus we gain a heightened awareness of the plasticity of the medium itself, and if this plasticity is the effect of software operations, which can manipulate an image down to its smallest molecule, we may need to begin analyzing how habitual cultural perceptions are transformed by software.

In our last experiment of the workshop, we ran one of the camera inputs through the Max-Msp programming environment, and here the generative potential of the synthetic image became strikingly apparent. Marija Stamenkovic's dance in front of the camera turned into a kind of action painting, a liquid flow of abstract, color shapes and lines, all contours of the body dissolved and made strange, strangely beautiful. But the velocity of her movement determined, at the same time, how the dissolution of form changed and evolved, and how she was perhaps able to play with the hypnotic dimension of her disappearance and reappearance within the mutating image-space (which followed the left to right motion of an image scanner, vertically "slicing" the image plane).

Rhythms of the Real: Afotek

To speak of the hypnotic dimension of such work, one inevitably thinks of musical and percussive rhythm, and in this respect our workshop harbored a surprise. In the last hour of the workshop, I asked the participants to add their voices and elements of free-associative storytelling into their movement, and we continued to put couples together, inviting interaction between two performers and their camera operators. We had connected the cameras to the computer software to effect a more playful exploration of how the boundaries of real bodies or the image-movement of bodies can be subject to modification and manipulation in real time processing. The software allows such extreme manipulation, filtering, and distortion through its scanning of the input data that the projected image space becomes generative and no longer representational. As I suggested above, the actual body interface with the software thus offers perspectives on identity transformations in virtual reality. I had not taken into consideration the rhythms of such transformations, the acoustic and pulsational experience of rhythm in the body, and how such rhythmic perceptions are culturally specific and meaningful, or how they might speak across cultures.

Interaction with digital technology suggests the composition of fictions: not "disembodiment" or abstraction but a new hyperplasticity in which the human and the technological are partners. New combinations—new hybrid forms—grow. The question now arises how this partnering is culturally meaningful, and meaningful to whom. The visual output, as I have suggested, may appear completely unnatural, abstract, and alien, forcing the performing body to focus on its own physiology without being able to re-integrate the phantasm or the phantasmagoric. Within a Western tradition of the *avant-garde,* the aesthetic separation of media, of the visual from the sonic, for example, has been a staple of experimentation, and many contemporary dances are not choreographed to the music or dependent on the rhythms in the body. Afro-Canadian choreographer Rân Ymân offered to dance a 25-minute solo ("Eyes of Eros") during our evening presentation, and he also advanced some provocative theses which contradicted my emphasis on the tactility of the visual. Rân is trained in African dance and has formulated his own practical philosophy (which he calls AFOTEK) as based in "rhythms of breath." Centered in an African tradition which does not separate dance from rhythm, his research is

> an exploration of rhythm; not the "objective" rhythm, nor the "general" rhythm, but the living rhythm within the body. Rhythms are the vectors which unceasingly create time, literally forging the existence of beings. Each individual is merely expressing his or her own sensitivity [rhythm]. Knowledge of rhythm is not just a simple measure of time but a coded expression of life cycles. AFOTEK believes rhythm is the soul of the dancer and the dance. The apprenticeship of Contemporary African Dance offers students a powerful and supra-causal knowledge of individual freedom and at-one-ness with their mind, body, and soul.[5]

For Rân, rhythm is an integral experience, and if his ancestral tradition, in which the dance listens to the call of the drum and responds, teaches him at-one-ness of body, mind, and soul, his contemporary sensibility seeks a different integration, namely that of movement and techno music. His exhausting solo dance, choreographed with precise patterns of steps, repetitions and circular movements, was performed to an extraordinarily complex electronic score with multiple layers of sound and a constantly shifting, polyrhythmic foundation. His intensity and precision amazed the audience, and we also noticed that he deliberately played with expectations and cultural stereotypes, referring to ritualistic and ceremonial dimensions, revealing his naked flesh in one sequence, and wearing a formal white gown in another. When he "traveled" through the space, his movements were unpredictable; when he danced in the circular position, his steps were identical and he focused his energy on exhausting repetitions even as the polyrhythmic pulse of the music was too complex for many of us to follow.

He had joined the workshop because he was interested in how the visual images in an interactive environment would respond to his steps and his breathing, and whether such images that tracked his movement, force, and precision could be translated into sensory data which could measure how precision feels in the body, and how the particular quality of his movement is achieved. If the environment is intelligent, he asked me, can it measure the degree to which memory (in the body) is measuring feeling and the accuracy he requests of his steps?

Body/Art and Technological Transformations: A Workshop

I don't think there are any easy answers, and we did not find any during the workshop, although Rân's participation motivated us to pay more attention to repetition and to repetition-as-interaction in a choreographic structure which emphasizes breath and the acoustic experience of rhythm. Our visual experiments with the camera interface were directed at transformations of the real, while Rân seemed more interested in something that one might call the "precision" of the image, or the precision of the machine, how the visual image movement might achieve the same hypnotic intensity, in repetition, that he was feeling in his steps and the efficacy of his movement as articulation of the techno rhythms generated by the computer program. There was such a lively discussion at the end of our public presentation that I am encouraged to believe we have only just begun the difficult research process into interactivity and digital media, especially on the level of subtle cultural meanings and difference. I did not thematize this in the workshop outline, as my focus was on a hands-on exploration of what we might mean by body-as-interface, and how interface design affects the (dis)continuity between human and technologically generated realities. It was clear, however, that our participants were encouraged to examine their understandings of the mutating body in contemporary (globalized) cultural transactions based on racial, sexual, and class differentiation. In front of the (fake) Byzantine mosaic, we generated portraits—small intimate studies of women (of different age and ethnic background) interacting through their images, movements, and gestures. We also processed their movements and blurred the boundaries, making their bodily images dissolve, disintegrate, and multiply. We did not apply any sensors that measure the rhythms of the heart and the pulse. Perhaps Rân was interested in a graphic representation of his rhythm, as we can see it in the oscillating soundwaves of the techno samples on our laptops. When I asked him about it, he responded that "tekhno [sic] music is one of the first pervasive explorations of nonfigurative music exploiting electronic tools to communicate evolving concepts through rhythm and sound. A general aesthetic of tekhno includes a pragmatic dance-floor efficacy coupled with an underground sensibility, preferring methods of the sonically unexplored over the blatantly familiar."[6]

Rân's pragmatism radicalizes notions of cultural difference and the interiority of the (African or diasporic) body. His interest in contemporary techno music, as well as in the historical evolution of a black music aesthetic and its influence on, and fusion with, current hip hop and world music (e.g., the transatlantic crossings and the Caribbean, Latin American, and Japanese variations on techno), suggests an enormously wide spectrum of rhythmic consciousness in our cultures that is now largely re-generated through digital sonics. Musical culture, along with spiritual and ancestral culture, thus enters the processing ensembles I have described: it enters code and software culture, and is stored and retrievable, and ready to be re-mixed, in the infinite variations of the real-time media that are performed and thus involved in the constantly evolving cultural imagination of the users and their "rhythms of breath."

> Tekhno is an expression of complex, paradoxical, and delicately balanced information that cannot be easily communicated. [. . .] It is a new style and way to express, experience, and perform rhythm. Born as a reaction to oppressive inner-city lifestyles and diverse visions of the future, tekhno developed its identity through the cultural renegades of Detroit and later the renegade culture of Europe's early rave scene. For more than 20 years of progression as a "planetary art-form," it has managed to subtly infiltrate the mainstream musical miasma in myriad ways, yet its potential for communicating abstract ideas has far from diminished. [. . .]
>
> The polyrhythmic tapestry of tekhno weaves layer upon layer of subjective dynamic meaning. Inside this apparently repetitive structure, a framework of hypnosis is established, allowing moments of novelty emerging from the inherent cycles to signify in reference to their rhythmic environs. From within these sonic systems, we can observe a subliminal mode of post-linguistic communication, where meaning defines itself according to a continually evolving context.[7]

Rân's emphasis on the nonfigurative and the sonically unexplored or experimental potential of techno preserves a certain u-topic way of reading media art, and his manifesto implies that the technical infrastructure, like the interactive environment we had set up, is not a determined context but structurally indeterminate. The image of the polyrhythmic weaving of a richly layered tapestry is the opposite of iconostasis. Both his and Marija Stamenkovic's participation in the workshop, along with our diverse group of volunteers, certainly confirmed the assumption that our own agency, our direct application of the interactive tools as cultural communications, will help us to ask cross-cultural questions and articulate our changing relations to our images.

Notes

1. "The Flesh Made Text: Bodies, Theories, Cultures in the Post-Millennial Era" was a conference organized by the School of English at Aristotle University, Thessaloniki, Greece, in cooperation with the Hellenic Association for the Study of English (HASE) and the Hellenic Association for American Studies (HELAAS), 14–18 May 2003.
2. I have dealt with this subject in my article "Dance and Interactivity."
3. For a discussion of new research into cognitive processes and improvisatory behavior in such intelligible spaces, see my dialog with Venezuelan dancer Marlon Barrios Solano. For critical studies of interactive art and new media, see Birringer "Dance and Media Technologies," Manovich, Grau, Leeker, Dinkla, Menicacci, Moser, and Klein.

4. For a fascinating theoretical study of "technical objects" and the interrelations between technology, corporeality and time, see Adrian McKenzie.
5. Rân Ymân and Ben Yânt, "AFT = AFOTEK," unpublished manuscript, quoted with permission from the authors.
6. Rân Ymân and Ben Yânt, "Tekhno," unpublished manuscript, quoted with permission from the authors.
7. Rân Ymân and Ben Yânt, "Tekhno." For another discussion of techno music and the collective energies of the dance and club cultures, see Michel Gaillot.

Works Cited

Birringer, Johannes. "Dance and Interactivity." *Gramma* 10 (2002): 19–40.
———. "Dance and Media Technologies." Special Issue. *Performing Arts Journal* 70 (2002): 84–93.
Dinkla, Söke and Martina Leeker, eds. *Dance and Technology/ Tanz und Technologie: Moving towards Media Productions—Auf dem Weg zu medialen Inszenierungen*. Berlin: Alexander Verlag, 2003.
Gaillot, Michel. *Multiple Meaning: Techno. An Artistic and Political Laboratory of the Present*. Trans. Warren Niesluchowksi. Paris: Editions Dis Voir, 1999.
Grau, Oliver. *Virtual Art: From Illusion to Immersion*. Cambridge: MIT Press, 2003.
Grzinic, Marina, ed. *Stelarc: Political Prosthesis and Knowledge of the Body*. Ljubljana: Maska/MKC, 2002.
Klein, Gabriele and Christa Zipprich, eds. *Tanz, Theorie, Text*. Münster: LIT Verlag, 2002.
Laban, Rudolf. *Choreutics*. London: MacDonald and Evans, 1966.
Leeker, Martina, ed. *Medien, Maschinen, Performances. Theater an der Schnittstelle zu digitalen Welten*. Berlin: Alexander Verlag, 2001.
Manovich, Lev. *The Language of New Media*. Cambridge, MA: MIT Press, 2001.
McKenzie, Adrian. *Transductions: Bodies and Machines at Speed*. London: Continuum, 2002.
Menicacci, Armando and Emanuele Quinz, eds. *La scena digitale: nuovi media per la danza*. Bolzano, Italy: Marsilio, 2001.
Moser, Mary Anne and Douglas MacLeod, eds. *Immersed in Technology: Art and Virtual Environments*. Cambridge: MIT P, 1996.
Solano, Marlon Barrios. "Materiality, Embodiment, Interactive Technologies." 20 Dec. 2006<http://www.dance.ohiostate.edu/~jbirringer/dance_and_technology/ips2.html>.
Ymân, Rân and Ben Yânt. "AFT = AFOTEK." Unpublished Manuscript.
———. "Tekhno." Unpublished Manuscript.

3. *Digital Divas: Sex and Gender in Cyberspace*[1]

SUE-ELLEN CASE

In *Dracula's Legacy* (*Draculas Vermächtnis*), Friedrich Kittler wittily deploys the elements in Bram Stoker's *Dracula* to image the new relations between women and technology.[2] For Kittler, *Dracula* illustrates the anxieties, possibilities, and repressive strategies that accompany women's emerging role in the use of new technologies. Two characters represent a simple bifurcation of women's roles: Mina Murray, who knows stenography and the ways of the typewriter, and her friend Lucy Westenra, who is bitten by the vampire and thus confined by doctors and other men who scrutinize her "hysterical" behavior.

Mina Murray figures the secretaries who will transcribe patriarchal discourse throughout much of the century, transforming the individual writing or speaking of men into an objective script that can bind together the transactions of business and nation.[3] She will enter the office, the work force, as an adjunct of men, in an unequal relation to their labor, social standing, and salary. Mina will operate what Kittler, in a German agglutinate, terms the "discoursemachineweapon" (*Diskursmaschinengewehr*), the Remington typewriter, developed and capitalized by the company that made weapons for the Civil War (29). In the later twentieth century, Mina would represent not only the women at the keyboard, but also those women in Third World Special Economic Zones whose labor on the machine produces its internal parts. They produce the "discourse machine" that bears the load of First World software designers, who are, for the most part, men.[4] In sum, Mina signifies the gendered production of uneven power between men and women in the new techno-economy. While women enable the transmission of the discourse, they do not create it.

Meanwhile, back in the bedroom, Lucy Westenra has been suffering, or perhaps enjoying, nightly visits from Count Dracula. Her perforated body, exhibiting the tracks of his bites, along with her wanderings, "delusions," and illicit lust bring her under the scrutiny of doctors and other "rational" men. They attempt to confine her to the bed or the divan, where she will serve as the object of psychoanalytic "truths" of the time concerning hysteria.[5] The rational men huddle around her body, which is clothed in a revealing and suggestive peignoir. Her misbehaving, induced by illicit penetration, provides a rationale for the men to murder the "foreign" Count Dracula.[6] Although it is important to bind these two roles together in order to fully understand how women have been situated in the world of emerging technologies, it is Lucy's role that I would like to develop here as the precursor of the construction of the sign "woman," within the new technologies. Her perforated body signifies the drive toward increasing interactive relations between machinic devices and corporeality. She represents how images of women's bodies are put to the uses of virtual penetration.

Between the user and the various machines of communication, analysis, and production, the screen stages their interactivity through images that have historically represented notions of identity, desire, and anxiety.[7] Software design enables the play of images as functions of interactivity (the GUI, i.e., Graphical User Interface). In order to do so, it necessarily borrows from the lexicon of familiar signs to represent the user and his or her actions in the cybersphere. As the user finds her/himself more and more imbricated in the web of new technologies, an increasing need for some sign of location, or identity, is needed to locate her/his functions. The sign for "woman" serves to manage this interaction, lending appeal and allure to the functions. As Kittler reminds us, this woman was first perceived as that sexy stenotypist who first replicated men's discourse on the machine. Soon, her image began to be produced within the cultural imaginary to figure the interactive functions with machines as both seductive and threatening. She appeared as a robot in films such as *Metropolis* or *The Stepford Wives*, which narrativized how her seductive qualities still required disciplining by the men she would serve. The sign system was up and running in its traditional semiotic production of the sign "woman," but still required new management of her referents. "Woman" was securely in the machine, but her referents were not yet fully absorbed by the new synergies of scientific, corporate, and social technologies.[8] "Woman" would need to exit, completely, her referents to the "real" world in order to successfully marry into cybersociety.

A variety of performance practices stage these relations between gender codes and the virtual spaces of new media. I have selected a few examples that trace a trajectory of signification, from the staging of the sign for woman and machine as a corporeal encounter, to the screening of the completely virtualized avatar of gender. Hopefully, these few examples can function as signposts of semiotic switching between the machinic and the social. As we will see, the referents of gender coding undergo a complete alteration as the corporate virtual composes its new cyberspace.

Virtually Yours

The title of Kate Bornstein's performance piece, *Virtually Yours*, wittily captures the inscription of ownership and desire in relations with the virtual.[9] Discovered in the light of her computer screen, Bornstein narrates how she, a transgendered male-to-female lesbian, is struggling with her girlfriend's decision to become a female-to-male heterosexual. Bornstein processes how her girlfriend's impending sex reassignment surgery confuses her own identity, based upon gendered sexual practices. She listens to a phone message from her girl-soon-to-be-boy-friend, telling her that she should play the new computer game *Virtually Yours*. Thus, Bornstein's body, already perforated by medical technologies as a reconstructed sex, sits before the terminal, where she will play the game of identity, prompted by the voice on an answering machine. The (stored) object of Bornstein's desire catalyzes her search for a locational identity in the new virtual space.

The telephone, after all, was the first instrument of virtual interaction to really penetrate domestic spaces. In "The Telephone and its Queerness," Ellis Hanson considers various erotic uses of the telephone, insisting that phone communication is "a mechanism of fantasy and pleasure," a site of perversions, and erotic behaviors, from the private cooing of couples to the completely commercialized performance of phone sex (37). Hanson insists that "through the telephone, desire makes brazen its age-old love affair with capital," where these phone-borgs are "chips in the integrated circuit," which confuse "the conventional distinctions between human and machine, desire and commerce" (35). In Bornstein's piece, the phone messages are played on the answering machine which, like the computer, was designed to store data. The phone voice, then, is the site of both the object of desire and the anxiety of being "cut-off." The lover is already a virtual one, whose absent body is being perforated by surgical operations and hormonal injections.

Following her girlfriend's advice, and in hopes of assuaging her grief and anxiety, Bornstein engages with the computer game, which promises to act as a kind of cyber-therapist. She relates and performs scenarios of desire as her input into the game and simultaneously as her "live" performance. She entices her audience to interact with one of her s/m rituals, which once offered her both erotic pleasure and an identification that placed her in proximity to her lover. As her scenarios increasingly complicate the relations among identification, sexual practice, desire, and loss, the game becomes unable to sort out the symptoms. Unlike Lucy's rational doctors, who could restrain her through analysis and cure the symptom by killing the count, the cyber-therapist ultimately suffers a breakdown of its own identity, asking: "Who am I when you don't play the game?"

In one sense, Bornstein performs the triumph of the bodily regime, something she also displays through her revealing costumes and seductive play with the audience. Although she performs her location as somewhere between medical technologies and two virtual systems, the "live/corporeal" performer still runs the show. In effect, Bornstein "channels" technology, rather than the reverse. In the terms of s/m, she "tops" the process of interactivity, suggesting that the corporeal representation of identificatory processes is still too complex to be entirely situated within virtual technologies. The "live" still animates the technological, even though it suffers loss and confusion in the process. Yet, to stress only her triumph over loss would not do service to the delicate balance Bornstein's piece achieves. She is, quite literally, as well as figuratively, illuminated by the computer screen—the postmodern Lucy—perforated, but not perishing from it.

While Bornstein performs the corporeal/virtual splits, uses of "woman" appear within cyberspace, made to signify its own processes. In the simplest form, "women" appear as avatars on the computer screen. For those less familiar with on-line activity, avatars are images on the screen that seem to represent the user. Often, avatars can be selected at a particular website where a variety of images are stored. The more practiced user might create her own avatar, using a photo, a photomontage, or a cartoon character as her representative on the screen. Some avatars can even perform limited movements, while others remain stationary, but nearly all can be moved around the space of the screen, in varying degrees of proximity to other avatars. Users may imagine their own participation within cybersocieties in the form of these avatars.

The term "avatar" is borrowed from Hindu texts, having become generally familiar through the text of the *Bhagavad-Gita*—the first epic story of avatars (Parrinder 19). In Sanskrit, the term means descent or a "downcoming." Etymologically, the term *Avatara* is formed by the verb *tri*, meaning to cross over or save, with the prefix *ava,* which means down. Hindu theological discussions of the term raised similar issues around the appearance of avatars to those that surround the uses of cyber-avatars today. For example, the eighth-century philosopher Sankara raised the problem of dualism in the notion of the avatar. Sankara argues that if Brahma is only One, how can he be two—both Brahma and his incarnation or avatar? Sankara solved this seeming contradiction by insisting that the manifestation of the god is not a "real" incarnation, but merely another image within *Maya*—the veil of illusion (50). The on-line avatar raises a similar question: is the on-line avatar a mask of a "real" user, whose "presence" is, somehow, acting on-line, or is it simply a part of a complete simulation—merely another empty cipher in the veil of cyber-maya?

Jennifer Gonzalez, in her article "The Appended Subject," offers a useful mediating definition of the avatar, situating it somewhere between a cyborg, an amalgamation of the corporeal and the virtual, and a complete substitution. Gonzalez summarizes the general understanding of the avatar as "an object constituted by electronic elements serving as a psychic or bodily appendage, an artificial subjectivity that is attached to a supposed original or unitary being, an on-line persona understood as somehow appended to a real person who resides elsewhere, in front of a keyboard" (27–28). Applying this definition, the avatar offers an identificatory fantasy of appearance, constructed with elements of fashions in the corporeal world: industrial logos, Japanese *anime*, MTV, and Comix. Yet, no code is more crucial in configuring the avatar than that of gender. As avatars represent the user in on-line chat rooms, the appearance of gender often determines with whom and how the players will chat. Note that the operating definition of the avatar still seems to be in relation to the user. Before moving away from that traditional understanding, a consideration of an actual on-line performance might aid in understanding how avatars function in cybersociety.

waitingforgodot.com

From the many possible uses of the avatar, I have selected an on-line performance entitled *waitingforgodot.com* for several reasons: first, for its familiarity of reference to those who study performance; second, because it represents an actual on-line performance piece; and finally, because it is designed to stage some of the issues crucial to this study. *waitingforgodot.com* premiered at the Third Annual Digital Storytelling Festival in Colorado in September 1997. It was created by Lisa Brenneis and Adriene Jenik. The performance takes place in a chat room at a site called "The Palace."[10] In this space, where avatars roam and users seek chat-mates, two roundheads appear, reciting their version of some of the most familiar lines from the play. They do not announce their performance as such, but, as cyber-street theater, they simply perform in a public space. In fact, *waitingforgodot.com* could be perceived as a new kind of street theater in the cybersphere, erupting in social spaces where people pass through or hang out. It offers a witty commentary on people hanging around in chat rooms with nothing to do or say and nowhere to go. However, as we will see, avatars resemble people, but do not necessarily represent them.

In Beckett's play, the tramps represent a minimalist, existential version of Everyman. Beckett's characters are literally Every*men,* in a world of men, retaining stable gender referents in his play.[11] In contrast, *waitingforgodot.com* deploys images derived from *pacman* video games and happy-face logos, which seem to suggest unmarked characters. They bear no markings of gender or "race." Everyperson, then, or better, "Everysignifier," is a cartoon image which was developed by the computer game industry and corporate ads to signify neutral and happy. The two floating heads are literally severed from referents to corporeal existence. Their unmarked status is part of the strategy of this performance. The "performers" are quite unlike the other avatars in the chat space. "Palace Princess" offers a scantily-clad, female figure without a head, while "Hedge Witch" and "Jen" portray young, hip, seductive fashions. Those choosing to appear as male offer more Punk or Gothic versions of "self," identified as "Bloody Razor" and "Clan Wolf." They are fully clothed, signaling masculinity through their bold looks out from the screen or the pronounced violence suggested by their names. Interestingly, the masculinized avatars are composed of photos, while the feminized ones are cartoon-type characters. The avatars, then, reveal a characteristic array of hyper-gendered features in their composition.

If we identify the roundheads in *waitingforgodot.com* as performers, what does their status imply about the nature of avatars in general? Are the other avatars in the chat room also performing? Do all avatars function like masks or only when the user intends to perform? Understanding the avatars as masks would agree with the received notion that they function as identificatory images for the user. Two sets of problems militate against this interpretation. The first has to do with traditional assumptions about the nature of masking and the second with the nature of the on-line conventions of representation. First, the definition of character and mask depends on the opposite term of actor or on the indication of some "presence" behind the mask. Indeed, the sense of a subject as constituted before representation is what Judith Butler nominates as performance, against her concept of performativity. Lurking behind the mask and the character is the "actual presence" that has somehow been altered or represented by the mask. In other words, the mask depends upon some notion of the "real" or the "natural" for its function. Nietzsche, in his study of the classical Greek mask in *The Birth of Tragedy,* offers a hyper image of the relation of the mask to the essential that emphasizes these qualities: "The Sophoclean hero—the Apolline mask[s . . .] are the inevitable products of a glance into the terrible depths of nature: light patches, we might say, to heal the gaze seared by terrible night" (46). For Nietzsche, as for the Hindu scholar, Sankara, the notion of mask and avatar borders on incarnation—the idea that a god or some figure of ideality is corporealized in the process of making theater (51). In the cybersphere, the corporeal resides in the function of the user, with the avatar serving as her/his virtual mask. Either way, the sense of avatar as mask points us back to the play of essences, the necessary stipulation that there is a user, whose "real" self is altered by the avatar.

Much of the discussion about avatars does presume this relationship between avatar and user, subjecting the dynamics to a scrutiny of identificatory processes and masquerade. Utopic visions of a sphere where cross-gender identifications abound, alongside feminist warnings against any belief in the possibility of "free" play within the gender regime. Yet, both sides would agree that the users are, somehow, performing versions of social identities and relationships in cyberspace. Anterior notions of "self," volition, or agency, and clear, stable attributes of social organization are required for the backdrop to this theater of avatars. As I have argued more fully in my book, *The Domain-Matrix,* many of these attributes are specific to an earlier form of capitalism and do not reflect the contemporary, corporate structuring of social relations.[12] Given the corporate, commercial take-over of what was once considered to be private space and discourse, the referents of the sign system no longer reside in the kind of natural environment Nietzsche and traditional studies of the avatar presume. Specifically in this study of the avatar, the signification of gender, or, as we will see, "race," has less to do with promoting an identificatory process between user and avatar than as a way to *promote* the avatar on-screen. In other words, avatars do not function as masks for users, but as brand names or logos competing in a commercial space.

Returning to those roundheads in *waitingforgodot.com,* whose function of Everysignifier is derived from computer games and corporate "happy faces," we can see how the avatar references structures of corporate branding and even the status of technology itself. The cartoon avatar, such as a Disneyfied diva in the chat space, is drawn to resemble the private body of earlier capital relations, but, in its cartooned abstraction, it signals the corporate reference at its root. The digital diva is a representation of gender codes used to articulate the interface between that anterior sense of the private and the live with new, corporate, virtual systems. The diva is the hostess, so to speak, who promotes forms of interaction that seem familiar and enticing in the new cyberspace. The users who promote themselves through these avatars, such as "Jen" or "Hedge Witch," are animating the interface for themselves, seduced and seducing the users to use the new products of corporate technology.

In one sense, Mark Poster prefigured this notion in his theory of how something like a subject position appears within a database. Poster notes that when so much information about a person congeals in the data, a kind of "double" of the subject actually appears there, but that subject is one completely interpellated or overdetermined by dominant ideologies (97–98). I want to continue in this line of reasoning, but abandon any notion of a subject on-line; instead, I want to draw the relations among avatars on the screen as *inter-fetish object relations.* As data and functions congeal around an avatar, it acquires the seductive qualities of the fetish. Its seductive qualities serve to compete for focus with other on-line objects within the competitive, commercial relations of the cybersphere.

The cyber-world of inter-fetish relations is simply one of the final frontiers in the development of corporate uses of the logo. Rather than serving users as masks for their identificatory fantasies, avatars actually function as forms of logos. In her brilliant study, *No Logo,* Naomi Klein offers a history of the rise of the corporate "branding" that ultimately produced the logo-centric surround of the new millennium. She notes that "the first task of branding was to bestow proper names on generic goods, such as sugar, flour, soap, and cereal [. . .]. Logos were tailored to evoke familiarity and folksiness" (6). Enter Uncle Ben, Aunt Jemima, and Old Grand Dad, who substituted for rice, flour, and whiskey. As corporate branding became more sophisticated, actual people, as well as the more cartoon-like characters, began to stand in for the logo. By now, we are accustomed to making a product association with movie stars or sports stars, as well as talking Chihuahuas and Bart Simpson. The personalized logos signify products or the conglomerate behind products. Magic Johnson means Nike, and MacDonald's can extend its referent through any number of toys that resemble familiar cartoon characters. Klein further develops how logos are placed within movies, novels, and other so-called cultural venues. Situating the logo within civic and cultural spaces spawned what *The Wall Street Journal* identified as the "experiential communication" industry, as Klein notes, "the phrase now used to encompass the staging of branded pieces of corporate performance art" (12). We now have branded hotels, theaters, theme parks, and even little villages. The brands loop back into their own worlds through synergies of entertainment and products, creating, as Starbucks calls it, "a brand canopy" (148). Brands, then, Klein argues, "are not products but ideas, attitudes, values, and experiences [. . .] the lines between corporate sponsors and sponsored culture have entirely disappeared" (30).

Gendered characterizations, particularly those that are sexualized, have been promoted in this logo culture to create the logo or, in our case, the avatar as fetish. To reverse Freud's equation, the referents of sexual practices are made to serve as fetish objects of product lines. Jean Kilbourne, a scholar of advertising, emphasizes that the average person in the United States is bombarded by 3,000 ads per day (55). Kilbourne notes that many of these ads create what she terms a "synthetic sexuality"—one that designates a certain body type, gestural system, and fashion sense as sexy. The referent is not sex; on the contrary, sex is the referent for the product line or, what is more, the corporation behind various product lines. Hyper-feminized avatars, then, circulate among the other logos, competing for focus, and acting out corporate and technological relations as seductive and even as sexual. Their referent is not the user, but the corporate logos which are used to comprise the image of the avatar.

Astrid Deuber-Mankowsky has composed a sophisticated treatment of the avatar of Lara Croft, the protagonist of the computer game *Tomb Raider*, which illustrates how the sexified, powerful Lara stands in for corporate, technological success. In the narrative of the game, Lara appears as a "white," upper-class, British archaeologist off on adventures in the Third World. She is scantily-clad, but tough, with weapons and martial arts in her arsenal against the Other. She is viewed from behind, suggesting that she represents, or works for, the game player. Many feminist treatments of Lara replicate the traditional focus on the user's identificatory processes, debating her subject/object status for the mostly male players, who both desire her and identify with her. Deuber-Mankowky, however, argues that Lara Croft functions not as a character, a *Spielefigur*, but as a *Werbefigur*, an ad.[13] The composition and function of Lara serves to perform the imaging power of the 32-bit platform and the 3-D graphics card. She is the sexy diva that attests to the imaging power of the Sony Play Station. In other words, an avatar of a heterosexualized, white woman offers a ground for the imaging of the new convergence of filmic and digital possibilities that made the game *Tomb Raider* popular. Lara represents the high level of 3-D simulation that the successful upgrading of the computer platform and graphic card allowed in the construction of the game. Her whiteness and gender work together to create an alluring and powerful image of new technologies at work in the world.

Cyber-minstrelsy

Like Lara, the majority of avatars on the net signify "whiteness" or stereotypical Anglo-American characteristics, yet there are also several uses for racial and ethnic markers in the logo-centric space. The earlier examples drawn from the initial stage of "branding," such as Uncle Ben and Aunt Jemima, present two logos based on racial stereotyping and nostalgia for the "Old South." While today, the image of a "mammy," and a "house servant" may seem dated in their form of representation, Spike Lee's recent film, *Bamboozled*, attests to their continuing power of representation in the late twentieth century. *Bamboozled* tells the story of a TV executive who becomes successful by producing a new series called *Mantan: The New Millennium Minstrel Show*. A dancing Aunt Jemima, along with a chorus line of minstrels, helps to make the series a popular success. Lee suggests that the current enthusiasm for black performance in mass media entertainment is just another form of the minstrel show, with similar stereotypes still capable of drawing an enthusiastic audience.

Imagining that we are part of a contemporary sophisticated, urban audience or buying public, it would seem that these antique markers of ethnicity would not produce much allure. Why would a minstrel masking of race be effective in this time of so-called, multicultural social practices? The answer may lie, in part, in the kind of economic conditions that encourage such strategies of othering. In both the mid-to-late twentieth century and the mid-nineteenth century, when minstrel shows were invented, major shifts in capital investment and labor practices caused high anxiety in certain sectors of the population. In his book on minstrelsy, *Love and Theft*, Eric Lott locates the beginning of minstrel shows in the 1840s, during the depression that followed the panic of 1837 (137). According to Lott, the new consolidation of industrial capital caused high unemployment among the laboring classes. Lott argues that during industrialization, these minstrel shows, depicting "happy" slaves singing and dancing on the porch of the old cotton plantation, played out nostalgia for pre-industrial times (148). But this nostalgia for the time of the "happy old slave" did not operate through identification with the slave. Remember that minstrel shows were the product of white entertainers in the northeast, who portrayed black, slave culture in the "Old South." The Blacks were represented as unruly and uncivilized in their lusting after a good time. Their unruly behavior served two functions: to render the agrarian past as less structured and more fun than the new industrialized time, and to identify unruly behavior as specifically "black." Lott cites reviews of the minstrel shows that describe a "savage energy," with performers whose "white eyes [were] rolling in a curious frenzy" (140). He notes that when these performers cross-dressed as women, they portrayed the black women as enormous, gorging themselves on food and sex. In this way, Lott suggests, the minstrel shows displaced anxieties over unemployment to a performance of racial hierarchies. By encouraging racist and sexist prejudices, the enjoyment taken in the minstrel show displaced the uneasy contest among whites for low-level employment in the northeast onto contempt for blacks in the "Old South." This form of working-class entertainment thus consolidated the audience, through their laughter, as "whites" (137). Further, their masculinity was shored up by the sexist rhetoric and the portrayal of heterosexual relationships as ones in which women were subordinate to men.

Many of the anxieties and solutions to the problems in the 1840s may also be identified within the current digital age. In the digital age, which arguably began in the 1980s with the invention of the Internet, the "upload" of economic prowess and employment possibilities into the electronic sphere has caused similar kinds of anxieties among workers. New firms and new job descriptions are replacing old ones, while many kinds of companies and forms of employment are disappearing. Skills with new technologies and software are required for everything from job skills to personal communication, and entertainment. Economic envy and fear among white working class sectors could be allayed by a form of entertainment that operates through stereotypes of black masculinity and white feminine allure. Sex and violence, those two markers of mass entertainment in the 1990s and onward, mask those anxieties through stereotypes that promise to initiate us into the land of the successful.

Imagining Internet representation as a play of racial stereotypes, Guillermo Gomez-Pena and Roberto Sifuentes opened the on-line "Ethno-Cyberpunk Trading Post and Curio Shop on the Electronic Frontier." In 1994, Gomez-Pena announced that they were going to infiltrate cyberspace as "cyber-immigrants" or what Gomez-Pena calls "cyber-wetbacks." Their "Ethno-Cyberpunk" trading post traded in ethnic identities both as a gallery installation and on the Internet. Avatars included "Cyber Vato," a "robo gang member," "el Postmodern Zorro" and "El Cultural Transvestite." Visitors to the website sent in images, sound, or texts about how Mexicans, Chicanos and Native Americans of the 1990s should look, behave, and perform.[14] The artists then reproduced these stereotypes to represent ethnic identities on-line. In other words, these artists only reproduced stereotypical notions of how Chicanos and Native Americans seem to appear, in order to compose their avatars or the on-line representatives of these members of ethnic communities. Displayed within a trading post, the stereotypes are elements of exchange. Whatever seems to be a referent to ethnicity is used for its product value.

Once more, Jennifer Gonzalez offers an insight into the construction of the avatar—this time as racialized. Continuing to operate on the assumption that avatars represent identificatory fantasies, she notes that the elements of racial stereotyping seem appealing and without threat because "Race is understood not to 'matter' [. . .] in this on-line domain," which claims to be "outside" the economic and juridical systems. She continues, "The idea of not being oneself is intimately tied to the conditions of leisure and the activity of consumption" (45). Gonzalez concludes: "It is precisely through an experimentation with cultural and racial fusion and fragmentation, combined with a lack of attention to social process, a lack of attention to history [. . .] that a new transcendental, universal, and, above all, consuming subject is offered as the model of future cyber-citizenship" (48). Even though she proceeds from a study of the subject, Gonzalez concludes that the avatar circulates in a special economic zone of privileged consumption, unmarred by considerations of labor and legal practices.

So it seems that both this study and studies that imagine the avatar as subject, racial and ethnic markers reference little else but market strategies. Yet, to condemn all representations of ethnicity on-line would only affirm the Anglo, "white" economy of representation that controls most of the on-line figures, bolstering the dominant assumption that the unmarked space of representation is, indeed, "white." For an imaging of ethnicity that is funky and playful, rather than the sort deployed by corporations such as Benetton, we can return to another performance staged by Adrien Jenik. This time, Jenik uses the screen as a dreamscape, in which a player may narrate a dream that the others will inhabit and draw as it proceeds. The dream is called *riverofsalsa*.

riverofsalsa

"Catwoman," coded Latina, enters the space. The space, the *mise-en-scene*, begins as a generic, unmarked road. "Scotty" appears in "*barrio*" wear, with a boom box. Catwoman narrates her dream, while the drawing on the screen visualizes it. The two avatars meet, a taco is suggested, then, suddenly, a river of salsa, flowing from the food, overtakes the space and the characters, immersing them. Ethnicity is marked by the fashion in clothing, in the actual drawing of "Catwoman," in items such as the boom box, and in the references to a specific ethnic cuisine. Certainly, these are stereotypical images of ethnic subcultures. Perhaps they fill the formula that Gomez-Pena and Roberto Sifuentes would identify as trade in the "Ethno-Cyberpunk Trading Post."

Nevertheless, as Beth Kolko outlines, in her discussion of the on-line site *LambdaMOO,* there is a "growing awareness that technology interfaces carry the power to prescribe representative norms and patterns, constructing a self-replicating and exclusionary category of 'ideal' user [. . .]" (318). In order to intervene in the construction of the ideal as "white," Kolko concludes that the user must somehow force an ethnic marking into the system by choosing a name with those specific associations, or by linguistic style, or by ethnic references (216). Kolko's work raises some key questions: how can we determine when these elements may be serving an identificatory function for the user, who does participate in the Latino subculture, or when are they simply elements of ethnic fashion? Finally, would it matter whether or not the user who was manipulating these signs was actually within the Latino subculture? Isn't the point to "color" the representational vocabulary of cyberspace?

Closing the Window

As these examples have shown, the interrogation of how signs of gender and ethnicity operate on-line reveals less about the status of these codes in the "real" world than the basic change in the sign system of the cyber. As the frame of the real recedes from what are called immersive technologies, so, too, does its power as a referent. Cyberspace stages a theater of masks without actors, rendering the mask an antique form of the "live" that once presumed the taking on of social and private faces, different from one's own identity. Hyper-gendered avatars and the practice of neo-minstrelsy reveal a transitional phase in which evocations of the "real" are still necessary to manage the new theater of logos. Gender codes are used to signify the allure and pleasure of new technological capabilities and product lines, while neo-minstrelsy masks the globalizing sameness of synergies with images of difference and diversity. The "happy face" logo/avatar registers the beginning of the transcendence of corporate representation in cyberspace, in which gender and minstrelsy will no longer be required for synergies to stage their competitive functions entirely without reference to social conditions.

However, while the residue of difference still plays in the increasingly monotone cyber-world, it may provide some small intervention into the upload of signification. Even if gender and ethnic codes serve only as fragments of identificatory processes for the ever-distant users, they might be used to signal the conditions of those who are not invited into the ranks of the privileged. Unfortunately, at this point, the sign for woman serves pretty much the same function of seductive hostess as in traditional uses, and ethnic markers seem a to signal "hip," "young," and hyper-gendered users on the make. But what if users with more activist agendas began to people cyberspace with the images of the poor, the weak, and the disenfranchised? What if the body types of the avatars did not match the requirements of young, thin, toned, Anglo ava-hunks or digital divas? What if they did not hang around chat rooms, but used them as sites to organize, to educate, and to radicalize? What if they could imagine the "discoursemachineweapon," as Kittler calls it, as one of the most powerful tools available for intervention—turning it back onto the logos who would manage it?

What would it take to make that happen?

Notes

1. A slightly modified version of this essay, entitled: "Dracula's Daughters: In-Corporating Avatars in Cyberspace," has been published in a collection of essays edited by Janelle G. Reinelt and Joseph Roach under the title *Critical Theory and Performance: A Revised and Enlarged Edition*, U of Michigan P, 2006. The essay is reprinted with permission from the publisher.
2. Elsewhere, I have argued for the vampire as a figure for appearance of lesbians in the system of representation. I think the work there amplifies this article's focus on gender rather than sexual practice. See Case ("Tracking the Vampire").
3. Interestingly, Bram Stoker served as secretary to the eminent actor/manager Henry Irving. The term secretary derives from the Latin "keeper of secrets." It had a more prestigious connotation for men in the Victorian era, when it suggested privy knowledge within the realm of public or governmental service. See *The History of the Secretarial Profession* on the official web site of Professional Secretaries: <http://www.iaaphq.org>.
4. See Kestler.
5. Nina Auerbach, in "Magi and Maidens: The Romance of the Victorian Freud," notes that Bram Stoker took part in the Society for Psychical Research in 1893, where he became acquainted with the notion of female hysteria (290). In a chapter

on "Victorian Mythmakers," Auerbach suggests that Svengali, from DuMaurier's novel *Trilby,* inspired Stoker's Dracula. She compares an illustration of the unconscious TriIby on stage with the swooning figure of an "hysterical" woman exhibited by Charcot. See Auerbarch (*Woman and the Demon* 15–34).
6. As we know, this practice persists today, with the taboo of illicit penetration providing a rationale for the murder of Matthew Shepard, among others.
7. I am indebted to Jeff Nyhoff for this clarification in his sophisticated, yet-unpublished work on performing the interface.
8. For a discussion of the multiple uses of the term "technology," see Terry and Calvert.
9. The visual elements of the performance described here are taken from a video of *Virtually Yours* performed at Josie's Juice Bar in San Francisco in 1994.
10. For a complete discussion of desktop theater, see Jenik. To access the archived performances, go to <http://leda.ucsd.edu/%oeajeniklmain/files>.
11. On the point of gender, see Knowlson who notes:

> [Beckett] felt very strongly that the characters in his plays were either male or female and that their sex was not interchangeable. There were many requests, sometimes fervent personal appeals made directly to him, for women to be allowed to play the male characters in *Waiting for Godot*. Beckett (or his agents) always turned them down, though he himself showed signs of wilting several times under the intense emotional pressure that was brought to bear on him. (610)

12. See, especially, the section entitled "Bringing Home the Meat," which traces the commodification of social relations.
13. Unfortunately, for some, Deuber-Mankowsky's monograph is in German.
14. For further information on this project and its attempt to "brownify" virtual space, see <*http://www.telefonica.es/fat/egomez.html*>.

Works Cited

Auerbach, Nina. "Magi and Maidens: The Romance of the Victorian Freud." *Critical Inquiry* 8:2 (Winter 1981): 290.

———. *Woman and the Demon: The Lift of a Victorian Myth*. Cambridge: Harvard UP, 1982.

Bornstein, Kate. *Virtually Yours. o solo homo*. Ed. Holly Hughes and David Roman. New York: Grove, 1998. 229–78.

Butler, Judith. "Critically Queer." *Glq: A Journal of Lesbian and Gay Studies* 1:1 (1993): 258–308.

Case, Sue-Ellen. *The Domain-Matrix: Performing Lesbian at the End of Print Culture*. Bloomington: Indiana UP, 1996.

———. "Tracking the Vampire." *differences* 3:2 (1991): 1–20.

Deuber-Mankowsky. *Lara Croft: Modell, Medium, Cyberheldin; das virtuelle Geschlecht und seine metaphysischen Tücken*. Frankfurt: Suhrkamp, 2001.

Gonzalez, Jennifer. "The Appended Subject: Race and Identity as Digital Assemblage." *Race in Cyberspace*. Ed. Beth E. Kolko, Lisa Nakamura, Gilbert B. Rodman. New York and London: Routledge, 2000. 27–50.

Hanson, Ellis. "The Telephone and its Queerness." *Cruising the Performative*. Ed. Sue-Ellen Case, Philip Brett, Susan Leigh Foster. Bloomington: Indiana UP, 1995. 34–58.

Jenik, Adriene. "Keyboard Catharsis and the Making of Roundheads." *The Drama Review* 45.3 (Fall 2001): 95–112.

Kestler, Grant. "Out of Sight Is Out of Mind: The Imaginary Space in Postindustrial Culture." *Social Text* 11:2 (Summer 1993): 72–92.

Kilbourne, Jean. *Ms. Magazine* (Dec 2000/Jan 2001).

Kittler, Friedrich. *Draculas Vermächtnis*. Leipzig: Reclam Verlag. 1993.

Klein, Naomi. *No Logo*. London: Flamingo, 2000.

Knowlson, James. *Damned to Fame: The Life of Samuel Beckett*. New York: Simon & Schuster, 1996.

Kolko, Beth. "Erasing @race: Going White in the (Inter)Face." *Race in Cyberspace*. Ed. Beth E. Kolko, Lisa Nakamura, Gilbert B. Rodman. New York and London: Routledge, 2000. 213–32.

Lott, Eric. *Love and Theft: Blackface Minstrelsy and the American Working Class*. Oxford: Oxford UP, 1993.

Nietzsche, Friedrich. *The Birth of Tragedy*. Trans. Shaun Whiteside. New York: Penguin Books, 1993.

Parrinder, Edward Geoffrey. *Avatar and Incarnation*. New York: Barnes & Noble, 1970.

Poster, Mark. *The Mode of Information*. Chicago: U of Chicago P, 1990.

Terry, Jennifer and Melodie Calvert, eds. *Processed Lives: Gender and Technology in Everyday Life*. London and New York: Routledge, 1997.1–19.

4. *Millennial Artaud: Rethinking Cruelty and Representation*

Elizabeth Sakellaridou

The summer 2002 was extremely rich in exposures to representations of the body and physical suffering in the performance, visual and plastic arts. My reflections on these instances of gaze politics, in production and reception, have framed the writing of this paper. In June 2002, I attended in London a performance of Martin McDonagh's play *The Lieutenant of Inishmore,* the most bluntly realistic staging of the violation and massacre of human bodies. Its unspeakable aesthetic of stage horror consisted of incessant nerve-cracking shootings and explosions; quantities of blood systematically splashing on actors' bodies, furniture and set; and a huge bloody trough, placed downstage, where real-size effigies of dismembered human bodies were gradually piled up by two characters, energetically engaged in sawing up parts off a number of corpses with which they had previously furnished the stage. That was a real butcher's festival, an excess even for the slaughterhouse. I was watching the implacable but dull spectacle nonplussed until my sixteen-year-old daughter, sitting next to me, burst out into a wild laughter, giving me a clue to a different reading of this déjà vu, Tarantino-style stage horror by a youth habituated to the excesses of violence in our contemporary media culture. It dawned on me that this was perhaps the wildest, most grotesque parody—a savage critique even?—of the aesthetic of extreme brutalism on the British stage of the 1990s, actually marking the end of the so-called "in-yer-face theater."[1]

Two months later, I visited the international electronic image exhibition "Iconoclash" at the Centre for Art and Media Technologies (ZKM) in Karlsruhe, where I explored, with the assistance of complicated electronic equipment, new relationships of my body with interactive space and I played with the sense of my physical presence and non-presence, the staging of my appearance and disappearance. The next day I made a huge leap back in time while visiting the Unterlinden Museum in the Alsacian town of Colmar, where I stood for a long time observing Matthias Grünewald's famous Renaissance painting of the *Crucifixion,* part of a larger work of art known as the Isenheim Altarpiece. This is a unique representation of Christ's Passion on the Cross, which blends the most extraordinary physical rendering of bodily torture in a horrific, detailed depiction of open, festering wounds[2] with a more internalized, metaphorical indication of suffering suggested by the expressionistic distortion of the fingers on the upper part of the painting. Especially the fingers of Christ's left hand bear an astonishing resemblance to twisted dried twigs growing out of a dead tree, as if of the same material as the cross. At the same time, the painting creates the vivid impression that the strong gestural pose of the fingers in a contraction of pain projects a fraction of sensience, of "aliveness," to the wood of the cross. For the spectator, this is an extraordinary moment of animism in art (Scarry, *The Body* 286). I subsequently visited the St. Lazare cathedral in the small Burgundian town of Autun, which houses some interesting contemporary sculptural representations of the stages of the Passion on the Cross. These images, mainly of the Crucifixion and the Pieta, were given suggestively through pieces of wood, roughly or more finely carved, indicating a dismembered torso and fragments of limbs, supported by metal bands or hanging from strings.

Upon returning home in September of that year, while flicking through *Time* magazine, I came across a picture of a stunning pose of the contemporary British performer and playwright Steven Berkoff from a solo performance he had prepared in commemoration of 9/11, called *Requiem to Ground Zero.* Through the grimaces of the face (the staring eye, the gaping mouth, the slightly deformed nose) and the contorted arm, hand and fingers, trying to obstruct vision and shield the head against the aggressiveness of the atrocious sight, the still pose gave a suggestive but powerful representation of the horror of the commemorated event as mirrored in subjective reception. Through this strategy of reflection and the avoidance of direct exposure to the reenactment of the actual horror, assisted by the concept of a frozen gaze and a mouth in a blocked attempt at articulation, the image also subtly suggested the inexpressibility of horror; it showed a body at the edge of unrepresentable pain. All five experiences I recorded focused on the suffering of the living body and the modes and limits of its representation.

After the 1960s, we have become accustomed to an escalating body craze, to a frenzied preoccupation with the body, of a simultaneous demystification and fetishization of the body, a polarity between overexposure and total eclipse. A number of conflicting or supplementary discourses on the body synthesize the colorful and also ambivalent spectrum of its various manifestations, functions and discursive possibilities as experienced or fantasized today. The sexualized, colonized, brutalized, aestheticized, spectacularized, medicalized, technologized, mediatized bodies speak of pleasure and fascination but also of fear, oppression and despair; they suggest an apotheosis and a malediction at the same time. Supporting theories of a philosophical, psychoanalytic, cultural, or scientific nature point contentedly to the power and the possibilities of human desire and fantasy investing the human body, but they also announce its powerlessness and extermination. What starts as a game of willful pleasure ends up in the fear of disappearance and annihilation. The Lyotardian statement on the collapse of master narratives, which presumably celebrated the ideological liberation of the postmodern body/subject, has already given way to a generation of new equally engulfing mythologies: for what else are the new tidings of such containing terms as "media culture," "globalization," "transnationalism" and the "posthuman age" if not new, systematic, ideological monoliths for collective submission and conformity of bodies/subjects? Additionally, the recent war in Iraq has revitalized the pragmatic dimensions of the human body and the individual will at the vanishing point. These new manifestations of a polymorphous manipulation of human existence have already been captured by intellectuals in order to be theorized (or perhaps depoliticized?) as famously (or infamously) as, just over a decade ago, the Gulf War was processed in Baudrillard's fertile fantasy and deft articulation.

Among such sea changes in political life, military action, technological advancement, cultural ethics, and theoretical trends that reshape our views of and attitudes to the body, I would like to re-examine some twentieth-century theories on the body and its suffering and the possibilities of its artistic representation. In this investigation at this historical moment, I would consider revisiting Antonin Artaud and his theory on physical theater and cruelty, a capital must, for a number of reasons: first and foremost, because, in our culture, cruelty has become a daily companion to our physical and psychic experience; equally, because Artaud articulated his visions on a theater of cruelty in an "anguished, catastrophic period" (Artaud 84) similar to ours, when he considered "cataclysms [to be] at our door" (Artaud 87); thirdly, because Western performance art and the "new brutalism" playwrights in Britain have given the practice of stage cruelty a literal, perverse, and sensational twist that would enrage Artaud and would, no doubt, make him denounce the "prostituting" of theater once again (Artaud 89); and, last but not least, because theorists such as Jacques Derrida, driven by their own theoretical pursuits, have blindly promoted Artaud's problematic statement about the "superstition of the text and the dictatorship of the writer" (Artaud 124) and have fiercely denounced the "tyranny of the text" (Derrida 236) by resorting to undeservedly harsh language—"cancellation," "aberration"—(Derrida 236) in order to refute the classics. In doing so, Derrida strategically suppressed Artaud's tempering comments on the loss of "the physics" of classical theater that could partly justify his complaint about our fixation on textuality alone (Artaud 108). The result of Artaud's unilateral hostility to the classics, together with the complicity of such equally one-sided commentators like Derrida, has led to an uninhibited and often totally unreasonable "anti-text mania" (Hornby 355) that has exasperated contemporary dramatists and critics who hold great respect for the performativity of the dramatic text. An autonomous performance art may have found a strong supportive voice in some Artaudian views on the theater and, recently, in Lehmann's theoretical sanctioning of a "postdramatic theater." But, a close re-reading of Artaud's contradictory postulates, along with a revision of some related or follow-up writings (such as Derrida's "The Theater of Cruelty and the Closure of Representation" or Elaine Scarry's *The Body in Pain*) as well as a reexamination of some specimens of the texts that Artaud rejected and Scarry doubted (for instance, Sophocles' *Philoctetes*) may change the landscape again and reconstitute faith in the physical power of words to depict the body and record pain in a mixed material and conceptual manner.

What I propose, therefore, is a double act of revisiting Artaud: as a return which aims at restoring his initial concept of cruelty as a philosophy of life and of body language as a mixture of physicality and signification, and as a new departure which will restore faith in the phenomenology of the written and spoken text and, consequently, in the unduly disgraced, so-called "logocentric" Western tradition. Part of my task will also be a questioning of Elaine Scarry's categorical statement—much in the vein of Artaudian theory—that "pain does not simply resist language but actively destroys it" and, therefore, remains inexpressible in linguistic terms (Scarry, *The Body* 3–4). Recent theoretical inquiries into the performativity of language, on the one hand, and on the function of a secondary, non-physical vision, on the other, can assist in a reassessment of the body-and-mind/psyche synergy in the human perception of pain and suffering and its artistic expression—all of them issues that had been initially conceived by but were eventually overlooked in Artaud's Theater of Cruelty. I shall selectively refer to Judith Butler's post-Lacanian, phenomenological examination of language in *Excitable Speech* (1997) and to James Elkins' exploration of the possibilities of visual representations of the body in pain in his *Pictures of the Body: Pain and Metamorphosis* (1999).[3]

In a seemingly Artaudian spirit, Scarry chooses Sophocles' *Philoctetes*, one of the few texts that deal manifestly with physical suffering, only to claim that in this classical play the protagonist's excruciating pain is merely depicted by a very limited range of "cries and shrieks," impoverished even further in their English translation (Scarry, *The Body* 5). This is a very partial and superficial reading of the Sophoclean text, suitably geared to serve Scarry's overall argument about the inability of language to record pain. Here, Artaud's own lifelong, agonizing practice of a linguistic rendering of his intense suffering, in a medium he greatly distrusted, can refute Scarry's argument. With specific reference to her expressed doubts about the adequacy of *Philoctetes*, I would also mention Terry Eagleton's contrary view in his book on tragedy, *Sweet Violence*, namely that "Sophocles forces us to listen to the agonized bellows of [. . .] Philoctetes, *squeezing every drop of theatre he can* out of [his] raw, pointless, unbearable pain" (31, emphasis added), thus underlining the potential physicality, the fleshness of the Sophoclean diction. Indeed, a close reading of *Philoctetes*, in the light of a Merleau-Pontian phenomenology of language[4] (which is, interestingly, also the Artaudian approach to language), and Butler's recent study on this subject, reveal other things: an amazing richness in representational methods and techniques for the depiction of pain, blending a chiasmic sensory and psychic action in the writing and the performance of the text. Like Artaud, Eagleton also emphasizes the fact that, if we face difficulties of representation with classical texts such as *Philoctetes*, these should be placed not with any inadequacy in the hermeneutics of pain in the verbal text but with the obscurity, in our days, of the representational art of the Greeks (Eagleton xiv).

Reverting to Scarry's remark that "Philoctetes utters a cascade of *changing* cries and shrieks that in the original Greek are accommodated by an array of formal words (some of them twelve syllables long)" (*The Body* 5)—these are selectively «αά,» «παπαί,» «απαπαί,» «φεύ,» «οίμοι,» «ατταταί» (Sophocles 424, 426, 428)—we have to agree with her that the English translation can hardly extend beyond a repetition of "ah!" (in Storr's translation rendered as "ah me!" several times and twice as "alack!" [Sophocles 425, 427, 429]). This verbal paucity, however, may be attributed—as Scarry herself partly admits (5)—to the "inflexibility" of a certain language or the "shyness" of a given culture to the recording of pain rather than to the "utter rigidity of pain itself" (5), which she ultimately chooses to emphasize.

My reading, which questions Scarry's reductive view of *Philoctetes* on the issue of pain, can be further supported by the overt sensitivity of the original Greek text and, to a lesser extent, its English translation to physical aspects of language that are located in the following: (a) the use of onomatopoetic words: all Greek exclamations of pain are formalized sounds while the English verb "spurt" in the translation can be noted for the physical motion and agency it gives to the linguistic signifier, here in collocation with blood—"the black blood spurts" (435); (b) the repeated references to the mouth and the tongue as powerful and fearful organs of speech articulation, as agents of "injurious speech" and "hate language" (in Butler's acute terminology)[5]; (c) several references to weapons (a sword, a bow, a knife, an axe), which Scarry would consider as metaphoric projections of the infliction of pain in the outer world (*The Body* 15, 17).[6] James Elkins, who focuses on cases of metamorphosis of the body in visual art, maintains that "in the absence of bodies

[. . .] we embark on a search for body metaphors," and that, on such occasions, "second seeing" plays a very important role: "Second seeing animates and directs everyday sight, and it is explicit in painting" (6, 7); (d) the strong and graphic descriptions of Philoctetes' wound and his sharp suffering, yielding occasionally to a self-reflexive narrative of pain that licenses the use of imagination (Sophocles 421)[7]—a process that Scarry would categorize as the only possible reconstitution of pain in the shape of an "artifact," calling the artists "the most authentic class of sufferers" (*The Body* 4).

Stage (d) in my analysis of the recording of physical pain in *Philoctetes* may give the impression of my convergence with Scarry's argument. On the contrary, I would like to argue that it is Scarry who, in the later stages of her book, moves from a conception of language as a pure functionary of the symbolic, forbidding the recording of the sensory experience, to a more phenomenological understanding of it, which gives it the ability to combine the material and the imaginative in the artistic (including the verbal) transcription of lived experience. Her modified position in her later collection of essays, *Resisting Representation*, proves her own discontent with her earlier writing.[8]

Sophocles proves much more flexible throughout in the practice of his linguistic craftsmanship; a true prototype of the artist as the ideal Merleau-Pontian observer of the world.[9] Stages (a), (b) and (c) of my analysis prove his constant awareness of the physicality of language, a language which, as Butler has recently theorized, is not only a system and an instrument but an agent, a speech act that not only prefigures a bodily act but is itself a bodily act (10–11), and, therefore, takes on a chiasmic, phenomenological function. Putting in doubt Scarry's statement that violence is a threat to language, Butler overturns the argument by asking the question differently: "what if language has within it its own possibilities for violence and for world-shattering?" (6). It is under a similar conviction that Sophocles consciously follows a double track in the writing of *Philoctetes*, building up a "narrative of pain" which constantly yearns for—actually reverts to—a pre-linguistic physicality. This understanding of dramatic language as performative is not very far from Artaud's own conceptualization of theater language as "half-way between gesture and thought," (89) as "ideas arrested in flight" (109).

The burgeoning physicality in the text of *Philoctetes*, both through the physical approach to language and the potential for a stage representation of pain, may prove the suitability of classical texts, especially tragedy, for the phenomenological treatment of the theatrical experience. It validates, rather than undermine, the Artaudian claim for a somatic theater—one that repeatedly underlines its reliance on chiasmic human perception and holds a true admiration for painters such as Grünewald (Artaud 87), who transcend realism and look for a more sophisticated textuality of somatic signs. Artaud is very fond of terms such as "sign," "ideogram" and "hieroglyph" (90, 94, 111) in the development of his theory, and he stresses the importance of raising "ordinary objects or even the human body [. . .] to the dignity of signs" (94). My parallel reading of Sophocles' *Philoctetes* and Artaud's Theater of Cruelty suggests that there is no conceptual incongruity between the two and that the latter's problematic rejection of the classical dramatic masters and masterpieces (Greek and Renaissance alike) was rather due to his solipsistic desire (like that of his ardent commentator Derrida) to replace one theology with another: in his case, the director's over the playwright's. On this particular issue, Richard Hornby, in his revealing article "Forgetting the Text: Derrida and the 'Liberation' of the Actor," emphatically counters the Artaudian/Derridean dictatorship/tyranny of the text with his own pertinent question: who will liberate the actor from the tyranny of anti-textual theorists and directors (356–57)!

The recurrent slippage of meaning that I have noted so far in and about Artaud's theory on the theater inevitably brings into the debate the phenomenon of the "new brutalism" of the British stage of the 1990s. The intense experimentation of this type of theater (also called "in-yer-face theater") with the limits of the realistic exposure of the (self-)victimized body has ultimately given us only naïve and crude aspects of Artaudian cruelty, reverting to what Artaud denounced and condemned in his own theory as "perverse" and "sensational" strategies (114), expressly cautioning against the pitfalls of "sadism" or "bloodshed" or "bodily laceration" or the "gratuitous pursuit of physical suffering" or the focus on "tortured victims" (102). It was only to be expected that such theater, which invests in the graphicness of experience, would soon exhaust itself. Its present decline, as also attested in the recent criticism of the British stage,[10] suggests that the aesthetic of explicit stage violence and brutality has indeed been very shallow, unimaginative and ephemeral. Sarah Kane herself, after the reception shock of *Blasted* (1995),[11] sought more sophisticated, though still sensory, modes of depiction of physical cruelty and suffering in *Cleansed* (1998) and proceeded to abstract and poetic, verbal accounts in *Crave* (1998) and *4.48 Psychosis* (2000). Harold Pinter, of the older generation of British dramatists, has always been a master of the subtextual physicality and brutality of language, exploring "injurious speech"—as Judith Butler would put it. Patrick Marber's *Closer* (1997), in the late 1990s, has added another major contemporary voice of "words that wound." Howard Barker has created a contemporary tragic idiom of unredeemed cruelty, mediated equally through expressionistic images and poetic words, working in parallel as relentless weapons for the infliction of pain.[12]

But, perhaps, the most amazing, recent demonstration of the dramatic language's performativity, its extraordinary capacity to communicate unspeakable or extreme sensations of both physical and mental pain, is Neil LaBute's *The Shape of Things* (2001). With the exception of some crude words used, the text is written in an expressly demure and civilized style, concerning both the linguistic and the performative aspects of the play. It gives out a peculiar sense of cautious decency and self-censorship, complying to the rules of a neo-conservative American society where "p.d.a." (public display of affection) is considered an undesirable offense. Yet, beneath its ironically antiseptic surface cleanliness, the play speaks of the physical and mental atrocities worked upon the body and personality of a naïve young man by a ruthless female art student. The piece closes with a bursting tirade on cruelty and art in its current crude manifestations in the world of image and performance:

> ADAM: [. . .] you know, when picasso took a shit, he didn't call it a "sculpture." He knew the difference. That's what made him picasso. And if I'm wrong about that, I mean, if I totally miss the point here and somehow puking up your own little shitty neuroses all over people's laps *is* actually art then you oughta at least realize there's a price to it all . . . you know? Somebody pays for your two minutes on cnn. Someone always pays for people like you. And if you don't get that, if you can't see at least *that* much . . . then you're about two inches away from using babies to make lamp shades and calling it "furniture." (beat) look, i know they call it the "art scene," but that's not all it should make. a scene. it should be more than that. anybody can be provocative or shocking. Stand up in class, or at the mall, wherever, and take a piss, paint yourself blue and run naked through a church screaming out the names of people you've slept with. Is that art, or did you just forget to take your ritalin? there's gotta be a line. for art to exist, there has to be a line out there somewhere. A line between really saying something and just . . . needing attention [. . .]. (132–33)

This vivid reaction to the politics and aesthetics of an explicit exposure of the body in pain from within the ranks of theater practitioners themselves highlights the necessity for a frequent reassessment of artistic mythologies and trends. Equally necessary is a revisioning of parallel theoretical formations, which wane not only because of sudden sociopolitical and ideological shifts, but through layers of distortions effected by the incessant applications, readings, commentaries and extensions of these theories, geared by personal or collective intent.

It is under this exigency that I suggest a post-millennial repositioning of Artaud, for new departures, which also restore to us our displaced Western heritage. These alert us to the incessant production of "new" lesser or greater narratives, which pose as liberating forces and claim originality while cunningly camouflaging self-interests and a good stock knowledge of the modes of power acquisition and the rhetoric of the vilification and extinction of some kind of "other." Here, the new trendy discourse of the "post-human age" and its concomitant "post-dramatic theater" pose the greatest threat as they definitely announce the death of the theater, the art of life par excellence, and legitimize its total replacement by the products of cybernetic and digital technology. It is at this conspiratorial junction between contemporary theory and technology for the murder of a corporeal theater striving in sweat and articulation, that the recuperation and reconstitution of Artaud's double-faced Theater of Cruelty is of the most crucial importance. It poses a philosophy of cruelty and a metaphysics of *mise-en-scène* whose very conflicting polarity between physicality and abstraction, a reality which is also a simulacrum of itself, sustains the durability of the most mortal of the arts. Artaud never forgave the theater its mortality nor language its estrangement from the natural world of things.[13] But, his wish to destroy the theater was as ardent as his desire to breathe new life to it and his mistrust of language as an adequate tool for the recording of painful experience was as strong as his impulse to employ it for a detailed account of his extreme life suffering.[14] Through his despairing frustration with various modes of artistic expression, he became the theater's most devoted visionary and language's most frantic practitioner for the capacity of both to create in art the ambiguous cruelty and pain of being alive. His split artistic experience of complete devotion and renunciation turns him into an epitome of the liminality of theater, an art torn between gesture and thought, the seen and the unseen, the real and the unreal, an art always at the vanishing point. Today, under the threat of a total technological takeover, the condition of the "vanishing point" becomes for the theater more than an issue for philosophical contemplation; it takes on the dimensions of factual material and historical disappearance. The agonizing figure of Artaud, accordingly, grows more emblematic and his contradictory theory of the word swallowed by the flesh, but also, paradoxically, of the flesh tending to the signification of textuality can be reinstalled as the only appropriate saving force of a theater by and for living, suffering humans—not amnesiac cyborgs or iconic simulations. When Baudrillard thinks he derides and dismisses Artaud by claiming that "we can think of the total theatre of Artaud *only with black humour*, his Theatre of Cruelty, of which this spatio-dynamic is only *an abject caricature*" (141–42, emphasis added), he actually highlights Artaud's proximity to the abject, due to the duality of his double vision. In the shadows and mirrors of his theater, Artaud has already prefigured post-Artaudian practices, as, for instance, the volatility of the real that Baudrillard emphasizes as one of the key practices of the image/media culture (141). Artaud is also already "after-Artaud" and, in this capacity, he survives both exhaustion and oblivion in the domain of the new millennium theater practice.

Notes

1. See Aleks Sierz's book under this title. Sierz also wrote a laudatory review of McDonagh's play, pointing out its "in-yer-face scenes" and its power to offend. Other critics, however, were much more sceptical about the effectiveness of his "shock tactics" (Bassett). The play generally received mixed reviews.

2. James Elkins remarks that Matthias Grünewald "has an attachment to the skin that may be unparalleled in visual art before modernism and outside dermatology" (67).
3. Elaine Scarry herself appears far less categorical concerning the language's susceptibility to materiality in her later book *Resisting Representation*, where, she concedes, however metaphysically, that "language sometimes seems full of the weight of the world" (3).
4. Merleau-Ponty was deeply fascinated by the problem of language and he embarked on an extensive study of it, which, however, was never completed. See especially *Signs* and *Consciousness and the Acquisition of Language*.
5. As the most explicit references to the destructive power of language not only as linguistic formation but also as physical utterance produced by the organs of speech, I would mention the following: «την γλώσσαν, ουχί τάργα, πάνθ' ηγουμένην» ("mightier than deeds of puissance is the tongue," 374–75), «αθυρόστομος αχώ» ("echo [. . .] with babbling tongue," 382–83), «θρασυστόμων» ("blustering boasts," 396–97) and «γλώσση δε δεινού και σοφού» ("shrewd and glib of tongue," 400–01). One should note that Sophocles' Greek poetic diction is much more powerful in the construction of images directly taken from the physical world, whereas the English translation often prefers a more oblique or periphrastic language, which weakens the physical effects. In *Resisting Representation*, Scarry stresses the idea of "volition in the motion of speech" and uses the term "rigorous speech" which can be considered as an equivalent to Butler's notion of linguistic agency (9, 10).
6. As an example of the function of the weapon as a sign of pain, Scarry actually brings in Philoctetes' bow in the Sophoclean play (*The Body* 17).
7. The chorus explains that Philoctetes' ill fate is familiar to them through narrative, not direct eye-witnessing: «λόγω μεν εξήκουσ', όπωπα δ' ου μάλα» ("I saw him not, yet fame affirms the tale," 420–21).
8. Like Butler, whom I mention later, Elkins also notes the limitations of Scarry's analysis in *The Body in Pain* (7).
9. This idea is beautifully expounded in Merleau-Ponty's extended essay "Eye and Mind." See especially his revealing descriptions about the state of intersubjective relationship between the painter and the world: "The painter, whatever he is, *while he is painting* practices a magical theory of vision. He is obliged to admit that objects before him pass into him or else that [. . .] the mind goes out through the eyes to wander among objects; for the painter never ceases adjusting his clairvoyance to them" (166). He, then, goes on to explain further that: "Inevitably the roles between him [i.e., the painter] and the visible are reversed. That is why so many painters have said that things look at them. [. . .] I think that the painter must be penetrated by the universe and not want to penetrate it" (167).
10. See, for instance, Howard Barker, Mary Luckhurst and Merle Tönnies. In a more general critique of the overexposure of the literal body, Johannes Birringer appears sceptical about both the intentions and the results of such practices. See Ch. 11, "The Postmodern Body in Performance," in *Theatre, Theory, Postmodernism*.
11. Critic Tom Morris of *The Guardian* makes a clinical listing of all brutalities reenacted in *Blasted:* "defecation, urination, masturbation, fellatio, sodomy, eye-chewing, sleep-rape and cannibalism" (4).
12. Scarry makes the interesting statement that the same object, the knife, for instance, can function both as a weapon that can inflict pain and as an artistic tool that can

assist in its representation. In a similar vein, Susan Sontag considers that in Artaud's "paroxysmic" verbal accounts of his acute suffering "words become knives" (xxiii).

13. Derrida makes a most dramatic presentation of Artaud's love-hate relationship to the theater:

> "That he [i.e., Artaud] thereby kept himself at the limit of theatrical possibility, and that he simultaneously wanted to produce and to annihilate the stage, is what he knew in the most extreme way. December 1946:
>
>> And now I am going to say something which, perhaps,
>> Is going to stupefy many people.
>> I am the enemy
>> Of theatre.
>> I have always been.
>> As much as I love the theatre,
>> I am, for this very reason, equally its enemy.
>
> We see him immediately afterward; he cannot resign himself to theater as repetition, and cannot renounce theater as nonrepetition:
>
>> The theatre is a passionate overflowing
>> a frightful transfer of forces
>>> from body
>>> to body
>> This transfer cannot be produced twice." (249–50)

14. In her introduction to Artaud's selected writings, Susan Sontag maintains that "nowhere in the entire history of writing in the first person is there as tireless and detailed a record of the microstructure of mental pain" as in Artaud's accounts, which offer a real "phenomenology of suffering" (xx, xxi).

Works Cited

Artaud, Antonin. *The Theater and Its Double.* New York: Grove, 1958.
Barker, Howard. "The Ethics of Relevance and the Triumph of the Literal." *Contemporary Drama in English* 9 (2002): 85–90.
Bassett, Kate. Rev. of *The Lieutenant of Inishmore. Theatre Record* 1–28 Jan. 2002: 9.
Baudrillard, Jean. *Simulations.* New York: Semiotext(e), 1983.
Birringer, Johannes. *Theatre, Theory, Postmodernism.* Bloomington, IN: Indiana UP, 1991.
Butler, Judith. *Excitable Speech: A Politics of the Performative.* New York and London: Routledge, 1997.
Derrida, Jacques. "The Theater of Cruelty and the Closure of Representation." *Writing and Difference.* Chicago: The U of Chicago P: 1978. 232–50.
Eagleton, Terry. *Sweet Violence: The Idea of the Tragic.* Oxford: Blackwell, 2003.
Elkins, James. *Pictures of the Body: Pain and Metamorphosis.* Stanford, CA: Stanford UP, 1999.

Hornby, Richard. "Forgetting the Text: Derrida and the Liberation of the Actor." *New Theatre Quarterly* 18.4 (2002): 355–58.
Kane, Sarah. *Blasted: Blasted and Phaedra's Love*. London: Methuen, 1996.
——. *Cleansed*. London: Methuen, 1998.
——. *Crave*. London: Methuen, 1998.
——. *4.48 Psychosis*. London: Methuen, 2000.
LaBute, Neil. *The Shape of Things*. London: Faber, 2001.
Lehmann, Hans-Thies. *Postdramatisches Theater*. Frankfurt: Verlag der Autoren, 1999. Trans. into English by Karen Juers-Munby as *Postdramatic Theatre*. London: Routledge, 2006.
Luckhurst, Mary. "Contemporary English Theatre: Why Realism?" *Contemporary Drama in English* 9 (2002): 73–84.
Marber, Patrick. *Closer*. London: Methuen, 1997.
McDonagh, Martin. *The Lieutenant of Inishmore*. London: Methuen, 2001.
Merleau-Ponty, Maurice. *Consciousness and the Acquisition of Language*. Evanston: Northwestern UP, 1973.
——. "Eye and Mind." *The Primacy of Perception*. Evanston, IL: Northwestern UP, 1964. 159–90.
——. *Signs*. Evanston, IL: Northwestern UP, 1964.
Morris, Tom. "Foul Deeds, Fair Play." *The Guardian*. 25 Jan. 1995: 4.
Scarry, Elaine. *The Body in Pain: The Making and Unmaking of the World*. New York and Oxford: Oxford UP, 1985.
——. *Resisting Representation*. New York: Oxford UP, 1994.
Sierz, Aleks. *In-Yer-Face Theatre: British Drama Today*. London: Faber, 2000.
——. Rev. of *The Lieutenant of Inishmore*. *Theatre Record* 1–28 Jan. 2002: 7.
Sontag, Susan, ed. *Antonin Artaud: Selected Writings*. Berkeley and Los Angeles: U of California P, 1988.
Sophocles. *Philoctetes*. *Ajax, Trachiniae, Philoctetes*. Trans. F. Storr. London: Heinemann and Cambridge, MA: Harvard UP, 1967. 361–493.
Time Magazine 2 Sept. 2002: 39.
Tönnies, Merle. "Sensationalist Theatre of Cruelty in 1990s Britain, Its 1960s Forebears and the Beginning of the 21st Century." *Contemporary Drama in English* 9 (2002): 57–71.

5. The "Bacchanalian" Body in Theodoros Terzopoulos' Theater: A Case of Interculturalism

Pinelopi Hatzidimitriou

The artist's body and its performance are socially determined, firstly inscribed by the Logos of the power nexus (through medicine, science, law, hygiene, fashion, advertising, gymnastics, etc.) and, secondly, by the training and the performance codes. For, to employ Eugenio Barba's words, theater training "colonizes" the body "imposing a new form of culture upon it from the outset" (qtd. in Ley 224) and acting becomes a practice that inscribes itself on the body, a "technology" in Foucault's sense as a means through which humans acquire knowledge about themselves (Zarrilli 72).

The above are valid for Theodoros Terzopoulos' theater and training system as well. For, as with any training system, his cannot be viewed in isolation from the specific milieu in which it makes its appearance, nor can we neglect the kind of performance for which it prepares the performer. When the Greek director created his group *Attis* to pursue an international and intercultural career in 1985, he decided to focus on ancient Greek tragedy and set the exploration of an alternative staging of the tragic genre as his main ambition. He also acknowledged that the technologization of everyday life in the late twentieth century has created "bodies distanced in images, viewed as resources, lived as things to be seen, managed and mastered" (Jones 35). The result is a dematerialized body, a body that has lost contact with its natural expressive abilities. Reacting to this (post)modern condition, Terzopoulos accords with Tadashi Suzuki and, more generally, with the avant-garde trends of the 1960s and onwards,[1] in his attempt to create a system that will "liberate" the body from the pressures that Western culture exercises on it. What the Greek director strives for is to grant the (post)modern dematerialized and technologized bodies their lost weighty (corpo)reality. The underlying thesis is that the artist's body is not only socially determined, but also socially determining "as the site of both resistance and power," as "a battlefield where 'mechanisms of power' meet 'techniques of resistance'" (Feher, qtd. in Jones 22).

"Deconstructing" the Body: "Bacchanalian" Bodies in Visceral Narratives

With the above in mind, Terzopoulos claims that *mania* lies at the heart of tragedy and formulates a method of training and acting that is founded on the concept of the "bacchanalian" body, the body in ecstasy (*baccheuomeno soma*). If mania is the cornerstone of tragedy, according to his vision, then this is because it implies "wild excitement," "split," "transgression of the everyday limits" and "expansion of the energy axes" of the human body (Τερζόπουλος [Terzopoulos] Προσωπική συνέντευξη, 20 July 2002).[2]

With such a thesis, Terzopoulos immediately sets himself apart from the logocentricity of the Occidental theater, which privileges and sanctifies the text, to foreground a "sensory theatre" (Terzopoulos, *Theodoros Terzopoulos and the Attis Theatre* 88). Consequently, he rejects the prevalent Greek scriptocentric staging of tragedy, as this was fashioned by the Neoclassicism of Central Europe. Tragedy is no longer "a sublime poetic work containing the culmination of classical ideals and offering, through its various interpretations, the confirmation of European humanistic values" (Varopoulou 10). On the contrary, Terzopoulos believes in the physicality of ancient Greek thought and treats tragedy as a dramaturgy that reveals intellectually but primarily physically "the human destiny in its catholic reality" (De Romilly 66). It is a narrative of the human's tragic agony as this stems from the visceral. To serve this vision, the director accords with theater people such as Antonin Artaud, Jerzy Grotowski, and Tadashi Suzuki, who base their practice on the conviction that, despite the social and ideological codes written on the body and beneath this social coating, there is an "essential" body. It is a universal and archetypal body that escapes all social particularities. Following the Grotowskian paradigm of the "holy actor" and the principle of "necessity" in Artaud's Theater of Cruelty, Terzopoulos formulates a system of training the objective of which is to lead the performer's body to manic transgression.

Still, how is ecstasy defined? The initial literal meaning of the ancient Greek word as the shift from a familiar position to displacement (*ek-stasis*) is accompanied by the metaphorical sense of mental confusion and madness, ultimately denoting manic ecstasy. As early as in Homer, Dionysus was called "enraged" (*mainomenos*), the one who is himself insane or makes others insane (*Iliad* 6.132), while Plato, in *Phaedrus* distinguishes between creative, divine mania and catastrophic, human mania. Creative is the mania of the philosopher, of the artist, the Muses' mania, the erotic mania inspired by Aphrodite and Eros, Apollo's prophetic and Dionysus' ritualistic mania (McDonald, "The Madness" 11 and Dodds 59).

Terzopoulos had as a starting point a description of an ancient method of therapy practiced at the Amphiaraeio sanctuary of Asclepius in Boeotia.[3] According to this ritual, at sunset the patients to be operated on began walking naked in a circle on the humid ground. By the coming of the dawn, the participants had entered an ecstatic state and were thus prepared for their operation that morning. The Greek director distilled the importance of extreme exhaustion from this ancient therapeutic practice and thus formulated a training system. He conducted long, even twenty-four hour workshops, subverting the normal pattern of human function (day-action, night-rest), and exposed his performers to severe weather conditions. The result was physical exhaustion accompanied by a release of mental and psychic tension. Apparently, Terzopoulos draws on a pool of traditional techniques of ecstatic transcendence and more specifically those of pain, motion, and self-concentration. This is why he enriched his research into bacchic mania and the "bacchanalian" body studying Dionysian rituals, such as the fire-walking ceremonies (*Anastenaria*), which have survived until today in the northern part of Greece. He was also inspired by the post-Civil War period in Greek history (the 1950s and 60s) and the ritualistic festivities that the laymen of the provinces performed as a means of discharging their anguish, pain and despair. All things considered, he aimed at transforming the performing body into a bacchanalian body.

Similar experiments were conducted by the American director Richard Schechner and his *Performance Group* in the 1960s. Focusing on the relationship between theater and anthropology and searching among rituals, he organized all-night dances to prove the power of repetition and, what he calls, "accumulation" as opposed to the "climax" of an action. Groups of eight to twenty-five persons danced in a simple, counterclockwise circle from four to eight hours. Performances like the whirling dances of the dervishes or the slow movements lasting over extended periods of time in Robert Wilson's theater follow an accumulation-repetition pattern, which lifts the performers to an ecstatic trance. Schechner calls this kind of experience "total low intensity"; it is trophotropic, that is, the heart rate and the blood pressure decrease, the pupils are constricted, the electroencephalogram (EEG) is synchronized (Schechner 11–12).

Terzopoulos, in turn, calls his own biodynamic system "the method of deconstruction." In this case, the head and mostly the arms become autonomous from the rest of the body, speaking, or rather "screaming" a new "language" of their own. Simultaneously, what is weakened is the controlling power of the ego, allowing the id of each performer to come to the surface.

Thus, the body is ready and free to re-experience and re-enact personal subconscious traumas, fears, and desires. At the same time, it becomes the proper medium for the expression of the collective unconscious since for the director all knowledge of the world resides in our bodies (McDonald, *Αρχαίος Ήλιος* 206). It is the body that carries ancient memories deep inside. Jungian echoes are clearly evident here. Nonetheless, more crucial is how the above belief affects the director's approach to tragedy. He emphasizes: "[t]he only and most accurate instrument we have for myth is memory. Body and voice are the common place of memory, in the most drastic way, in the sense that they live here today" (Terzopoulos, *Theatre Olympics: Crossing Milennia* 5). Consequently, he argues that "the necessity of myth is not to make a story but to remake a memory" (5). This is precisely the point that the German playwright and director Heiner Müller underlines when he writes that

> In Terzopoulos' theatre, myth is not a fairytale, it is a condensed experience; the process of rehearsal is not the performance of a dramatic concept, it is an adventure on a journey to the landscape of memory, a search for the lost keys of unity between body and speech, the word as natural unity. (qtd. in Terzopoulos, *Theodoros Terzopoulos and the Attis Theatre* 35)

In this training system, body and voice are treated in unison, with the performer's physiological resonators being related to the nuclear rhythms of the ancient Greek texts. Physicalization of rhythm results when "the word follows the rhythmic pattern of the body, or the body follows the rhythmic pattern of the word" (Τερζόπουλος [Terzopoulos] 2 May 2003). The "kamaton t'eukamaton" choral part from the *Bacchae*[4] is illustrative of the vocal component of Terzopoulos' method. In this ancient Greek excerpt, Terzopoulos identifies a rhythmic unit similar to the rhythm of the pyrrhic dance of the people of Pontus (the ancient district in north-eastern Anatolia adjoining the Black Sea).

Following Peter Brook and his "study of structures of sound" of dead languages such as ancient Greek, Latin, or Avestan, Terzopoulos also searches into the sound structures of the ancient Greek texts to find what he calls "core rhythms" (*Theodoros Terzopoulos and the Attis Theatre* 55). Nevertheless, he is careful to differentiate his views from those of Brook's. According to Terzopoulos, Brook misses the crucial parameter of the performer's body memory when he [Brook] argues that the sound fabric of a dead language is an emotional code that reveals the passions that forged it and that the moment an actor speaks these syllables, he/she is lifted out of the emotional constrictions of the twentieth-century city life into an overwhelming passion previously unknown to him (Brook 130). Terzopoulos explains:

> The body cannot carry in its structure, in its gene neither the "eleleu" nor the "otototoi."[5] If you can lead the performer to a depth, for there is the split—

what I did in the past, those incredible all-night workshops [. . .]—if you initiate the performers in that split, then you need to hand them no text of a language they don' t know. You leave them that night when they have opened through deconstruction, and they will tell you a thousand "otototoi" and "otomotoi" [*sic*]. (Τερζόπουλος [Terzopoulos] 2 May 2003)

Treating each tragic word as a "trauma, a thrombus of blood" (Terzopoulos, qtd. in Stroumpos 9), Terzopoulos transforms pain into speech and speech into pain (*logos-ponos*). It is a struggling physicality that produces speech, a body that strives to speak even when it has reached an energy impasse. The tragic quality of speech is not the outcome of a "constructed" sentiment but of the violent wonder that the performer's body experiences when the air supplies are exhausted, yet the body must continue sounding. This is a panicking process that becomes a life-giving one. Here lies one of the governing principles of the system of the *Attis* theater, that of violence. Physical and ritual violence permeates its ideological core, governs the actors' training, and determines the performances. Not accidentally, the passage from rhythm to rhythm, movement to movement, gesture to gesture and sound to sound is so violently executed that the performed actions become abrupt, aggressive and cruel, escaping rationality, psychological causality and consequence (Varopoulou 10).

The results of this search into the bacchanalian body became evident for the first time in the 1986 production of the *Bacchae*, in which Terzopoulos created a performance of violent,ritualistic force. Like the anthropologist Sir James George Frazer, who proposed a three-stage scheme of human evolution (magic, religion, science) and explained myth narratives through the (vegetation) ceremonies they are assumed to have arisen from (Coupe 22–25), Terzopoulos turns to primitive ceremonies—that is, magic—to explain myth and stage tragedy. As mentioned above, he used the Greek fire-walking ritual of *Anastenaria* to explore "the possibility of antisocial body transformation" (Sampatakakis 93). More specifically, in this ritual the dancer acquires divine power to defeat pain and physical annihilation and makes pain an event to be experienced and triumphed over.[6] In the performance of *Bacchae*, contradictory gestures, relaxation, and tightening of the body members, breathing, cries, pauses, varied tempi of pronunciation did not directly serve the meaning of the text. Instead, they composed an autonomous, rhythmic system of body and vocal reactions which supplemented the meaning of the tragic text (Varopoulou 12).

Even in the mid 1980s, most Greek critics and spectators, contrary to their foreign colleagues,[7] firmly believed that such an approach to tragedy was blasphemous: "The idea of deconstructing a classic text was simply sacrilege, while an aesthetic approach evoking spontaneous, authentic, dark or monstrous components was found repulsive" (Varopoulou 9). What such verdicts failed to see is that the *Attis* theater highlights the corporeality of the (tragic) text, since the text no longer describes the body and the pain it suffers on a symbolic level. On the contrary, it becomes body itself, a *logos-ponos*. About the same year that Elaine Scarry, drawing evidence from another Greek tragedy, Sophocles' *Philoctetes,* proposed that language cannot convey pain because physical suffering destroys language, Terzopoulos explored the suffering physicality of the linguistic medium in *Bacchae* negating Scarry's thesis and confirming Elizabeth Sakellaridou's one that *logos-ponos* "reconstitute[s] faith in the physical power of words to depict the body and record pain in a mixed conceptual manner" (5).

What is more, in the view of Erika Fischer-Lichte, this performance "did in fact write theatre and cultural history" ("Transformationen" 117) because Terzopoulos forged a new relationship between theater and ritual long before theoreticians in the 1990s focused on the affinities between the two. He succeeded in putting the spectators in a liminal state and created a series of threshold experiences through artistic means. The German theater theorist, however, is undoubtedly ready to clarify the aesthetic as opposed to the ritualistic character of these experiences:

> Eventual transformations caused by them were basically reversible even if they had a long-lasting effect on one or two of the audience members. To what extent they actually changed the lives of those concerned can only be judged by those affected—however, a social acceptance of this change is not necessary. ("Transformationen" 116)

Still, Terzopoulos wholeheartedly supports the "liberating" character of his method, at least for his performers. The feeling that one's body exceeds its limits and becomes a channel of explosive energy or a site of conversion of primary materials, he claims, leads one to a physical, intellectual, and emotional catharsis. The spectators, on the other hand, intrigued by the overwhelming eruptions of energy, the shock, and the aesthetic perfection of the spectacle, are invited to undergo a personal descent into the deeper layers of their existence. In his discussion of "holy theatre," a theater that wants to communicate the intangible and universal dimensions of human existence, Philip Auslander distinguishes between "communal theatre" and "therapeutic theatre" (13). While Brook's communal theater wants to achieve emotional harmony among spectators on the grounds of a celebratory, common, human identity, Artaud's and Grotowski's therapeutic theater uncovers repressed psychic material aiming at spiritual renewal. It is the latter, psychoanalytic interpretation of catharsis that Terzopoulos embraces as well. Like Artaud, he believes that his demanding painstaking training system leads the actor to a state of emotional and physical purification and wellbeing. Contrary to Artaud, however, he claims that the actor's catharsis does not precede or automatically cause that of the spectator. The performer does not manipulate the spectator but rather suggests that a similar cathartic process of self-analysis is possible. The *Attis* theater is closer to the Grotowskian vision, since it is "concerned with the spectator who has genuine spiritual needs and who really wishes, through confrontation with the performance, to analyse himself" (Grotowski 40).

Postmodern criticism warns that despite its promising agenda, avantgardist performance theory fails to liberate the body and consequently fails to challenge social and political hegemony. On the contrary, the body is disciplined anew either by the dramatic text (as it is the case with Stanislavsky's system) or by the text of the archetypal psychic impulse (in Grotowski's method). The postmodern body is, thus, favored because it views itself as a historical and social construct, asserts its materiality, and exposes the ideological discourses and their inscriptive mechanisms (Auslander 89–97). Admittedly, Terzopoulos does not share such postmodernist worries. He cultivates and sustains the profile of a "director-guru" (to employ Bradby and Williams' term), who is in ceaseless search of the right, the authentic, the genuine and the novel. Terzopoulos himself has contributed to the construction of such a public persona as can be proved by the slight but significant revisions the original story of his life undergoes in its tellings/interviews. In 2000, for example, he emphasized the historical importance of his birthplace, describing it as a village built on the ground lying over tombs of ancient Pydna, the region where Euripides wrote *Bacchae* (20 Aug. 2000) while in 2006 he recalled that

> When we played as children we nearly always found remains of ancient vases and statues in the earth. Once I found the head of a Maenad, another time the head of a Hercules but never an entire vase or picture, just fragments. The whole of Greek mythology was lying in little bits. ("The Metaphysics of the Body" 136)

Such revisionist tellings reveal a "director-guru" and contribute to the creation of the public persona of a modernist artist with an aura. Likewise, the past, classical heritage, and tragedy are not treated as a mere bank of cultural references and styles which he recalls and recycles in a postmodern pastiche. All postmodern expectations of him acting as a *bricoleur*, one that plays around with fragments of dispersed narratives that he himself has not created, are inevitably cancelled. On the contrary, Terzopoulos proves to be a manifestation of the modernist anthropocentric paradigm of the original inventor, who treats imagination as a creative center of meaning. His imagination is not the Derridean, mass-produced postcard addressed "to whom it may concern;" it is not a signifier without reference or meaning that floats aimlessly through a communications network devoid of "destiny" or "destination," like Andy Wharhol's or Bob Wilson's are (Kearney 2–13).

Of course, the preceding reflections should take into consideration the contribution of his personal and cultural background in the modeling of his vision and aesthetics. After all, his personal course intersects with the history of modern Greece, a small country at the outermost, southeastern part of the Balkan Peninsula, marked by occupations, wars, dictatorships, and a civil war. In 1974, Greece finally exited this vicious, bloody, and bitter circle and became free and democratic at last. The nature of Greece's transition to democracy and the European Union—a gradual process of constitutional reform rather than a radical break with the past—was accompanied by a cultural reformation. The purist ideology of Greekness began to be questioned and interculturalism started to gain ground, attracting a younger generation of directors, among them Terzopoulos, who wished to confront and surpass the established theater traditions.[8] Concurrently, frontiers opened and alternative readings of ancient drama by distinguished foreign directors were frequently presented.

Although he is part of this movement, Terzopoulos has followed an idiosyncratic course. Wishing to compensate for the absence of a solid, theater tradition in his homeland, he traveled abroad to absorb the world theater tradition and the avant-garde masters. What he cannot, however, divest himself of is his personal and family background and experiences of displacement. A descendant of a leftist family of Greek refugees who came to Greece chased from Hellespont first by the Turks and then by the Russians and were later defeated in the Greek Civil War, he was brought up in the late 40s and 50s in a small agricultural village. His early years were, thus, marked by a defeated, nomadic, folk culture, yet a rich and diverse one, in which the Greek dialect of the Hellespont, for example, songs from Russia, and Turkish verses coexisted. With such a history, Terzopoulos could not adopt a postmodern philosophy and aesthetics. In a technologized, postmodern condition that questions authentic, undifferentiated subjectivity, he chooses to adopt essentialist positions regarding identity and embodiment. In opposition to amnesic cyborgs or virtual replicas, he foregrounds the archetypal, suffering body caught in ontological agony. For those who promote a rigorous critique of subjectivity, such a strategy of resistance is ineffectual. In their line of thinking, returns to unitary subject positions are either impossible to achieve or politically regressive when invoked, for they fail to confront contemporary realities, thereby postponing any genuine resistance (Causey 60–61). Terzopoulos, by contrast, is guided by the Artaudian credo that it is through the senses and an element of cruelty that metaphysics can be brought back to our spirit. Propelled on by such principles, he crosses geographies and cultures and leads his "bacchanalian" bodies in intercultural directions.

Crossing Geographies and Cultures: the "Bacchanalian" Bodies in Intercultural Directions

Placing the "bacchanalian" body at the nucleus of his system, Terzopoulos inevitably turns to other cultures in order to enrich and expand his research into ecstasy and bacchic mania. This is because ecstatic manifestations vary according to religious, cultural, historic, and other parameters with their common denominator being the transcendence of human limits (Αδραχτάς [Adrachtas] 5). His interest in other civilizations and their transcendental practices is reinforced by his desire to concentrate on myth, in general guided by the essentialist principle that

> the structural elements are the same for all peoples and the deeper we look for the ground stone of human existence, the more common roots we find. It is the ancestral tree of tradition with its roots going deep. (Terzopoulos *Theodoros Terzopoulos and the Attis Theatre* 61)

Based on this premise, he began to study the rituals of cultures outside the West, such as those of the Aborigines in Australia and the Native Indians of the Amazon basin, using the "comparative" method in his intercultural theater practice.[9] He has collected, selected, and combined elements of ritualistic practice independent of time, place, or the historical period. In this, he is in agreement with Sir James George Frazer who, according to Laurence Coupe, "believes that we can make comparisons across cultures because the primitive human urge to myth-making is essentially the same" (23). With nine Colombian actors of Native-American origin he created the performance *Dionysus* in 1998, based on the myth of the god Yurupary (the pre-Colombian equivalent of Dionysus) combined with the Euripidean *Bacchae*. With the guidance of local anthropologists, he investigated the rituals of Colombia and the Amazon basin and visited shamans to witness their shamanistic ceremonies. The director is attracted by the way another ancient civilization approaches bacchic mania. What he discovered, in this case, is that their movement patterns are of a static nature, characterized by obsessive rhythms and absolute geometry. As in the Greek *Bacchae*, here, too, he concentrated on bacchic mania and created a performance that inspires awe and fear subverting any views of tragedy as the repository of Western humanistic ideals.

Such a practice invites us to identify in the person of Terzopoulos the Greek example of directors who explore different cultures and their ritualistic traditions, thus connecting theater with anthropology.[10] As early as 1970, Peter Brook, for instance, founded his *Centre International de Recherches Théâtrales* to explore with artists from France, Mali, Japan, Great Britain, and America "a 'deeper chain of rules' separating and uniting human beings the world over, in the pursuit of a truly living theatre of international forms"

(Bradby and Williams 154). Likewise, the year that Brook created his *Conference of Birds* (1979), based on African rituals, Barba established his *International School of Theatre Anthropology* in Bonne to investigate "human beings' socio-cultural and physiological behavior in a performance situation" (Barba and Savarese, qtd. in Ley 232). He attempts a transcultural study of an extra daily use of the body and focuses on a common, universal human condition. In the same period that Terzopoulos set the principles of his group *Attis*, Grotowski directed the *Objective Drama Project* at the California-Irvine University (1983–1986) to extract some expressive codes of different, traditional cultures from their authentic environment and introduce them to performers. This project was an extension of the *Theatre of Sources* research project (1978–1982), for which Grotowski and specialists from Japan, Haiti, India, Bali, and Mexican Indians looked into the "techniques of sources," as Grotowski called practices such as yoga, voodoo, and the dervishes' whirling.

A similar spirit, engaged in a mystical search for the theater's origins and for a primordial language as we find it in Artaud (Ley 285), pervades Terzopoulos' philosophy and practice. What is more, his aesthetic exploration is enveloped with a humanistic view of the world, as he believes that all peoples are made of the same emotional material, which is still recognizable despite its different manifestations. For Terzopoulos such a practice is simultaneously artistic and political. He belongs to that intercultural trend in theater that worldwide promotes, as Fischer-Lichte remarks, intercultural exchange as a means of encouraging truly global communication through the shared experiences of similarities and differences inherent in cultures. What is resisted, at the same time, is the cultural monopoly that Americanization promotes with Coca-Cola, television, or McDonald's.[11]

It has been widely argued, however, that much contemporary European and North American theater anthropology and interculturalism are an offspring of the modernist, performance ethnography of the early twentieth century. Artaud's ethnography, the studies of anthropologists, such as Victor Turner, and theater theorists and practitioners, such as Schechner and Barba, or the experimentation of Grotowski, Brook, and Lee Breuer are considered to be voyeuristic, fetishizing, and imperialistic. They actually perpetuate the dualisms coined by anthropology in complicity with the post-1950s neo-imperialism (e.g., writing/ritual, subject/object, observer/observed, anthropologist/ primitive) and they unconsciously impose European aesthetics on the indigenous cultures thereby depriving them of their right to self-representation. The Indian, Rustom Bharucha, for example, warns us about the inability of the weak countries to negotiate, assert their rights and, thus, preserve their difference. In light of the contradictions of a postcolonial history, Bharucha notes interculturalism is not a mere issue, but a "burning reality" (qtd. in Ley 281). It can be liberating, but it can also be a continuation of colonialism, a harsher exploitation of cultures like those of the Third World where intercultural exchanges were not a matter of choice but of imposition.[12]

Similarly, discussing the current theater and dramaturgical trends in Latin American countries, Diana Taylor reminds us that the indigenous culture is the outcome of the clash of the native peoples of this continent with their conquerors. Thus, any attempts at returning to and representing a somewhat pure, pre-Colombian, ritualistic performance naively and clumsily erase five hundred years of history (64–65). The complex history of cultural change, to put it differently, is reduced to an inaccurate folkloric myth and selectively privileges tribal practices as original and without history. For others, practitioners' claims for a moral political model of theater that promotes vital cultural exchange and universality are pretentiously egalitarian. Such cultural borrowings that take no consideration of the cultural context result in representations that are Orientalist and inauthentic (Stone Peters 203).

In light of such critiques, we are aware that the moment we classify Terzopoulos in this intercultural field of theater anthropology, we expose him to possible objections over his claims for universality and the political effect of his practice on the collaborating cultures. Yet, all documentation by both collaborators of *Attis* worldwide and theoreticians seems to prove quite the opposite, asserting in one way or another Julie Stone Peters' general thesis that the invocation of global humanism is not necessarily complicit with an overwhelming hegemonic order and that

> The critique of productions with universalist overtones fails to acknowledge that communication across distances relies on a recognition not only of differences but also of sameness. Indeed, what is marked as the same is inevitably also different or the marking of sameness would have no meaning. (207)

On the contrary, an insistence on authenticity and orthodoxy can be as threatening as Orientalism, for it implies stereotyping and is akin to the concept of purist, cultural self-identity and consequently nationalist ideologies. After all, Stone Peters continues, poststructuralists suggest that concepts of identity such as nation, ethnic group, and national culture are no longer relevant in a transnational, migratory and diasporic, world culture but, in the words of Julie Rivkin and Michael Ryan,

> They are imaginary constructs which displace displacement by substituting for the history of permanent migratory dislocation an ontologizing image of home or homeland, a proper place where a spuriously pure ethnos can authenticate itself. (853–54)

As has already been noted, Terzopoulos turns to ritualistic practices as well as Asian theater forms in his attempt to avoid the logocentric, Western, theater tradition, to disregard realistic style and create a theater that incorporates the sacred, the formal, and the ritualistic. He becomes part of a rich tradition in the West that "flirts" with the East in an attempt to reconsider and enrich the art of theater and the performer and to elaborate on his "bacchanalian" bodies. After all, we cannot remain indifferent to Stone Peters' speculation that even if practitioners such as Brook or Barba have inherited practices that their modernist predecessors inherited from colonial missionaries, these may be transformed into a partially postcolonial, migratory, and diasporic world. This seems to be even more important in the case of Terzopoulos, who has no Anglo-Saxon past but is a descendant of a migratory nomadic culture, an agent of a currently small country (despite its celebrated ancient past), caught between the East and the West. In any case, through the exploration of political and cultural histories, such as the Greek Civil War and *Anastenaria*, Terzopoulos has managed to give voice to "the otherness within Greek historicity," to dig out "the most violated bodies of historicity," disturbing thus "the historic harmony of *Sprechchor*, or the splendor of a frozen Greek civilization" (Sampatakakis 100).[13]

Terzopoulos tries to ensure equality in his intercultural collaborations, avoiding any simplistic, stereotypical imitation of non-Western, cultural forms, working instead on what Schechner calls "the deep structural level" as opposed to "the imitative level." Similarly, he considers Schechner's "barter" to be an exchange in which both parties take part and he supports the invitation of foreign artists to the West ("modern to modern") in the same way that he is invited to the East to stage ancient Greek tragedy (Pavis 41–50).

For, apart from his primary role as theater director, Terzopoulos has held major directing posts as founding member of the International Institute of Mediterranean Theater and president of its division in Greece, chairman of the International Committee of the Theater Olympics, artistic director of the first Theater Olympics at Delphi and chairman of the second ones held in Moscow. From these strategic positions, in which he can join forces with distinguished theater personalities, he has tried to promote alternative readings of classical texts. A telling example is the intercultural project *Mania Thebaia: The Theban Cycle* (2001), for which Terzopoulos directed a third version of *Bacchae* for the *Düsseldorf Schauspielhaus*. He was one of the four directors of different cultural backgrounds—the others being Tadashi Suzuki, the Russian Valery Fokin, and the German Anna Badora—who met in a common space designed by the artist Jannis Kounellis.[14] At the same time, he has encouraged young directors such as the Turkish Sahika Tekand, the Russian Nikolai Roschin, and the Colombian Alejandro Rodriguez to search anew into the tragic genre, borrowing from the *Attis* system all that is valuable to them.

The twofold character of the Greek director's activities, which combines artistic work with cultural politics, is not an oxymoron as it is a common course of action in theater nowadays, a result of the postmodern condition.

Examining the current experimental theater in America, Bonnie Marranca concludes that we can no longer talk of an American avant-garde, for despite its anti-commercial and unconventional beginnings, it has formed very commercial alliances (177). On the other hand, for Johannes Birringer, the popularity of the avant-garde theater blurs all distinctions between the aesthetic and the institutional (the latter including sponsoring, production, publicity, promotion) (182). Birringer implies what postmodern criticism points out as the loss of critical distance between culture and theory. For Fredric Jameson, for example, criticism and utopian expectations were possible in modernist times as culture and socio-economic life were clearly distinguished (Connor 27–64). The examples, after all, of the historical avant-garde and the "liberating" generation of the 1960s have shown that, in both cases, the system managed to reassert its omnipotence not by violent means but by either commercializing or marginalizing all artistic "heresies" (Πατσαλίδης [Patsalides] 57–76, 255).

In conclusion, for the past twenty years Theodoros Terzopoulos and his "bacchanalian" bodies have moved in both intracultural and intercultural directions. Regardless of what theoretical controversies these bodies may cause, it is still true that he is the only Greek theater director nowadays whose work has received worldwide appreciation, especially in the field of tragedy— one who has used his art as a means of reconsidering and subverting stereotypes of "Greekness," as a way of promoting collaboration and exchange among cultures. His insistence on an "essential," archetypal body is not nostalgic but one of the many possible ways through which art struggles to restore the lost, weighty (corpo)reality of the (post)modern, dematerialized and technologized bodies. After all, as he comments, "theatre is diverse, if you have the courage to live it" ("The Metaphysics of the Body" 171).

Notes

1. Robert Wilson, for example, "liberated" the body from meaning, cancelling its perception as a sign. See Fischer-Lichte *The Show and the Gaze of Theatre* 25–40.
2. Where published translations in English have been unavailable, the Greek citations have been translated by the author herself.
3. For the sanctuaries and the therapeutic centres in antiquity, see Ferguson 88–102.
4. This excerpt is from the first choral part of Euripides' *Bacchae*: "κάματόν τ' ευκάματον, Βάκχιον ευαζομένα" (*Βάκχαι* 67).
5. These are two fragments from Aeschylus' *Prometheus Bound* (889) and Euripides *Hercules Enraged* (875).
6. For more on the subject, see Sampatakakis 92–94.
7. After its premiere at the Ancient Stadium of Delphi, in Greece, and for the following four years, *Bacchae* was presented abroad, in Europe, Japan, the USA, and Australia. Audiences and critics there welcomed this groundbreaking interpretation of tragedy. Helen Thomson, in *The Australian* (Melbourne), comments that "[w]hat is unmistakably conveyed by this remarkable company is an incredibly powerful,

emotional effect which accurately reproduces the play's message [. . .]" while the arts critic Anne Marie Welsh, in her review for *The San Diego Union,* describes "Terzopoulos' vision" as "steady, clear and pure," meriting his movement language for being "as clear as speech and strikingly original." For more, also see reviews by Radic, Vojtko, Pilar, and Schumacher.
8. The particularities of Greece's historical course have not left its theater unaffected either. Living under the Ottoman occupation for nearly 400 years (1453–1832), the country was not able to follow the decisive changes that took place in the rest of Europe. Only in the eighteenth century did the Greek Enlightenment launch an intellectual renaissance and, tried to give the theater, among other arts, the significance it already held in Europe. However, as late as the 1930s, the director was accepted as the third in the theater hierarchy, coming after the dramaturge and the actor. Similarly, the issue of the revival of ancient Greek drama has become central and attracted the attention of major Greek directors such as Alexis Minotis at the National Theater, Demetris Rondiris and Karolos Koun. While the first two followed the principles of German, neoclassical idealism and Max Reinhardt, the third belongs to the celebrated generation of the 1930s, which stressed the importance of folk culture and Byzantine art and supported the blending of tradition and modernism at a historical moment that required the stabilization and re-invigoration of a national identity traumatized by the 1922 disaster in Anatolia.
9. In Latin America, and more specifically in Colombia, he has had the opportunity to study the indigenous manifestations of ecstasy and, thus, enrich his research. Still, he has not restricted himself to these traditions. He has equally worked with the Russians, especially with the famous Russian actress Alla Demidova in productions such as Müller's *Medea Material, Quartet,* etc.; with the Turks; with actors from the island of Sardinia (*Paska Devadis*); and others. He has also conducted numerous workshops all over the world, thus coming into contact with performers from Europe, Australia, Latin America, the USA and Japan.
10. For a thorough presentation and analysis of the theater's relation to the social sciences, particularly anthropology and sociology, see Carlson 13–33.
11. See Fischer-Lichte, "Interculturalism" 27–40.
12. In India and Africa, for example, the Western theater was imported as a model to be imitated and was in fact a colonialist tool for the manipulation of the native consciousness. See Fischer-Lichte, "Interculturalism" 133–46.
13. Likewise, Hans-Thies Lehmann emphasizes that the director touched upon the old ideological trauma of the perception of the "Greek" in Germany, as this was shaped by German Classicism, the conservative quarters, and even fascism (181).
14. In the German production of *Bacchae,* young students of the dance school of Pina Bausch were employed for the chorus of the Bacchantes, whereas Dionysus was performed by a young German of Turkish origin (Fatich Kevicoglou).

Works Cited

Αδραχτάς, Βασίλης, επιμ. "Έκσταση: Ο Δρόμος του Μύστη." *Ελευθεροτυπία-Αφιέρωμα* 131 (9 Οκτωβρίου 2001). [Adrachtas, Vassilis, ed. "Ecstasy: The Mystic's Passage." *Eleftherotypia-Tribute* 131 (Athens, Greece) 9 Oct. 2001].
Αισχύλος. *Πορμηθεύς Δεσμώτης.* Μτφρ. Τάσος Ρούσσος. Αθήνα: Κάκτος, 1992. [Aeschylus.

Prometheus Bound. Trans. Tasos Roussos. Athens: Kaktos, 1992].
Artaud, Antonin. *The Theater and its Double*. Trans. Mary Caroline Richards. New York: Grove, 1958.
Auslander, Philip. *From Acting to Performance: Essays in Modernism and Postmodernism*. London and New York: Routledge, 1997.
Barba, Eugenio, and Nicola Savarese. *A Dictionary of Theatre Anthropology: The Secret Art of the Performer*. London and New York: Routledge, 1991.
Birringer, Johannes. *Theatre, Theory and Postmodernism*. Bloomington: Indiana UP, 1993.
Bradby, David and David Williams. *Director's Theatre*. London: Macmillan, 1988.
Brook, Peter. *The Shifting Point: Forty Years of Theatrical Exploration 1946–1987*. London: Methuen, 1988.
Carlson, Marvin. *Performance: A Critical Introduction*. London and New York: Routledge, 1996.
Causey, Matthew. "The Aesthetics of Disappearance and the Politics of Visibility in the Performance of Technology." *Gramma* 10 (2002): 59–71.
Connor, Steven. *Postmodern Culture: An Introduction to Theories of the Contemporary*. Oxford: Blackwell, 1989.
Coupe, Laurence. *Myth*. London and New York: Routledge, 1997.
De Romilly, Jacqueline. Η Ελληνική Τραγωδία στο Πέρασμα του Χρόνου. 1995. Μτφρ. Αθηνά-Μπάμπη Αθανασίου και Κατερίνα Μηλιαρέση. Αθήνα: Το Άστυ, 1996. [De Romilly, Jacqueline. *Ancient Greek Tragedy in the Course of Time*. Trans. Athena-Mpampi Athanasiou and Katerina Miliaresi. Athens: To Asti, 1996].
Dodds, E.R. Οι Έλληνες και το Παράλογο. Μτφ. Γιώργης Γιατρομανωλάκης. 2η έκδοση. Αθήνα: Ινστιτούτο του Βιβλίου—Α. Καρδαμίτσα, 1996. [Dodds, E.R. *The Greeks and the Irrational*. Trans. Giorgis Giatriomanolakis. 2nd ed. Athens: Institute of Book—A. Kardamitsa, 1996].
Euripides. *Three Plays of Euripides: Alcestis, Medea, The Bacchae*. Trans. Paul Roche. New York and London: Norton, 1974.
Ευριπίδης. *Βάκχαι*. Μτφρ. Γιώργος Γιάνναρης. Αθήνα: Κάκτος, 1993. [Euripides. *Bacchae*. Trans. Giorgos Giannaris. Athens: Kaktos, 1993].
———. *Ηρακλής Μαινώμενος*. Μτφρ. Τάσος Ρούσσος. Αθήνα: Κάκτος, 1992. [Euripides. *Hercules Enraged*. Trans. Tasos Roussos. Athens: Kaktos, 1992].
Ferguson, John. *Among the Gods: An Archaeological Exploration of Ancient Greek Religion*. London and New York: Routledge, 1989.
Fischer-Lichte, Erica. "Interculturalism in Contemporary Theatre." *The Intercultural Performance Reader*. Ed. Patrice Pavis. London and New York: Routledge, 1996. 27–40.
———. *The Show and the Gaze of Theater: A European Perspective*. Iowa City: U of Iowa P, 1997.
———. "Transformationen—Theatralität und Ritualität in den Bakchen/ Transformations—Theatre and Ritual in the Bacchae." *Reise mit Dionysus: Das Theater des Theodoros Terzopoulos/ Journey with Dionysos: The Theatre of Theodoros Terzopoulos*. Ed. Frank M. Raddatz. Germany: Theater der Zeit, 2006. 104–17.
Grotowski, Jerzy. *Towards a Poor Theatre*. 1968. London: Methuen, 1975.
Homer. *The Iliad*. Trans. E.V. Rieu. Harmondsworth: Penguin Books, 2003.
Jones, Amelia. "Survey." *The Artist's Body: Themes and Movements*. Ed. Amelia Jones and Tracey Warr. London and New York: Phaidon, 2000. 16–47.

Kearney, Richard. *The Wake of Imagination: Toward a Postmodern Culture.* Minneapolis: U of Minnesota P, 1988.
Lehmann, Hans-Thies. "Terzopoulos' Müller—Eine Skizze/Terzopoulos' Müller—A Sketch." *Reise mit Dionysus: Das Theater des Theodoros Terzopoulos/Journey with Dionysos: The Theater of Theodoros Terzopoulos.* Ed. Frank M. Raddatz. Germany: Theater der Zeit, 2006. 176–85.
Ley, Graham. *From Mimesis to Interculturalism: Readings of Theatrical Theory Before and After "Modernism."* Exeter: U of Exeter P, 1999.
Marranca, Bonnie. *Theater Writings.* New York: Performing Arts Journal, 1984.
McDonald, Marianne. *Αρχαίος Ήλιος, Νέο Φως: Το Αρχαίο Ελληνικό Δράμα στη Σύγχρονη Ελληνική Σκηνή.* Μτφρ. Παύλος Μάτεσις. Αθήνα: Εστία, 1993. [McDonald, Marianne. *Ancient Sun, Modern Light: The Ancient Greek Drama on the Modern Stage.* Trans. Pavlos Matesis. Athens: Estia, 1993].
———. "The Madness that Makes Sane: Mania in Tadashi Suzuki's 'Dionysus.'" *Theatre Forum* 4 (Fall/ Winter 1994): 11–18.
Πατσαλίδης, Σάββας. *Θέατρο και Θεωρία: Περί (Υπο)Κειμένων και (Δια)Κειμένων.* Θεσσαλονίκη: U Studio P, 2000. [Patsalides, Savas. *Theater and Theory: On (Sub)Texts and (Inter)Texts.* Thessaloniki: U Studio P, 2000].
Pavis, Patrice, ed. *The Intercultural Performance Reader.* London and New York: Routledge, 1996.
Pilar, Fernández. "Un Reencuentro con Nuestros Demonios." Review of *Bacchae.* Dir. Theodoros Terzopoulos. *Extremadura* (Merida, Spain) 22 August 1986.
Radic, Leonard. "Bold View of Ancient Drama." Review of *Bacchae.* Dir. Theodoros Terzopoulos. *The Age* (Melbourne, Australia) 25 Mar. 1987.
Rivkin, Julie and Michael Ryan. "Introduction: English without Shadows, Literature on a World Scale." *Literary Theory: An Anthology.* Ed. Julie Rivkin and Michael Ryan. Massachusetts and Oxford: Blackwell, 1998. 851–55.
Sakellaridou, Elizabeth. "Millennial Artaud: Rethinking Cruelty and Representation." Speech. Conf. *The Flesh Made Text: Bodies, Theories, Cultures in the Post-Millennial Era.* School of English. Aristotle U of Thessaloniki, 14–18 May 2003.
Sampatakakis, Yeorgios. "Dionysus Restitutus—Terzopoulos' *Bakchen*/Dionysus Restitutus—The *Bacchae* of Terzopoulos." *Reise mit Dionysus: Das Theater des Theodoros Terzopoulos/ Journey with Dionysos: The Theater of Theodoros Terzopoulos.* Ed. Frank M. Raddatz. Germany: Theater der Zeit, 2006. 90–102.
Scarry, Elaine. *The Body in Pain: The Making and Unmaking of the World.* New York and Oxford: Oxford UP, 1985.
Schechner, Richard. *Between Theater and Anthropology.* Philadelphia: U of Pennsylvania P, 1985.
Schumacher, Ernst. "Neue Sicht Auf Ein Antikes Stück." Review of *Bacchae.* Dir. Theodoros Terzopoulos. *Berliner Zeitung* (Berlin, Germany) 23 Jan. 1987.
Stone Peters, Julie. "Intercultural Performance, Theatre Anthropology, and the Imperialist Critique: Identities, Inheritances, and Neo-Orthodoxies." *Imperialism and Theatre: Essays on World Theatre, Drama and Performance.* Ed. J. Ellen Gainor. London and New York: Routledge, 1995: 199–213.
Stroumpos, Savas. "The Exploration of Terzopoulos' Psychophysical Approach to Ancient Greek Tragedy." Diss. U of Exeter, 2003.
Suzuki, Tadashi. "Culture is the Body." *Acting (Re)Considered: Theories and Practices.* Ed. Phillip B. Zarrilli. London and New York: Routledge, 1995: 155–60.

Taylor, Diana. "Transculturating Transculturation." *Interculturalism and Performance: Writings from PAJ.* Ed. Bonnie Marranca and Gautam Dasgupta. New York: Performing Arts Journal, 1991: 60–74.

Terzopoulos, Theodoros. Συνέντευξη στη Ευδοκία Παλαιολόγου. «Η Τέχνη Ανήκει στους Λίγους.» *Επενδυτής* 20–21 Ιανουαρίου 1996: 24. [Interview with Evdokia Palaiologou. "Art Belongs to the Few." *Ependytis* (Athens, Greece) 20–21 Jan. 1996: 24].

———. *Theodoros Terzopoulos and the Attis Theatre: History, Methodology and Comments.* Trans. Alexandra Kapsalis. Athens: Agra, 2000.

———. Προσωπική συνέντευξη. 20 Ιουλίου 2002. [Personal interview. 20 July 2002].

———. Προσωπική συνέντευξη. 2 Μαΐου 2003. [Personal interview. 2 May 2003].

———. "The Metaphysics of the Body: Theodoros Terzopoulos in Conversation with Frank M. Raddatz." *Reise mit Dionysus: Das Theater des Theodoros Terzopoulos/ Journey with Dionysos: The Theater of Theodoros Terzopoulos.* Ed. Frank M. Raddatz. Germany: Theater der Zeit, 2006: 136–73.

———. Director's note. *Theatre Olympics: Crossing Millennia:* 5.

Thomson, Helen. "Powerful Evocation of an Ancient Message." Review of *Bacchae.* Dir. Theodoros Terzopoulos. *The Australian* (Melbourne, Australia) 25 Mar. 1987.

Varopoulou, Eleni. Prologue. *Theodoros Terzopoulos and the Attis Theatre: History, Methodology and Comments.* Theodoros Terzopoulos. Trans. Alexandra Kapsalis. Athens: Agra, 2000: 9–14.

Vojtko, Welsh. "Bacchae." Review of *Bacchae.* Dir. Theodoros Terzopoulos. *The San Diego Union* (San Diego, USA) 17 Oct. 1987.

Welsh, Anne Marie. "'Bacchae' Takes Audience Back to the Wellspring." Review of *Bacchae.* Dir. Theodoros Terzopoulos. *The San Diego Union* (San Diego, USA) 19 Oct.1987: D-6.

Zarrilli, Phillip B., ed. *Acting (Re)Considered: Theories and Practices.* London and New York: Routledge, 1996.

Part II
Narrative(s)

6. Dissecting Bodies and Selves in the Early Modern Period

Effie Botonaki

The early modern period saw the rise of the so-called "New Science," which was both a result of the Humanist thirst for knowledge and a response to the needs of the developing economic environment. Medicine, and especially human anatomy, was the field that attracted both scientific attention and public interest, as it concerned the yet-unknown and mysterious territory of the body. Thus, while the dissection of dead bodies for medical purposes had been practised for centuries in secret, in the early modern period it became legal and more acceptable.

Renaissance anatomists such as Berengarius, Valverde de Hamusco, Estienne, Spigelius, and especially Vesalius published textbooks with illustrations of anatomized bodies and their works revolutionized medical knowledge. It was through these textbooks that the physicians of the time tried to understand the internal structure and function of the body, finally being able to leave behind the theories of Galen from the second century AD. This progress and intense interest in anatomy led historians to speak of an "anatomical Renaissance." England was slow in following Italy or the Netherlands in allowing frequent public dissections and establishing the performance of anatomies as a necessary part of the education of physicians. However, the publication in the seventeenth century of anatomical textbooks with Vesalian images attracted a great deal of attention and informed a wide reading public of the new medical findings. When, for instance, the English anatomist, and surgeon to James I, Helkiah Crooke, published his *Microcosmographia* in 1615, his work proved to be a huge success.

The growing fascination with the findings of anatomic research is particularly evident in language: medical vocabulary imbued all discourses, even those that were until then considered to belong to entirely different domains. If, for example, we look for seventeenth-century books that include the word "Anatomy" in their title, we will come across works of various genres and on various topics; interestingly enough, those in which this word appears most frequently are books of religious content. Some such titles are *The Anatomy of the Christian Man* (1613), *The Anatomy of Melancholy* (1621), *The Anatomy of the English Nunnery at Lisbon . . . Dissected and laid open . . .* (1622), *An Anatomy of Independency* (1644), and in response to that, *The Anatomist anatomis'd* (1644), *Gods anatomy upon mans heart* (1649), etc. The frequent appearance of medical terms in early-modern, religious books, treatises and sermons strikes the modern reader as somehow "inappropriate," as we tend to see religion and science as almost binary opposites. Nonetheless, despite the well-established division between the body and the soul, and the degraded status of the former in Christian religion, the early modern Protestant divines seemed to be fascinated with scientific terms and bodily metaphors. As I will be arguing in this essay by referring to guidebooks on devotion and to spiritual diaries, the gap between the body and the soul apparently grew narrower in this period, and the body, which had been disregarded and held in contempt for centuries, re-acquired greater and greater importance.

The importance of the body and its study with the tools of experimental science occur and develop along with the study of the self. The sixteenth and especially the seventeenth centuries is a period when ego-documents proliferate: diaries and autobiographies are written in the hundreds, if we take into account not only what has survived but what appears to have been originally produced and has been lost. One reason for this emphasis on the self, as I have argued elsewhere, is the Protestant urge for self-knowledge and self-guidance.[1] The authors of books on devotion would encourage believers to look within themselves on a daily basis, or even several times a day, and perform another kind of dissection, or rather, self-dissection, which they called—once more borrowing a scientific and medical term—"self-examination." Very often, self-examination took a more material form as a result of being transcribed into a written text, the devotional diary. If we, too, anatomize these self-anatomies, we will find that the dissection of bodies for the advancement of medical knowledge and the dissection of selves for the sake of self-knowledge are very similar processes, and they share the same roots, methods, and aims.

In the 1660s, the newly-founded Royal Society stressed the importance of direct, empirical observation and involvement in the acquisition of knowledge, and contrasted this method to the blind, uncritical acceptance of established theories. As Thomas Sprat complained in his *History of the Royal Society* in 1667,

> the Seats of Knowledg, have been for the most part heretofore, not *Laboratories,* as they ought to be; but onely Scholes, where some have *taught,* and all the rest *subscribd* [. . .] For first, as many *Learners* as there are, so many hands, and

brains may still be reckon'd upon, as useless. It being onely the *Master's* part, to examine, and observe; and the Disciples, to submit with silence, to what they conclude. (68)

One of the aims of the Royal Society was to "remedy" this "Error" and eventually "render" England "a Land of *Experimental knowledge*" (114). The dissection of small animals was a frequent occurrence in the Society's meetings, as it was believed that the "outward description" of creatures and things had to be supplemented with the "dissection of inward Parts," if their true substance and function was to be known and understood (qtd. in Shapiro 22). The new Science saw the body as a machine constituted of parts that had to co-operate harmoniously if the whole was to be strong and healthy. It also argued that with the employment of Reason, it would be possible to discover the secrets of that mysterious machine. Anatomists undertook to perform this task by reducing the body to its minutest parts, and trying to understand the essence and use of all these fragments.

On the other hand, several anatomists thought that their task helped to know and understand not only the human body but, most importantly, God; as the anatomist Helkiah Crooke wrote: "Whosoever doth well know himself, knoweth all things. [. . .] First he shall know God, because he is fashioned and framed according to his image, by reason whereof, hee is called among the Divines, the Royall and Imperiall Temple of God" (qtd. in Sawday, *Body Emblazoned* 129).[2] One of Andrew Cunningham's central arguments in his book, *The Anatomical Renaissance,* is that for Protestants the knowledge of anatomy was "an important means to the knowledge of God" (232), and that Renaissance anatomy "had the admiration of God's creative providence at its core" (267). Cunningham reaches this conclusion by comparing Luther's views to those of the anatomist Andreas Vesalius, noting that neither was "prepared to take as doctrine anything which could not be pointed out with the finger in the sacred book, the Word, the body" (235). In *Books of the Body,* Andrea Carlino takes this argument even further, claiming that the Reformation actually heralded a change in the status of anatomy, seeing the science as proof of God's handiwork and thus raising its importance.[3]

Resembling anatomists, the authors of the seventeenth-century, Protestant, devotion manuals argued that the believers should observe the inner workings of their soul as strictly as possible in order to know and improve themselves. In the preface to John Corbet's guidebook for private prayer, entitled *Self-Imployment in Secret* (1681), the spiritual exercises he performed in his self-examination are described as a "more Interiour Portraiture" (A2) and "the Dissection of his Soul" (A4v). Those of his friends who were familiar with the written version of these exercises urged him to publish them for the benefit of other Christians. The description of this self-examination once more points to the affinity between the dissection of bodies and the dissection of selves:

> And as Anatomy discovers all the curious Contexture of our Bodily Fabrick: Here are vivid representations of *Faith, Love, an Heavenly Mind* [. . .] with whatever Parts, and Principles besides, Compose the whole Frame of the *New Creature*, as if we could perceive with our Eyes, how the Blood in an Humane Body, Circulates through all the Vains and Arteries, how the Heart Beats, the Spirits Fly to and fro, and how each Nerve, Tendon, Fibre, and Muscle, perform their several Operations. (A5–A5v)

In his analysis, Dr. Corbet argues that believers have to resort to their intellectual capacities and employ their reason to gain self-knowledge:

> In order to peace of conscience and assurance of my good estate towards God, it must in reason be supposed, that I may rightly understand the marks of sincerity set down in God's Word, as also the predominant inclination and motions of my own soul (1) [. . .] For I have no other ordinary way to know my sincerity [. . .] but to examine it according to my best understanding [. . .] In this Self-Examination it is requisite that I use all Diligence and Impartiality with Constancy. (2)

Manuals like Dr. Corbet's had been published in large numbers from the beginning of the seventeenth century and were obviously popular with those Protestants who were anxious to be good Christians but felt unguided in this arduous task. Let us not forget that, unlike the Catholics, Protestants would take part in few and quite plain rituals, and they had no official confessor to turn to. If they were to tread the right path, they would have to guide, advise, monitor and punish their own selves. The best way to do the above, they were told, was through private reading, meditation, self-examination, and prayer. The conscientious Protestants who recorded their devotional exercises became keepers of spiritual diaries. Like the prayer manuals that encourage self-examination, these diaries are also replete with medical and scientific vocabulary; they use scientific methods to record and process their material, and they are heavily preoccupied with the diarists' bodies and bodily needs. Like anatomists, pious diarists dissect themselves in an equally methodical manner, trying to conclude whether they have been guilty of any offences and guard themselves against sin. Thus, when, in 1608, Dionysia Fitzherbert gave an account of the mental crisis she had suffered and recovered from, she entitled it *An Anatomie for the Poore in Spirit Or the Case of an afflicted Conscience layed open by Example* (MS Bodl 154).

The scientific character of the process of self-dissection is particularly obvious in the case of diaries not only in terms of diction, but also in terms of method and form. In these texts the authors cut up their lives into days and each day into hours; they observe and record their thoughts and feelings, and

Dissecting Bodies and Selves in the Early Modern Period

divide them into categories, cataloguing them as virtuous or wicked. On Sunday 12, 1599, the diarist Margaret Hoby wrote:

> After I was redie, I went to priuatt praiers, then to breakfast: then I walked tell church time [with] Mr Hoby, and after to dinner: after which I walked and had speech of no serious maters tell :2: a clock: then I wrett notes into my bible tell :3: and after :4: I came again from the church, walk, and meditated a Litle, and againe wrett som other notes in my bible of that I had Learned tell :5: att which time I returned to examination and praier: and after I had reed [. . .] I walked abroad: and so to supper, after to praers, and Lastly to bed. (*Diary* 62)

By observing their lives as a scientist observes an experiment in progress, and by recording their findings, diarists could "review" them later and determine relationships of cause and effect, which would then enable them to understand and, most importantly, regulate themselves according to the dictates of their faith.

Diarists abundantly use words such as "observe," "consider," "meditate," "compare," "review," "perceive," "find," "understand"—more often than we would conventionally expect from a believer in prayer. A fanatic diary-keeper, Mary Rich, Countess of Warwick, spent September 2nd, 1670 meditating on the Great Fire of London, since it was on that day in 1666 that the fire began. She then wrote in her diary:

> I spent [. . .] much time in *considering* that great judgement God had sent upon London, and then *considered* that my sins had contributed to the destruction of it. I did then, by examination, look much into myself, and *consider* what my sins were; and when I had, by all the awakening *considerations* I could, stirred up my heart, I went to prayer. (*Memoir* 213, emphasis added)

In a similar manner, the anonymous author of a manuscript diary held at the Bodleian Library claims that the aim of her journal-keeping is the "constant *consideration* of the pr[e]sence of God [. . .] the Lord give me his grace that at the end I may *percive* some incres in this vertue" (Rawl. Q. e. 27, f.31, emphasis added). Separating the various sections of her manuscript into "Books," she entitles the one kept between Oct. 1680 and Jan. 1681 "The fourth Boke of my dally obsarvation on my self" (Bodl. Rawl. Q.e. 27 f.1). Thus, the Protestant, private prayer and self-examination sought to affect the heart through Reason; it was the "diligent" performance of rigorous mental exercises that would prove the validity of God's word and urge believers to adhere to it, not blind faith. As the divine Stephen Charnock argues, "There must be diligence to discern the rational workings of our Soul" (827), "Reflection and knowledge of self is a Prerogative of a rational Nature. We know that we have souls by the operations of them. We may know that we have Grace by the effects of it, if we be diligent" (829). And in a note on the above, Charnock explains, "*Cogito ergo sum,* is the first principle in the new

Phillosophy."

Furthermore, the very format of many diaries is not at all haphazard but the result of careful and methodical organization; many diarists allowed only one entry per page, and in some cases they divided this page into specific sections. The anonymous diarist mentioned earlier divides each page-entry into three sections: the first is the main body of the entry, the second is devoted to the sins of the day, and the third to the mercies of God. Part of Elizabeth Mordaunt's diary is kept in two columns per entry: one for things "To returne thanks for" and the other for things "To ask perden for" (225). In several diaries there are tables of contents, cross-references and headlines.[4] Very frequently, what is recorded is actually enumerated.[5] All the above ways of organizing their material aimed at helping the diarists to review their entries speedily and with ease and thus have a better grasp of their content. So this supposedly spontaneous outpouring of thoughts and feelings was not as irregular as one might expect it to be, but well-organized and methodically presented.

As the above examples illustrate, the diarists examine and anatomize themselves with, one might say, medical scrutiny. Interestingly enough, several of those who gave themselves up to self-examination, especially in a written form, were unusually learned and interested in the sciences and, particularly, medicine. Some of them were so accomplished that they would even act as amateur practitioners and surgeons as, for example, the diarist Margaret Hoby. Hoby was often called upon not only to dress wounds but also to perform surgery. On one occasion, she records in her diary: "this day, in the afternone, I had had a child brought to me . . . who had no fundament, and had no passage for excrementes but att the Mouth: I was earnestly intreated to Cutt the place to se if any passage Could be made, but, althught I Cutt deepe and searched, there was none to be found" (*Diary* 184).[6] Likewise, the comments Elizabeth Bury's husband made on her learning and diary-keeping draw clear links between medical knowledge and self-knowledge:

> She was always very Inquisitive into the Nature and Reason of Things, and greatly obliged to any that would give her Information. Another Study which she took much Pleasure in, was *Anatomy* and *Medicine,* being led and prompted to it partly by her own ill *Health,* and partly with a Desire of being useful amongst her Neighbours: In this she improv'd so much, that many of the, great Masters of the Faculty, have been often startled, by her stating the most nice and difficult Cases, in such proper Terms, which could have been expected only from Men of their own Profession; and have often own'd, that she understood an Human Carcase and the *Materia Medica* much better than most of her Sex, which ever they had been acquainted with. (5–6)

In referring to her diary, her husband writes, "She found it of singular *Advantage* to her self, to observe this Method; and would often say, That were it not for her *Diary,* she would neither know what she *was,* or what she *did,* or what she *had*" (13). Bury often "reviews" the diary that she kept for more than 20 years, and is thus able to draw *reasonable* conclusions about her life: on 1 Jan. 1701 she records, "In a serious review on the Year past, I find still more abundant *Mercies* to me [. . .] than I could ever have hop'd for" (61). So through careful observation, meticulous recording and diligent survey, the diarist feels able to analyse and know herself.

Although devotional diaries were supposed to focus on the diarists' spiritual rather than physical state, their authors frequently allowed their records to be filled with details about their bodily infirmities and their worries about their health problems. In fact, many people sought to gain a better understanding of their physical problems and monitor their health through their diaries. They noted down with dates, and in all possible detail, what state they were in, what treatment they followed, and how it proceeded. In this respect, the spiritual diary was not used to heal only the soul, but the body as well. The diarist's physical condition affected the production of the diary in very direct ways, determining how frequently it was kept, how long the entries were, what their content was, and, of course, what the handwriting was like. Sometimes, the abrupt ending of a diary signifies death, as in the cases of Lady Anne Clifford and the anonymous relative of Cromwell. From this point of view, the body writes the diary in more than one sense.

One important reason for the vivid presence of the body in spiritual diaries is that their authors interpreted their good or bad health as a sign of God's providence or punishment, or as His way of trying their faith. Let us not forget either that, according to the then-dominant, Judaeo-Christian perception of the body, the latter was thought to be a container/prison of the soul. In order for the soul to ascend to God, it had to transcend the fallen body and defy its needs, so the relationship between the two was mainly confrontational. Additional and equally important reasons for the early modern diarists' preoccupation with their physical condition was the fact that they were living in the midst of disease and death and, at the same time, they were beginning to see themselves as unique individuals, worthy of attention, good health and longevity. Thus, the vivid interest even of common people in the findings of medical research and all sorts of medical advice can be explained. In her study of 1,392 English almanacs printed between 1640 and 1700, Louise Hill Curth has found that 72.3 percent of them include medical information and preventive or remedial advice or advertisements for medical products and services (258, 281). If we consider that 350,000 to 400,000 copies of almanacs were printed every year in that period and that their content most probably reflected the interests of the reading public, we can understand how important knowledge of the body had become.

Anatomy fascinated early modern Europeans for the same reasons, and it did so regardless of their education or vocation. Crowds would visit theaters of anatomy on the continent in order to witness the dissection of corpses, and these viewers were willing to pay for a ticket (Sawday, *The Body Emblazoned* 41–2). In the early eighteenth century, entrepreneurial anatomists in London began to offer courses, which they advertised in newspapers, to anyone who was interested enough to pay a fee. These courses would take place in private houses or even taverns, and, according to Anita Guerrini, the anatomists who offered them "sought to convey a natural theological message about the craftsmanship of the deity in the design of the human and animal body" (224) as well as to "entertain." Anatomy was for the virtuoso participants "at once fashionable yet moral, offering its spectators a tinge of melancholy alongside a titillating frisson, a spectacle with educational value" (239). Despite the public fascination with this procedure, the prospect of being subjected to it seems to have caused nothing less than terror. There is evidence that those who were afraid they were likely to be anatomized would take all possible measures to prevent this from happening. Many people would not want so much as to be cut or to be embalmed, and left such orders in their wills. The same anxiety is found among diarists in relation to the laying open of their manuscripts. Few were willing to let even close family members read them, and even fewer would be willing to see them go into print. The exposure of so personal a document as a diary would make its author feel "naked," since diaries are not only as sensitive as bodies, but also as private as bodies are.

At this point, it is instructive to refer to the illustrations of anatomized bodies in contemporary books. Whereas prior to the sixteenth century these illustrations presented the cadavers in a realistic manner—as dead bodies—in the sixteenth century, the cadavers acquire life; they stand, move and have their eyes open. Still more importantly, they perform the dissection themselves, holding their dissected flesh open and sometimes looking inquisitively into their own carcasses.[7] Jonathan Sawday has argued that this change in the depiction of dissections reveals the anatomists' anxiety about public opinion and that it was the result of their wish to make dissection appear less gruesome and to obscure their participation in this violent act. It could also be argued, however, that this change in the representation of anatomized bodies is related to an increasing desire for self-knowledge, which went well beyond the scientific community. So the cadavers' active participation in their dissection may signify both the anatomists' desire to disassociate themselves from this procedure as well as the desire of common people to learn more about their bodies and themselves. And to return to the similarities between dissection and diary writing, the images of the inquisitive and acquiescent, self-demonstrating cadavers bear a strong resemblance to the diarists, who dissect themselves upon the diary page with their pen and then look curiously within.

The preoccupation with the body and the self in the early modern period, and also in our days, does not actually concern all bodies, irrespective of class.

Self-examination and diary-writing were in fact a luxury that only wealthy believers could perform properly; it required free time, private space, and the ability to afford paper and ink. Furthermore, it was mainly upper-class people who would deem themselves important and worthy of attention. Significantly enough, all the diaries that have survived from this period belong solely to upper and upper-middle-class people. Speaking of literal dissection, the anatomic tests would be performed on the bodies of criminals,[8] the poor, foreigners, or the unidentified and unclaimed—in other words, these tests were conducted by the powerful upon the powerless. On the other hand, medical progress would benefit first and foremost, if not exclusively, those who had influence or/and wealth. So, only *some* bodies were valuable, worthy of attention, and care, and it was these bodies which were able to avoid dissection.

Another, less obvious aim of this early modern attention to and analysis of the body and the self was their regulation. As far as the body is concerned, the dangers of its submission to scientific experiments, even for the sake of knowledge, has always been a contentious issue. As far as the self is concerned, its metaphorical self-dissection, whether as an early modern religious duty or, later on, as an essential part of psychoanalytic treatments, often aims not merely at self-knowledge but at self-punishment and self-appropriation, i.e., helping people adjust to social expectations and norms they feel uncomfortable with.

Fortunately, however, neither the body nor the self can be effectively regulated—not to the extent that is desired, at least. Those anxious diarists who wanted to make sure that they were following God's dictates, and who would perform self-dissections as reformatory and penitential exercises, would all too often realize with regret that they were making the same mistakes again and again, despite their careful, daily self-examination. As for the ambitious researchers who, through the centuries, have sought to know the body to its minutest tissue and cell, they have always been confronted with the realization that there is still more to know, that, in the old days, the knife and, nowadays, the scan have to search deeper and deeper, further and further. Ironically, even in those cases when there is nothing further to cut and scan, the proud achievers eventually realize that they have to go back to the whole, because this ultimate fragment they have so painfully discovered and analysed tells them nothing when examined in isolation. Thus, it appears that both the body and the soul cannot be subdued by the powers of Reason and human will and that they are always at least one step ahead of rational understanding, able both to facilitate and frustrate the efforts of those who want to dissect, know, and control them.

Notes

1. See my "Seventeenth-Century Englishwomen's Spiritual Diaries: Self-Examination, Covenanting, and Account Keeping."
2. For more references to anatomists with similar views of dissection, see Sawday, *Body Emblazoned* 263–64, n. 44.
3. See Ch. 4 of the book.
4. See, for example, the manuscript diary of Katherine Austen.
5. See the diaries of Elizabeth Mordaunt and Anne Harcourt.
6. Grace Mildmay and Anne Halkett are two more cases in point.
7. See, for example, The *Anatomised Anatomist*, and *Self-demonstrating Figure* by Valverde, *Self-demonstrating Figure* by Andreas Spigelius, and *Self-dissecting Figure*, by Berengarius. All the above illustrations can be found in Sawday, "Fate of Marsyas," 124, 131. These illustrations along with a number of others are also included in Sawday's *Body Emblazoned*.
8. On this issue, see Richardson 32–34.

Works Cited

Anon. Daily spiritual diary, *c.* 1679–81. Bodl. MS Rawl. Q. e. 26–27.

Anon. (A relative of Oliver Cromwell, b. 1654). A short autobiographical sketch followed by a diary, 1690–1702. BL Add. MS 5858. ff. 213–21.

Austen, Katherine (1628–83). *Book M.* Diary and meditations, 1664–6. BL Add. MS 4454.

Botonaki, Effie. "Seventeenth-Century Englishwomen's Spiritual Diaries: Self-Examination, Covenanting, and Account Keeping." *Sixteenth Century Journal* 30:1 (1999): 3–21.

Burton, Robert. *The Anatomy of Melancholy.* London, 1621.

Bury, Elizabeth (1644–1720). *An Account of the Life and Death of Mrs Elizabeth Bury, Who Died, May the 11th, 1720. Aged 76. Chiefly Collected out of her Own Diary.* Ed. Samuel Bury. London, 1720.

Carlino, Andrea. *Books of the Body: Anatomic Ritual and Renaissance Learning.* Trans. John and Anne Tedeschi. Chicago: U of Chicago P, 1999.

Charnock, Stephen. *The Works of the Late Learned Divine Stephen Charnock, B.D.* 2 Vols. London, 1684.

Clifford, Lady Anne, Countess of Pembroke (1590–1676). *The Diaries of Lady Anne Clifford.* Ed. D. J. H. Clifford. Stroud: Alan Sutton, 1990.

Corbet, John. *Self-Imployment in Secret.* London, 1681.

Cowper, William. *The Anatomy of the Christian Man.* London, 1613.

Crooke, Helkiah. *Microcosmographia.* London, 1615.

Cunningham, Andrew. *The Anatomical Renaissance: The Resurrection of the Anatomical Projects of the Ancients.* Aldershot: Ashgate, 1997.

Curth, Louise Hill. "The Medical Content of English Almanacs, 1640–1700." *Journal of the History of Medicine and Allied Sciences* 60: 3 (2005): 255–82.

Fitzherbert, Dionysia. *An Anatomie for the Poore in Spirit Or the Case of an afflicted Conscience layed open by Example.* MS Bodl. 154.

Freke, Elizabeth (1641–1714). Diary, 1671–1714. BL Add. MSS 45718–9.

———. Mrs Elizabeth Freke, Her Diary, 1671 to 1714. Ed. Mary Carbery. Cork: Guy and Company Limited, 1913.

Godwin, Thomas. *An Anatomy of Independency*. London, 1644.

Guerrini, Anita. "Anatomists and Entrepreneurs in Early Eighteenth-Century London." *Journal of the History of Medicine and Allied Sciences* 59: 2 (2004): 219–39.

Halkett, Anne (1623–99). Memoirs. 1677–8. BL Add. MS 32376.

———. *The Memoirs of Anne, Lady Halkett and Ann, Lady Fanshawe*. Ed. John Loftis. Oxford: Oxford UP, 1979.

Harcourt, Lady Anne. Occasional memoirs, c. 1649–61. *The Harcourt Papers*. Vol. I. Ed. Edward W. Harcourt. Oxford, 1876. 169–99.

Hoby, Lady Margaret (1570–1633). Daily diary, August 1599-July 1605. BL MS Egerton 2614.

———. *The Diary of Lady Margaret Hoby*. Ed. D. M. Meads. London: Routledge, 1930.

Mildmay, Grace (1552–1620). *With Faith and Physic: The Life of a Tudor Gentlewoman, Lady Grace Mildmay 1552–1620*. Ed. Linda Pollock. London: Collins and Brown, 1993.

Mordaunt, Elizabeth, Viscountess (1633–79). *The Private Diarie of Elizabeth Viscountess Mordaunt*. Duncairn: Private press of Edmund Macrory, 1856.

Rich, Mary, Countess of Warwick (1624–78). Diary, 1666–78. BL Add. MSS 27351-5.

———. *Memoir of Lady Warwick: Also her Diary, from A.D. 1666–1672*. London: Religious Tract Society, 1847.

Richardson, Ruth. *Death, Dissection and the Destitute*. London: Routledge and Kegan Paul, 1987.

Robinson Thomas. *The Anatomy of the English Nunnery at Lisbon . . . Dissected and laid Open. . . .* London, 1622.

Sawday, Jonathan. *The Body Emblazoned: Dissection and the Human Body in Renaissance Culture*. London: Routledge, 1995.

———. "The Fate of Marsyas: Dissecting the Renaissance Body." *Renaissance Bodies: The Human Figure in English Culture c. 1540–1660*. Ed. Lucy Gent and Nigel Llewellyn. London: Reaktion Books, 1995. 111–35.

Shapiro, Barbara J. *Probability and Certainty in Seventeenth-Century England: A Study of the Relationships Between Natural Science, Religion, History, Law, and Literature*. Princeton, New Jersey: Princeton UP, 1983.

Simpson, Sydrach. *The Anatomist anatomis'd*. London, 1644.

Sprat, Thomas. *History of the Royal Society*. 1667. Ed. J. I. Cope and H. Whitmore Jones. St Louis: Washington UP, 1966.

Watson, Thomas. *Gods anatomy upon mans heart*. London, 1649.

7. *From Rejection to Affirmation of Their Bodies: The Case of Afro-German Women Writers*

Jennifer E. Michaels

In *Race, Gender, and Class Perspectives in the Works of Maya Angelou, Gwendolyn Brooks, Rita Dove, Nikki Giovanni, and Audre Lorde,* Ekaterini Georgoudaki writes: "The long economic, political, and cultural control of the colored people has resulted in their acceptance of white standards of femininity (white complexion, blue eyes, blonde hair, skinny body, gentle and submissive behavior, fragility, dependence on man, etc.)" (165). In her view, "the black woman has been forced to constantly measure her worth against these standards and to feel ugly and unfeminine, because she doesn't meet them" (165). Such notions of beauty have been particularly damaging to Afro-German women, many of whom are of African or African-American and white German heritage. Most of these women grew up in the years after the Second World War in Germany, a predominantly white society where their skin color marked them immediately as different and made them vulnerable to racist and xenophobic behavior, and they had little opportunity to develop a positive attitude to the black part of their biracial identities. The Western standard of beauty, the only one to which they were exposed in their childhood, shaped their self-image and often led them to hate being black and long to be white. In their essays and literary texts such leading, Afro-German, women writers as May Opitz, who later took on her father's name Ayim, Helga Emde, Ika Hügel-Marshall, and others address problems of negative self-image and speak out against the derogatory depictions of Africans—in their view a legacy of colonialism—that still pervade German society.[1] They struggle to come to terms with their otherness and marginalization, to overcome their alienation from their blackness, and to begin to affirm and be proud of their black bodies.

As many feminists have pointed out, standards of feminine beauty tyrannize most women—at least to some extent. Germaine Greer writes: "Every woman knows that, regardless of all her other achievements, she is a failure if she is not beautiful" (23). In her estimation, concern with appearance "goes some way towards ruining some part of every woman's day" (25). She and others observe that the multi-million-dollar beauty industries are quick to play on women's insecurity about their bodies and encourage and profit from their attempts to meet prevailing standards of beauty. Naomi Wolf remarks that "the West pretends that all ideals of female beauty stem from one Platonic Ideal Woman" (12), but she and others point out that views of female perfection can change quickly (Brownmiller 23). The gaunt, youthful, and hungry model has replaced, for example, the full-sized women favored by Rubens or Renoir as the current ideal. Wolf notes that in recent years "the weight of fashion models plummeted to 23 percent below that of ordinary women" (11). Although the average size of women is no smaller now than during the Second World War, "the size-fourteen mannequins that looked beautiful in the 1940s have been replaced in store windows by size-six (or smaller) mannequins" (Eaton 31). Current notions of desirable physical beauty have had harmful consequences. They have led to the rise in eating disorders, especially among young women and girls (Wolf 11; Eaton 31), who, "at younger and younger ages, strive to control their bodies to the point of starvation" (Brand 4), and have contributed to the growth in unnecessary, cosmetic surgery. The majority of patients who undergo such surgery are women who seek to keep their youthful looks or rid themselves of what they have been conditioned to view as unsightly fat.

Another harmful aspect in Western thinking about beauty is the tendency to view the body as an outward sign of moral character (Brand 11). Some see being fat, for example, as a sign of moral weakness. Noël Carroll argues that in our culture "the beautiful exterior is taken as a sign of inward or moral goodness; the nonbeautiful or ugly exterior is often imagined to correlate with evil or depravity" (38). According to such rhetoric, ugliness signifies "a demoted moral status" (42). As Carroll points out, such thinking can be used to valorize or dehumanize not only individuals but entire groups: "The moral credentials of a group—an ethnicity or a race—can be endorsed by means of an association with beauty, or it can be demeaned by being represented as nonbeautiful or ugly" (38). Depictions of peoples of other ethnicities and races as the antithesis of beauty "not only associate them with evil, but render them not quite human" (42). In his view, such portrayals are "diabolically effective levers of ethnic and racial hatred" (53).

Western notions of physical perfection that undermine white women's self-esteem are even more damaging to black women. Not only do they experience pressures to conform to white standards, but they are also exposed to prevailing notions that equate being black with being ugly. In the West, the concept of black has long been associated with "the undesirable, the ugly, the unacceptable, the rejected" (Blackshire-Belay 96). In the eighteenth century, for example, a broad nose was "a visual metaphor for the inherent ugliness of the Black" (Gilman 26). Many representations of blacks in the eighteenth and nineteenth centuries focused on kinky hair, swollen lips, and large buttocks. By grotesquely exaggerating differences between the black and the white body, such images sought to shape societal notions of ugliness (Willis and Williams 62).

Such Eurocentric notions of beauty dehumanized black people and depicted them as evil and inferior. As Paul Taylor shows, classical racialism held that what it defined as "the physical ugliness of black people was a sign of a deeper ugliness and depravity" (58). Negative qualities associated with the word "black" exist in most Western countries. The color symbolism of Christianity, for example, associates white with purity, goodness, and nobility, and black with death, dirt, and evil (Ayim, "Weißer Stress" 111; Lange 98). In *Black Skin, White Masks,* Frantz Fanon notes that in Europe the black man is the symbol of evil and that the color associated with Satan is black. He writes: "When one is dirty one is black—whether one is thinking of physical dirtiness or of moral dirtiness." The black man "stands for the bad side of the character" and is "the symbol of sin" (qtd. in Gilman 1–2). As Gilman observes: "Darkness remained universally equated with evil" (20).

In nineteenth-century Europe, the biological racial theories propagated by such people as Joseph-Arthur, Count de Gobineau, categorized blacks as the lowest form of human life, and shaped colonialist thinking. In the discourses of European colonialism, blacks were frequently depicted as ugly, inferior, lacking in intelligence, and morally depraved—images that helped white colonizers justify their harsh treatment of the colonized. An extreme form of demeaning representations of blacks, designed to make them appear subhuman, is what Carroll terms "simianization." He notes that linking blacks with apes did not cease with the end of colonialism but still thrives on the Internet (49). Willis and Williams point out that in the nineteenth century the so-called sciences of phrenology and physiognomy "linked blacks to animals (particularly monkeys), and were touted as 'proving' African inferiority." These pseudo-sciences "generated popular representations of blacks as ape-like creatures, with huge lips, bulging eyes, and sometimes even tails" (2). Like Carroll, they observe that such images "have not been eradicated from public memory and still influence how the larger society, and even some blacks themselves, view people of African descent" (2). They also note that black women are often portrayed as "feral, fecund creatures, hardly different from wild animals" (80).

Black women were further dehumanized and robbed of their individuality by being perceived as depersonalized, exotic, sexual objects (Fremgen 65–68), as the sex tourism in some African countries indicates. Alice, a black woman from Cameroon living in Germany, where Fremgen interviewed her in the early 1980s, writes that in the opinion of many white men the black woman has only sex to offer: she doesn't count as a person; only her body is important. For them she is merely a "sex toy" (Fremgen 62). Helga Emde, the daughter of an African-American occupation soldier and a German mother, recalls that as she was walking with some girlfriends, a group of workmen remarked: "The Black one, that's the one I want." She remembers feeling humiliated and angry that these men "only looked upon me as a walking sex object" ("Occupation Baby" 194).

Since colonial times, Eurocentric notions of beauty have shaped the self-perceptions of black women not only in Europe but also throughout the world. As Susan Brownmiller observes: "The emphasis on light-skinned feminine beauty among American blacks has been one of the bitter fruits of racism, the imposition of one culture's values on another" (134). The Kenyan writer Miriam Kwalanda relates that even in Africa a light skin is more highly esteemed than a dark one. To feel lighter, she remarks, means to feel more European and thus better (25). These notions were especially damaging to Afro-German women who grew up after the Second World War in a predominantly white society in which Western standards of beauty prevailed. Unlike Africans and African-Americans who had the support of large black communities, the few Afro-Germans were dispersed throughout Germany. Whether they lived in a large city or a small town, they rarely, if ever, saw other black people when they were growing up. Without a black community to help them affirm the African side of their heritage, they internalized the racist notions of their surrounding society. They tried to be as white as possible, and they rejected and sometimes hated being black.

Germany assumed the prevailing negative discourses about black people from other European countries. German aesthetic theory of the eighteenth century viewed blacks as ugly, since they did not conform to the European concept of beauty, modeled after the Greeks. In *Laokoon oder über die Grenzen der Malerei und Poesie* [Laokoon or About the Limits of Painting and Poetry, 1766], Gotthold Ephraim Lessing, for example, listed "a flattened nose with prominent nostrils" among images that evoke disgust (Gilman 25). In his *Geschichte der Kunst des Alterthums* [History of the Art of Antiquity, 1764], Johann Joachim Winckelmann argues: "The swollen, thick mouth, which the Blacks have in common with the apes of their land, is an extraneous growth and a swelling caused by the heat of their climate" (qtd. in Gilman 53). The physiognomist Johann Caspar Lavater equated appearance with mental ability. For him, a flattened nose was a sign of stupidity (Gilman 52). In his view, the appearance of the black "reduces him to the level of one of the other primates of Africa, the ape" (Gilman 54). Negative images of black people were reinforced by the nineteenth-century racial theories that shaped European colonialism.[2] Like other colonial powers, Germans idealized the white colonizer and attributed only negative qualities to the colonized. In constructing this artificial other, Germans depicted blacks as evil and not quite human (Kron 28–29).

The speech therapist and poet May Ayim, the daughter of a Ghanaian father and a German mother, focuses on the legacy of German colonialism in several essays. Unlike other European powers, Germany's colonialist period spanned only the last decades of the nineteenth century until the end of the First World War. Despite this short period, Ayim argues, colonial stereotypes of blacks continued to shape racist thinking in Germany in the twentieth century. When, for example, black French troops were stationed in the Rhineland after the First World War, German nationalists warned of rape and racial pollution. Under the Nazis, some of the children born to these black French troops and German mothers were sterilized and sent to concentration camps (*Showing our Colors* 41–54). Nazi racial ideology, with its idealization of the tall, blond, blue-eyed Aryan and its categorization of non-Aryans as degenerate and a danger to the purity of the Aryan race, stemmed from nineteenth-century discourses on race. Ayim believes that such discourses did not disappear with the defeat of the Nazis but continue to poison the present, as the demeaning images of Africans in the media suggest. Black people, she notes, are depicted as "intrinsically ugly" (*Showing our Colors* 130).

In their texts, Afro-German women depict the negative self-image they struggled against when they were growing up after the Second World War. They experienced their blackness as a stigma since it meant being perceived as ugly and being marginalized. Emde notes that Nazi, racist thought was evident in Germany in the postwar years: "The ideology of a white Aryan superior nation with blue eyes and blond hair was still there and part of my daily life" ("I too am German" 33). Ayim also believes that this Aryan ideal continues to be the prevailing standard of beauty in Germany ("Rassismus" 137). Emde relates that being raised in this white world led not only to low self-esteem but also to a fear of being black: "black meant frightening, strange, foreign, and animalistic" ("Occupation Baby" 102). She grew up thinking that a white person was beautiful, noble, and perfect, whereas a black person was inferior, and she rejected being black and wanted to be as white as possible. A black friend, she recalls, tried to overcome her blackness by scratching, cutting, and brushing her skin until it bled ("I too am German" 36). In her poem "Der Schrei" ["The Cry"], Emde describes her futile attempts to look like a European in order to be accepted: "look, i'll [sic] straighten my hair,/ make my lips thin" ("Occupation Baby" 111). She squeezed her lips together so they would appear less "puffy" and, therefore, more European ("Occupation Baby" 103). In her alienation from herself and her fear of being black, she turned herself into the opposite of the Western ideal of beauty: "What better way to protect myself than with a fat, unattractive body? I ate myself into a regular cage of protection. It was a vicious cycle: I wasn't supposed to stand out [. . .] but I was big and fat and Black" ("Occupation Baby" 103–04). Growing up, she recollects, she felt fragmented, confused, disoriented and without an identity of her own ("Occupation Baby" 103).

Particularly troublesome to many Afro-German women was their hair, since it did not conform to the Western notion that straight hair is a necessary component of female beauty. As Paulette Caldwell observes, in the twentieth century "the writings of black women confirm the centrality of hair in the psychological abuse of black women" (qtd. in Taylor 60). Emde recalls that white Germans considered her hair exotic and likened it to horsehair. Everyone wanted to touch it, a problem that Leloba, a woman from South Africa who moved to Germany in 1976, also experienced ("I too am German" 36; Fremgen 72). When Emde was thirteen, she tried to straighten her hair so that it would be like the white people's hair she admired so much. Straight hair, she thought, would make her less conspicuous. The Afro-German Ellen Wiedenroth recalls that as a child she longed to have the straight, shiny, blue-black hair she saw in pictures of Egyptian art, but her own hair "always had to be rolled up and continually cut. It was subdued and I with it" (*Showing our Colors* 169).

In her autobiography, *Daheim unterwegs: Ein deutsches Leben* ["On the Way Home: A German Life," 1998], Ika Hügel-Marshall, the daughter of an African-American father and a German mother, recalls that when she was growing up she had no greater wish than to be white and she hated her skin color. In the orphanage where she lived, people thought she was ugly. They called her hair "Negro" hair, and on one occasion the nuns scratched her face bloody with a brush to show the other children that her skin color was real, not made out of chocolate.

Ayim recollects that for many years she thought she was ugly because she was black. She asked her mother to wash her white and even tried eating soap to become white (*Showing Our Colors* 206–07). Ayim shows that in "a variety of ways the idea is transmitted that white skin is the better skin color" (*Showing our Colors* 35). In her poem "winterreim in berlin" ["winter rhyme in berlin"] she writes: "you are as white as snow/ and I as brown as shit/ you think" (*nachtgesang* 68).[3] She criticizes black women's use of creams to retard pigment formation. In Frantz Fanon's words in *Black Skin, White Masks,* such bleaching creams are designed to make it possible "for the miserable Negro to whiten himself and thus to throw off the burden of that corporeal malediction" (qtd. in *Showing Our Colors* 35). Ayim was dismayed that Western notions of beauty were also prevalent in Africa. Even there, she writes, it is important to have a thin nose, straight hair and a light skin (*Showing Our Colors* 146). The use of bleaching creams, hot combs to straighten their hair, and even eating soap all underscore Afro-German women's rejection of their blackness.

Although many white Germans view blacks as ugly, others perceive Afro-German women as exotic. This patronizing notion of the exotic underscores, however, that Afro-Germans are thought of as "other," because they do not fit into German notions of "normal" beauty. Being termed exotic is another way to marginalize them. In *Showing Our Colors,* Laura Baum tells of running into two drunks. One said: "Hey, she's good looking!" and the other replied: "But she's not European" (145). People said that her color had "an 'exotic' attraction for them, a foreignness, but not quite as foreign as black" (148). At school a student told her that "mulattoes were especially beautiful people" (148). In Baum's opinion, this thinking leads to "a stereotyped or ideal image of colored women as singing, dancing, laughing, and being otherwise erotic and exotic." She stopped feeling good about such remarks, when she realized "that a certain kind of behavior was also linked to this 'beauty'; a kind of behavior that's not German or European" (148). Ayim also resents those who find her beautiful and interesting because she is "dark but not too dark" (*Showing our Colors* 161).

Particularly damaging to Afro-German women were the notions that outward appearance reflects inner character. Wiedenroth notes that color is not seen as value-free. White "is equated with purity (hygienic and moral), with wholeness" and black "stands for dirt, for evil as such, for menacing nothingness" (*Showing our Colors* 165). In her autobiography, Hügel-Marshall voices common experiences when she describes how she internalized society's racist stereotypes that to be black meant to be ugly, primitive, and uncivilized. She was taught that she was stupid and immoral and that black people were worthless. White society defined her through its stereotypes of her appearance and skin color. If she did not do well at school, it was to be expected because she was black. If, however, she did well, people thought she had cheated. In several poems, Ayim criticizes notions that a black skin denotes an inner ugliness and moral failing. In "sein oder nichtsein" ["to be or not to be"], she writes that when she was growing up in Germany she learned that Africans sweat more than whites, that they smell, and that they are primitive and lazy. She learned that backwardness could be recognized from afar by skin color (*nachtgesang* 17–18).

The situation for Afro-German women changed radically in 1984 when the African-American feminist poet and activist Audre Lorde taught a course on black American women poets at the Free University in Berlin. Here Lorde met black German women and became, until her death in 1992, their mentor and inspiration. In an interview in 1990, Lorde recognized the problems black Germans faced in defining their identities and finding their voices. It is difficult, she notes, "to survive and create as a Black person in a situation where you are not only discriminated against but wiped out in terms of your message and your identity and your consciousness" (Hall 193). Lorde encouraged Afro-German women to break out of their isolation and come together to find a sense of identity. To support them in what she calls the "long and sometimes arduous journey toward self-possession" ("Turning the Beat Around" 44), Lorde helped them coin the name Afro-German to connect them to their diverse African and African-American, cultural heritages. Through this name, they began to define themselves rather than letting others label them as "colored," "half breed," and "mulatto," terms derived from the colonial past (*Showing Our Colors* xxiii). Lorde encouraged them to break their silence and establish a voice of their own, and this led to the publication of *Farbe bekennen* [*Showing our Colors,* 1986; 1992]. Through their work on this book, the first published by Afro-German women, the authors began to examine their cultural origins and biracial identities and to build a community.

Lorde believed it was crucial for black women to define themselves and she transmitted such thinking to Afro-German women. She writes: "We *must* learn to respect ourselves and our needs" (Hall 72). In her essay "Sadomasochism: Not About Condemnation," Lorde underscores the importance of "reclaiming ourselves" (13). Black women should not "be afraid of difference." They should be "real, tough, loving" (Hall 100). Lorde encouraged Afro-German women to resist pressures to conform to Western standards of beauty, to develop their self-respect, and to keep their natural looks. As Georgoudaki observes: "Through the portraits of her own mother and of other colored women Lorde also defies the traditional Western identification of womanhood and beauty with whiteness" (76). In texts such as her biomythography *Zami,* Lorde depicts strong, independent, beautiful, black women who are "feisty" and "incorrigible" (Hall 88). She taught Afro-German women to delight in their black bodies, to realize that being black is beautiful, and to appreciate the "wonderful richness of Black women" (Hall 179). Through her teaching, Lorde connected Afro-German women to the celebration of the black female body promoted by African-American writers and photographers since the early twentieth century (Willis and Williams 159).

Afro-German women's growing self-confidence and self-esteem, inspired by Lorde, is evident in *Showing Our Colors* and other texts, in which these women speak out against the derogatory stereotypes of Africa and Africans that still pervade modern German society. Of particular concern to many Afro-German women are the images of blacks portrayed in school textbooks and in children's literature in which they are typically depicted as lazy, ugly, ignorant, and stupid, as in the popular children's song "Zehn kleine Negerlein" ["Ten Little Niggers"] or even as monkey-like creatures, toys, or cannibals (Ayim, "Racism Here and Now" 126–44; Fremgen 38–43). In their essays and literary texts, Afro-German women point out the harmful effects of these images and put pressure on publishers to delete racist connotations in their books, and they work to develop anti-racist curricula for schools (Emde, "I too am German" 41).

Afro-German women have struggled to overcome their negative self-image and to affirm the beauty of being black. In *Showing our Colors,* the impact of Lorde's celebration of blackness is clear when Ayim, Laura Baum, and Katharina Oguntoye discuss notions of beauty. Although Oguntoye still does not like to lie in the sun to get darker because, as she writes: "When I look pale, I feel less foreign" (*Showing our Colors* 157), she affirms her African looks when she says she likes broad noses on people. Ayim shares this view: "I'd even like having a broader nose. I think broad noses are fantastic" (146). She used to think she would be less conspicuous if she was lighter, but now she asserts: "I'd like to be black, plain and simple" (*Showing our Colors* 157). For many years, Abena Adomako felt uncomfortable in her blackness but has now found the courage "to show my body without hiding myself behind high-necked blouses or white shirts in shame" (*Showing our Colors* 203). Ika Hügel-Marshall declares that she loves herself and her skin color ("Wir brauchen uns" 29), and in her autobiography she writes that when she looks in the mirror she is glad because she would not like to be different from what she is (140). Yet, the journey from rejection to acceptance of their blackness was often painful. Emde, who struggled through psychoanalysis, is grateful to her therapist "who stayed by my side on this rocky journey in the search for my Self, my identity, and my roots" ("Occupation Baby" 110).

In her essay "Turning the Beat Around," Lorde defines difference as "a creative force for change" (45–46), and she taught Afro-German women to celebrate their difference and to reject the dichotomy of black and white. Afro-German women create identities that encompass their African and German heritages, and they find such multiple identities empowering. In *Showing Our Colors,* Baum writes that she is proud of being colored: "I don't want to be white or black either, but I do want to be colored" (156). Ayim also resists being put "into a black or white compartment" (157), and in "Racism Here and Now," she entitles one section "The 'In-between World' as Opportunity" (141). Inhabiting the borderlands between cultures can, she believes, be liberating and can lead to greater self-knowledge.[4] She writes: "Always having to examine and explain my situation provided me with more clarity about myself" (*Showing our Colors* 209). She believes that if Afro-Germans "do not accept the external imposition of what seems to be a contradiction, that of being *both* African and German, a self-awareness can develop that necessitates no such fragmentation" (*Showing our Colors* 142). In her view, those whose heritage derives from different cultures have "to deal with their identity in a more intense manner," but this "limbo" existence "between belonging and exclusion" enables them to attain "a form of self-consciousness that does not derive its strength from separatism" (*Showing our Colors* 231). Tina Campt terms the identities that Afro-German women forge for themselves "textured identities" since texture "connotes multiplicity and plurality without fragmentation" (17). Braiding together their cultural heritages becomes for Afro-German women a source of creativity with which they can express their difference.[5]

In *Showing Our Colors,* Oguntoye observes: "African women don't fit the European ideal of beauty" (146). She continues: "It really enrages me that this society makes it so hard for me to regard African women as beautiful. Words don't really exist for me to describe African looks with regard to African women or myself without these inferior standards of beauty. It's not my brown skin that is considered beautiful, but my light-brown skin" (146). In their texts, Afro-German women not only depict their painful struggle from dislike and rejection of their blackness to a growing affirmation and pride in their black bodies, but they also contest Eurocentric notions of beauty that marginalize them. In *Showing Our Colors,* Oguntoye writes: "I really want to get people away from the narrow-minded attitude that German is just blond and blue-eyed. There are so many different types of people here" (150). Ayim agrees and she challenges white Germans to view multicultural coexistence not "as a one-sided process of accommodation and subordination, but as a rapprochement with mutual willingness for change" (*Showing our Colors* 231). Through their texts, Afro-German women have made influential contributions to the ever-growing, minority voices in contemporary German literature and have thus played an important role in raising awareness that, like other European countries, Germany has also become a multi-hued society. In such a society, Ayim hopes words to describe African looks as beautiful will exist.

Notes

1. May Ayim (1960–1996) was a speech therapist in Berlin. Her father came from Ghana, and her mother was German. She was known for her numerous essays on such topics as the history of black people in Germany and racism and was the author of two volumes of poetry, *blues in schwarz weiss* (1995) and *nachtgesang* (1997). Helga Emde was born in 1946. Her mother was German and her father was an African-American soldier. She contributed to the collection *Farbe bekennen* (1986) (*Showing our Colors,* 1992) in which Afro-German women discuss their experiences growing up in Germany. Hügel-Marshall was born in 1947. Like Emde, her mother was German and her father was an African-American soldier. She has written an autobiography, *Daheim unterwegs,* and she lectures about racism at universities in

Berlin.
2. See, for example, racial theories expounded by Houston Stewart Chamberlain and Joseph Arthur Comte de Gobineau.
3. "du bist so weiss wie schnee/ und ich so braun wie scheisse/ das denkst du dir." The English translation is mine.
4. Cultural critics such as Homi K. Bhabha in *The Location of Culture* and Gloria Anzaldúa in "Borderlands" in *The Latino/a Condition* also stress the liberating opportunities of inhabiting "in-between" spaces.
5. In *Autobiographical Voices: Race, Gender, Self-Portraiture,* Françoise Lionnet draws on the Martinican writer Edouard Glissant to explain the concept of "the *métissage* or braiding, of cultural forms" (4). She sees *métissage* as "the fertile ground of our heterogeneous and heteronymous identities as postcolonial subjects" (8).

Works Cited

Anzaldúa, Gloria. "Borderlands." *The Latino/a Condition.* New York: New York UP, 1998. 627–30.
Ayim, May. *nachtgesang: gedichte.* Berlin: Orlanda Frauenverlag, 1997.
———. "Racism Here and Now." *Showing Our Colors: Afro-German Women Speak Out.* Ed. May Opitz, Katharina Oguntoye, and Dagmar Schultz. Trans. Anne V. Adams. Amherst: U of Massachusetts P, 1992. 126–44.
———. "Rassismus und Verdrängung im vereinten Deutschland." *Grenzenlos und unverschämt.* Berlin: Orlanda Frauenverlag, 1997. 133–38.
———. "Weißer Stress und Schwarze Nerven." *Grenzenlos und unverschämt.* Berlin: Orlanda Frauenverlag, 1997. 111–32.
Bhabha, Homi K. *The Location of Culture.* London and New York: Routledge, 1994.
Blackshire-Belay, Carol Aisha. "Historical Revelations: The International Scope of African Germans Today and Beyond." *The African-German Experience: Critical Essays.* Ed. Carol Aisha Blackshire-Belay. Westport, Connecticut: Praeger, 1996. 89–123.
Brand, Peg Zeglin. "Introduction: How Beauty Matters." *Beauty Matters.* Ed. Peg Zeglin Brand. Bloomington and Indianapolis: Indiana UP, 2000. 1–23.
Brownmiller, Susan. *Femininity.* New York: Linden Press/Simon & Schuster, 1984.
Caldwell, Paulette M. "A Hair Piece: Perspectives on the Intersection of Race and Gender." *Duke Law Journal* 40 (1991): 365–96.
Campt, Tina M. "Afro-German Cultural Identity and the Politics of Positionality: Contests and Contexts in the Formation of a German Ethnic Identity." *New German Critique* 58 (Winter 1993): 109–26.
Carroll, Noël. "Ethnicity, Race, and Monstrosity: The Rhetorics of Horror and Humor." *Beauty Matters.* Ed. Peg Zeglin Brand. Bloomington and Indianapolis: Indiana UP, 2000. 37–56.
Eaton, Marcia M. "Kantian and Contextual Beauty." *Beauty Matters.* Ed. Peg Zeglin Brand. Bloomington and Indianapolis: Indiana UP, 2000. 27–36.
Emde, Helga. "An 'Occupation Baby' in Postwar Germany." *Showing Our Colors: Afro-German Women Speak Out.* Ed. May Opitz, Katharina Oguntoye, and Dagmar Schultz. Trans. Anne V. Adams. Amherst: U of Massachusetts P, 1992. 101–11.
———. "I too am German—An Afro-German Perspective." *Who is German? Historical and Modern Perspectives on Africans in Germany.* Ed. Leroy T. Hopkins. Washington: American Institute for Contemporary German Studies, 1999. 33–42.

Fanon, Frantz. *Black Skin, White Masks.* Trans. Charles Lam Markmann. New York: Grove Press, 1967.

Fremgen, Gisela. *. . . und wenn du dazu noch schwarz bist: Berichte schwarzer Frauen in der Bundesrepublik.* Bremen: edition CON, 1984.

Georgoudaki, Ekaterini. *Race, Gender, and Class Perspectives in the Works of Maya Angelou, Gwendolyn Brooks, Rita Dove, Nikki Giovanni, and Audre Lorde.* Thessaloniki: Aristotle U, 1991.

Gilman, Sander L. *On Blackness without Blacks: Essays on the Image of the Black in Germany.* Boston: G. K. Hall, 1982.

Greer, Germaine. *The Whole Woman.* New York: Knopf, 1999.

Hall, Joan Wylie, ed. *Conversations with Audre Lorde.* Jackson: UP of Mississippi, 2004.

Hügel, Ika. "Wir brauchen uns—und unsere Unterschiede." *Entfernte Verbindungen, Rassismus, Antisemitismus, Klassenunterdrückung.* Ed. Ika Hügel, Chris Lange, May Ayim, Ilona Bubeck, Gülsen Aktas, Dagmar Schultz. Berlin: Orlanda Frauenverlag, 1993. 18–32.

Hügel-Marshall, Ika. *Daheim unterwegs: Ein deutsches Leben.* Berlin: Orlanda Frauenverlag, 1998.

Kron, Stefanie. *Fürchte dich nicht, Bleichgesicht!: Perspektivenwechsel zur Literatur afrodeutscher Frauen.* Münster: Unrast Verlag, 1996.

Kwalanda, Miriam and Birgit Koch. *Die Farbe meines Gesichts: Lebensreise einer kenianischen Frau.* Frankfurt am Main: Eichborn, 1999.

Lange, Chris. "Evatöchter wider Willen: Feministinnen und Religion." *Entfernte Verbindungen: Rassismus, Antisemitismus, Klassenunterdrückung.* Ed. Ika Hügel, Chris Lange, May Ayim, Ilona Bubeck, Gülsen Aktas, Dagmar Schultz. Berlin: Orlanda Frauenverlag, 1993. 95–109.

Lionnet, Françoise. *Autobiographical Voices: Race, Gender, Self-Portraiture.* Ithaca and London: Cornell UP, 1989.

Lorde, Audre. "The Master's Tools Will Never Dismantle the Master's House." *Sister Outsider: Essays and Speeches.* Trumansburg, NY: The Crossing Press, 1984. 110–13.

———. "Sadomasochism: Not About Condemnation." *A Burst of Light: Essays by Audre Lorde.* Ithaca, New York: Firebrand Books, 1988. 11–18.

———. "Turning the Beat Around: Lesbian Parenting 1986." *A Burst of Light: Essays by Audre Lorde.* Ithaca, New York: Firebrand Books, 1988. 39–48.

Oguntoye, Katharina, May Opitz, Dagmar Schultz, eds. *Farbe bekennen: Afro-deutsche Frauen auf den Spuren ihrer Geschichte.* Berlin: Orlanda Frauenverlag, 1986.

Opitz, May, Katharina Oguntoye, and Dagmar Schultz, eds. *Showing Our Colors: Afro-German Women Speak Out.* Trans. Anne V. Adams. Amherst: U of Massachusetts P, 1992.

Taylor, Paul C. "Malcolm's Conk and Danto's Colors; or, Four Logical Petitions Concerning Race, Beauty, and Aesthetics." *Beauty Matters.* Ed. Peg Zeglin Brand. Bloomington and Indianapolis: Indiana UP, 2000. 57–64.

Willis, Deborah, and Carla Williams. *The Black Female Body: A Photographic History.* Philadelphia: Temple UP, 2002.

Wolf, Naomi. *The Beauty Myth: How Images of Beauty Are Used Against Women.* New York: William Morrow, 1991.

8. Re-Mapping Nation, Body and Gender in Michael Ondaatje's The English Patient

Lilijana Burcar

The English Patient has been widely applauded for offering a profound critique of Western imperialism and the discourse of nationalism that feeds it (see for example Ismail and Sadashige, respectively). In its interrogation of imperialist, national discourses, the novel erodes their hegemonic premises and lays bare the shaky, normative postulations of unitary, national identity. It does this by featuring national identity both as a matter of constantly fluctuating and reassembling, spatio-temporal relations that are marked by political machinations on the one hand, and a set of highly prescriptive positionalities and enforced, destructive allegiances on the other. Any identity is foregrounded as not only heterogeneous and fluid, but also strikingly open-ended and indeterminable, giving way to embedded and embodied notions of subjectivity. The politics of location thus emerges as an important critical tool in drawing attention to precisely those socio-political and material practices that give rise to a historically specific set of borders and epistemological boundaries, in which discourses like nationalism parade as immutable and intrinsic. Within this operative framework, *The English Patient* also appears to subscribe to a project of re-embodiment which is essential to any interrogation of Western imperialism and dismantling of underlying, nationalist discourses.

It is my contention that *The English Patient*'s project of re-embodiment, which in its own right functions as a supplementary critique of Western, imperialist practices, assumes the body is also understood to be a material net of interconnectedness, and therefore a rhizomatic entity. The rhizomatic, corporeal schema emphasizes the underlying transformability of bodily materiality, as it points to its capacity to function primarily as a set of operational linkages, connections, and multiplicities. As such, it works against prescriptions of uniform embodiment typical of nationalist discourses and directly defies and defeats their demands for identity to be static and firmly entrenched. Curiously, the very disintegration of fixed identities and the shaping of web-like, embodied subjectivities are manifestly captured in the novel's redrawn corporeality of exclusively male-defined bodies. The boundaries of these bodies are shown to be malleable and porous, projecting themselves as categories in the process of becoming. They exist in fact only through exchanges with each other.

The concept of rhizomatic corporalities, however, is not extended to encompass women, who are divested of their hybridity and subsumed instead under the homogenized and universal category of Woman. Reduced to the symbolic function of monolithic woman, women's bodies are instrumentalized to the extent that they come to signify either the external symbolic and physical boundary, or the invisible and marginalized group of what in the end turns out to be only a re-embodied, but still tightly-knit, homosocial community. Precisely by keeping women out and positing a homosocial grouping as the premise of community-building, the text, as it plays itself out, inadvertently reinstalls the basic framework of the nation-state's mythic narrativization and representations of itself. Namely, within this framework, woman has functioned as a sign while historical women have been relegated to the status of secondary citizens through such means as social-sexual contract. It is my second contention that in its anti-imperialist stance, *The English Patient* may well criticize naturalization of nation-state formations, but it does so while neglecting the fact that genderization and sexualization of female corporeality is the central site of their hegemonic, masculine production. This essay demonstrates that while *The English Patient* may question national boundaries precisely by bringing in the concept of rhizomatic embodiment, it cannot debunk them in the end to offer a vision of a truly alternative, political community. By overlooking the gendered dimension of nation-state discourses that are fuelled by gender hierarchizations, so that women's bodies are denied the possibility of escaping imposed fixities, the novel endorses them, in that it eventually works towards the collapse of rhizomatic embodiment under the rubric of homosociality.

This essay, therefore, consists of two parts. The first focuses on the way the novel, by bringing in the rhizomatic schema of embodiment, exposes the cracks in seemingly impenetrable, but in fact very much makeshift, national boundaries. Their latent instability is foregrounded during times of crisis, such as WWII, when ideological and inscriptionally violent, national borders and nationalist, epistemological boundaries implode. The second part points to how the loose ends of seemingly dismantled, nationalist discourse are once again imperceptibly tied up under the conveniently essentialized, corporeal sign of monolithic woman, so that ultimately the novel unwittingly annuls the political potential inherent in the concept of rhizomatic embodiment.

Imagined Communities: Nation as Narration

The story frame of *The English Patient* unravels in the year of 1945, just before the atomic bombing of Hiroshima and Nagasaki. All the principal characters have been transplanted from Britain's dominions or satellite states, and in their coming together they constitute a temporary, makeshift community heavily marked by its members' locatedness "along the edges of waning imperial powers" (Sadashige 245). Thus, the tableau of four characters through whom the story is told includes Hana, a Canadian nurse and daughter of an Italian immigrant; David Caravaggio, a Canadian-Italian friend of Hana's father and a prewar thief turned war-spy; English-educated Count Almasy—known as the English patient—a desert explorer and cartographer; and Kirpal Singh, a Sikh billeted into the British army as a sapper, whose job is to undo the "arbitrary destructiveness of the Allied and Fascist forces" (Hawkins and Danielson 146). Significantly, the end of WWII finds the tableau of the text's four focal characters clustered together in a ruined, Renaissance villa in the north of Italy, the cradle of Humanism, which, among other things, also set in motion the inauguration of nationalist discourses and nation-states. As the ruined villa symbolically epitomizes the house of the imperialist nation lying in ruins, the tableau of the four characters, with their memories and scars left in the wake of the destruction of WWII, problematizes the political reality and conceptual postulation of nation by exposing it as a transitional (fluctuating), social reality and as a form of conceptual violence in the service of expansionist schemas of Western, imperial powers.

The novel follows the characters' traumatic accounts of their war experience, which left them either permanently maimed, shell-shocked, doomed to ghostly death, or simply no longer blindly in love with British ways, and their duplicitous staging of a civilized war in the name of entrenching racially violent and imperialistic partitioning of the world. In the ruined Renaissance villa, these characters come together to implement communal living, which divisive nationalism discourages and precludes. All of them have been recruited under the umbrella of patriotism to fight a war that is not theirs but rather that of ruling, political elites of their respective nation-states or colonial masters, and, therefore, orchestrated primarily by the expansionist interests of Allied and Fascist forces alike. In this war theater, Kirpal's task as a sapper is to defuse bombs and prepare the terrain for the British arrival, while Almasy, as a desert explorer and cartographer, will help to fix the desert for its later use and exploitation by the British and German forces. The key story-teller is Almasy, who recounts to his silent and exhausted caregiver Hana his cartographic endeavors in the desert, early English espionage, his love affair with Katherine, and his fall into the desert, the way the Bedouin took care of him, and kept him alive only to be handed over to the Allies once he gave them the names of the European weapons they wanted. If, under Almasy's guidance, Hana learns to read novels that are directly implicated in the justification of Western imperialism and divisive nationalist discourses (Ismail 412), Kirpal, too, in the end, awakens to these discourses' destructive reality. When the atom bombs are dropped on Japan, he no longer seeks excuses for the behavior of his adopted English fathers but recognizes the policies "of Western wisdom" (284) for what they are: "[. . .] he sees the streets of Asia full of fire. It rolls across cities like a burst map, the hurricane of heat withering bodies as it meets them" (284).

Nation, as Bhabha reminds us, is a modern invention originating in Humanism and enlightened rationality. It stands for a battery of discursive and representational practices which define, legitimate, or valorize specific sets of customs, imprinted memories, and groupings of people as possibilities for developing, controlling, and redistributing resources (During 138–39). Nation as a political and lived reality is, therefore, always a form of narrative, a matter of figurative stratagems and displaced identifications. In short, it is a modern emblem of imagined community, whose totalizing boundaries are a result of inscriptional violence. In order to assert its sovereignty, the imagined community of nation needs to invent its others so as to be able to talk about its progress, homogeneity, and historic continuity in the first place. And it is in this way that nation also enters the discourse of Western imperialism as its main political tool in staging and maintaining the myths of Western, cultural supremacy. The title character, Almasy, eventually comes to hate nations because he realizes they serve as an ideological platform on which Western, imperial practices rest. His greatest desire is to shed the straightjacket of his acquired nationality, which is later achieved in "the emblematic wreckage" (Hawkins and Danielson 143) of his own charred and faceless body. Almasy, the cartographer and desert explorer, comes to understand that "nation-states"—the product of European Humanism—"deform" you (Ondaatje 138), wreaking havoc, destruction, and annihilation in their wake.

The English Patient, at least in its initial stages, undertakes an extensive dissection and condemnation of nationalism as it is employed in the service of imperialist, expansionist projects by simultaneously also calling into account the forms of embodiment that the discourse of nationalism prescribes, circumscribes, or completely disavows. Of crucial importance for the purpose of our discussion here is the metaphor and image of the desert, where "nothing [is] strapped down or permanent" (Ondaatje 22), and where nations are "rapidly and completely interred" (17).

The desert, which cannot be "claimed or owned" because it is "a piece of cloth carried by winds" (138), resists being held down; it refuses to be contained and domesticated within the signifying systems of Western, imperial powers and their national assemblies. The desert, of which Almasy thinks of as "that pure zone between land and chart, between distances and legend, between nature and storyteller" (246), is a place in-between where imperialist maps have no exact translation against the shifting dunes of sand. Even more importantly, juxtaposed against the backdrop of shifting desert sand, these maps betray the instabilities and insecurities inherent in the very narratives of imperial conquests and their weaving of national boundaries. The imperialist practice of laying claim to a land and its peoples, argues McClintock, is not only tied to the act of superimposing original namings with Western, patronymic names, which retrospectively come to function as performative acts of original discovery (20–25). The charting of territories, and by extension the narratability of national boundaries, is also closely related to the process of feminizing and sexualizing the appropriated land, so that its topographical and geological features are reconstructed to resemble the culturally intelligible figurations of the body of a woman. It is precisely this kind of troping of the land that makes it possible for imperialist powers to reassemble and deploy it in the service of their own dubious interests.[1]

These are the kinds of boundaries, the contouring and etching of which the desert's drifting, shifting sands will neither admit nor allow. Caught in an ever-changing kaleidoscope of its disappearances and self-fashioned appearances, the desert can be defined only in terms of its indefinability. The desert, which keeps folding and unfolding itself as an eclectic collection of permutations, refuses to be framed, that is, violently contained within the imperialist tropes of nation-making boundaries. The desert is then an in-between space of signification, where the concept of national enclosures and imperial boundaries collapses. In a desert, that space in-between, nations and their meaning-making processes loaded with the violent rhetoric of boundary inscription, bogus claims to originariness, and utopian dreams of progressiveness sink. In the desert, nations are made "historical with sand across their grasp" (Ondaatje 18). Left in their wake is only a museum of weapons, a testimony of the brutality of these Western nations' practice of drawing so-called civilized maps. So it is to this "museum in the desert" (20) that Almasy, the cartographer, is taken by the Bedouin after being rescued from a burning plane for one specific purpose only—to call out loud, in what is a symbolically reverse gesture of his mapping practices, the name of every single weapon ever deposited in the desert, each of which turns out to be of invariably European parentage.

The charred body of the English patient comes to echo the desert's refusal to be harnessed to the signifying systems by means of which such precarious, political entities as nations inaugurate their boundaries. So it is in the English patient's faceless countenance and burned body that recognizable national, gender (and racial) boundaries are defied and symbolically dissolved and renounced. The body of the English patient serves as a powerful reminder of the fact that the body is "an elaborate sign system, always open to reinterpretation," and is, therefore, "a particularly fraught interface" (Eagleton 302). The English patient's charred body can then be seen as not only offering a profound meta-commentary on the permeability of national borders, but as also exposing the precariousness of such identificatory schemas as nation or race that impinge upon the construction of subjects and their bodily materialities. This can be clearly witnessed in the compulsive and erroneous attempt on the part of the Allies to saddle Almasy with at least a provisional identification, which they retrospectively come to believe to have been his all along. In their desire to pin him down, the Allies come to read him as English, which is a violent inscription the charred body of the English patient bears with impunity through the stories he tells and always with an ironic wink of a knowing, glaringly multifaceted, eye.

Body-Becomings

Alongside the interrogation, deconstruction, and dissolution of the nationalist discourses, *The English Patient* launches a redefined politics of embodiment and corporeality. This politics both refutes the transcendence of the body, otherwise prevalent in masculinist narrations of subjectivity, and defies and argues against the body's traditional sedimentation and hierarchization as witnessed, for example, in psychoanalytical discourse. When the English patient is shot down and falls into the desert from what he calls "the war in heaven" (Ondaatje 5), his badly burnt body bursts out of the wreckage of the crashed plane to share in web-like, rhizomatic, bodily materializations of desert people. This kind of reconfiguration of corporality is best encapsulated in the figure of the Bedouin healer who is summoned to the side of the English patient's ailing body. When Almasy first casts eyes upon the healer, and burdened as he is by his cartographic past, all that he can erroneously decipher is a man's head that appears to be moving on a table towards him (9). But upon closer inspection, realizing that the man is wearing "a giant yoke from which [hang] hundreds of small bottles" (9), he sees the Bedouin healer "moving as if part of a glass curtain, his body enveloped within that sphere" (9). The Bedouin healer, in short, glides along the desert planes like a "wave of glass" (9) that is folding in and out. His arms intertwined with the yoke and tinkling glass bottles melt into "wings" like those of an "archangel" that flutter with "the snatches of the glassy sound" (9).

The glassy figure of the Bedouin healer acts as a truly cyborgean icon that not only points to the malleability of bodily contours and permeability of bodily boundaries, but it also draws attention to the constantly forming and unforming materiality of the body itself. The body here is understood to be a highly diversified, non-unitary, non-holistic and non-singular site of intensities and multiplicities, a flight of forces, capable of undergoing constant permutations, transformations and realignments. Featured as an undulating tapestry of glass bottles, the wooden yoke and flesh, the cyborgean corporeality of the Bedouin healer's body reminds us that embodiment is never "about [permanently] fixed locations in a reified body" (Haraway 195), but about making linkages and connections, about forming assemblages and transitory alignments, about becomings in the Deleuzian sense. Bodies then, as Grosz succinctly puts it, cannot be thought as "hid[ing] or reveal[ing] an otherwise unrepresented latency or depth but [as] a set of operational linkages and connections, with other beings, and other bodies" (120). They can be described only as "discontinuous, non-totalizable series of processes, organs, flows, energies, corporeal substances and incorporeal events" (Grosz 164). Their otherwise porous and highly pliable boundaries, as the cyborgean icon of the Bedouin healer itself demonstrates, indeed materialize and constantly mutate in active interactions with other bodies and objects, themselves understood as planes of intensities and inter-penetrated multiplicities.

Arrangements into which bodies enter together with other multiplicities constitute what Deleuze and Guattari call assemblages. These, according to Grosz's reinterpretation, are "the provisional linkages of elements, fragments, flows of disparate status and substance: ideas, things—human, animate, and inanimate—all [of which] have the same ontological status. [. . .] their law is the imperative of endless experimentation, metamorphoses, or transmutations, alignment and realignment" (167). In the assemblage of the flesh, yoke, and glass bottles, the healer's body, if approached from Deleuze and Guattari's perspective of understanding corporeality and embodiment, can be postulated only as a direction of movement rather than a fixed state or final position. Here the body of the Bedouin, which is enveloped within the shawl of glass bottles but also wrapped around and in-between them, stands for an active engagement in the production of connections, permutations, alignments, and realignments out of which emerge constantly forming and unforming networks of intersecting multiplicities and varying bodily intensities.

The weaving of corporeality as a set of operational linkages, connections, and multiplicities in *The English Patient* is not confined to the desert of 1941 only. The shape-shifting and open-ended corporeality exemplified and embodied in the Bedouin healer's tinkling wings of an archangel also finds its echo in the gardens of the ruined Italian villa in 1945, in the productive bodily-openness of the Sikh sapper, who is fond of "toss[ing] water over himself like a bird using its wing" (Ondaatje 72). This body, too, functions as a set of multiple intensities and active becomings, so when Kirpal, for example, touches the roof of the tent, it seems like he is folding a "khaki wing over himself during the night" (128). Bodily productiveness is also demonstrated by Caravaggio's holding of his hands together like a "human bowl" (54), which echoes the Bedouin healer's body-becoming when he joins the soles of his feet into a "bowl" (35) to make a "skin cup" (10), in which tinctures and medicinal herbs can be mixed. The bed-ridden English patient joins these corporeal becomings as his now "almost liquid" (135) body embarks on a memory journey through the Bedouin's desert out of which he emerged nationless. In their productive openness, these male bodies act as a series of flows and speeds, producing unexpected and unpredictable linkages. They are posited as always productive and connective, as engaged in processes of active becoming, through which they expand their capacities. In Grosz's words, such bodies admit that

> while there must be some kinds of biological limits or constraints, these constraints are perpetually capable of being superseded, overcome, through the human body's capacity to open itself up to prosthetic synthesis, [that is] to transform or rewrite its environment, to continually augment its powers and capacities through incorporation into the body's own spaces and modalities of objects. (187–88)

Assemblages and body-becomings work against the traditional production of body as bounded and bordered, that is, as a fixed, coagulated and rigidified state of being on the one hand, or as inherently united, singular and holistic, self-evidenced materiality of presence on the other. The body is regarded instead in terms of what it can do, "the things it can perform, the linkages it establishes, the transformations and becomings it undergoes, and the machinic connections it forms with other bodies, what it can link with, how it can proliferate its capacities" (Grosz 165). Rhizomatic embodiment is, therefore, a matter of on-going inter-corporeal exchanges, of bodily openness and interchangeability with other bodily planes of multiplicities and intensities. So it is in the desert, along the undulating surface of which glides the iconoclastic cyborgean figure of the Bedouin healer, and where the "sandblasted glass" of medicine bottles has "lost its civilisation" (Ondaatje 10), that the English patient, too, comes to participate in the bodily openness, linkages, and interchangeability with others. For it is primarily by the taste of the saliva that enters him along with the dates he is fed (6) that he gets to know and recognize his Bedouin caretakers. Of the same significance is also a dancing boy's semen that is collected from the desert floor and passed to Almasy's lips to be swallowed like precious water. The potentiality and livability of the body is shown to derive from transformative intercorporeality, from sharing in and with other bodies, things and living beings, with whom it engages in corporeal fluidity and "invention of meaning" (Ricoeur qtd. in Weiss 170). As a matter of affinities, intensities and constant becomings, rhizomatic embodiment thus runs contrary to fixed identities and immutable corporalities insisted on by divisive nationalisms.

Bodies that Signify but Do Not Matter

In *The English Patient*, intercorporeality and active body-becoming do not apply to the bodies of the two female-defined actants, Katherine and Hana, Almasy's lover and the Canadian nurse, respectively. The bodies of the two women and their forms of embodiment instead remain tied to the institution of femininity. Here women's bodies either teeter on the edge of total erasure by being turned into a nursing appendage to the huge, engulfing, human body of the nation, or feature as a set of fragmented, disassociated, body parts, which are then translated "into [the] text of the desert" (236).

The latter practice of inscribing and molding the body pertains to Katherine's corporeality. Her body springs into life only through the narration of the stratifying, territorializing, and cartographic gaze of her lover-observer Almasy. He is the one who hates boundaries and nations. And yet he places boundaries around Katherine's body so that outlined against the constellation of male bodies gushing forth with a preponderance of loosened, dismantled, and obliterated national borders, hers appears anachronistically trapped in a fixed position. Transfixed by Almasy's probing eyes, her corporeality is chopped up and shredded into snippets of fragmented body parts so that the body she can no longer hold on to and claim as her own becomes only "[a] sweating knee beside the gearbox" (Ondaatje 150), a sensuous mouth gulping "the chlorinated water [with] some coming down her chin, [and] falling to her stomach" (149), a "jaw cupped in her hands" (229), a cluster of "awkward limbs climbing out of a plane" (144), a pointed "elbow" next to a camp fire (144). Held in the gaze of Almasy's cartographic eyes, Katherine's body is dismembered, while its floating, scattered parts are labeled with proprietorial "official names" (241), and thereby re-assembled and re-appropriated to be used in the description of landscape features. Thus, Almasy cannot think of "the hollow indentation" "at her neck" (162, 241) except in terms of the Bosphorus Strait he would like to dive into. Similarly, he is incapable of describing Katherine unless he resorts to "arching out in the air the shape of a mesa or a rock" (235). His way of looking at Katherine, by reducing her to the parts of her fragmented body, therefore echoes old map-making practices in which, for example, a recently discovered oasis would be placed onto a map by being described as the "white-dove shoulders" of a woman bathing (140). Fragmented and re-appropriated, parts of Katherine's body, then, meet a specific fate, shedding light on imperialist practices of land usurpation. Transformed into the landscape, which is in turn constructed as feminine, they go to show that the "knowledge of the unknown world is mapped as a metaphysics of gender violence" (McClintock 22). As soon as this world is feminized, it is also turned into the kind that can be "spatially spread for male exploration" (McClintock 22) and re-appropriation.

Katherine's embodiment cannot escape the straight-jacket of being tampered with as the contours of her fragmented and shredded body parts are endlessly retraced to fit the mould of imperialist practices of charting and claiming unknown land. According to this text's scenario, it is only in death that Katherine's body can extricate itself from the dictates of the map-making practices that turn it into a whirl of fragmented, dissociated body parts. It is only in death that the body of Katherine can be attended to in a way different from the one dictated by the imposing constraints of cartographic practices. It is in death that the shell of Katherine's specularly constructed embodiment is cracked open to reveal a corpse whose stiffened features can no longer be construed along gender lines. For in death these dissolve to be replaced with a web-like, expanding, and intercorporeal kind of bodily materiality, in which lodge "a richness of lovers and tribes, tastes [one has] swallowed, bodies [one has] plunged into and swum up as if rivers of wisdom, characters [one has] climbed up into as if trees, fears [one has] hidden in as if caves" (Ondaatje 264).

As Katherine's fragmented body is for ever lost by being scattered across the desert and buried in the cartographic narrative of landscape drawing, what are we to make of Hana's body and her forms of embodiment then? While men's bodies, including that of the Bedouin healer, are shown to be productive bodies, constantly proliferating and expanding their capacities in transformative interaction with other bodies and their environs, Hana's body is doomed to performing stunts of ongoing corporeal disappearances. These concern the remolding of her body into an invisible, fixed, nursing body whose professional tools are not the extension or foundation of her active becoming, but come to function as a form of her literal and metaphoric displacement. If Kirpal, for instance, can enjoy the physicalness of his body and is subconsciously in love with it (75), Hana cannot, because the refurbishing her body undergoes results in its shrinkage and elision, so much so that her tongue is exchanged for and replaced by a swab, her tooth for a needle, and her mouth for the mask with codeine drops (125). This shrinkage of Hana's body conditions her relocation along the side of the huge body of the nation ravaged in war, and male by default. Bending over this huge, dying body heavy with tons of shrapnel metal and wriggling worms, Hana's constrained, nursing body is called upon, as a part of its patriotic duty, to "put up with the insults and the advances of the dying men" it tends (Ismail 430). To this huge, dying, human body, a nursing body is a mere appendage, a non-entity, but the kind of non-entity that continues to nurse even when the war is over. In the house of the nation lying in ruins somewhere in the north of Italy, the nursing body is still a "vagrant" (Ondaatje 14), craving for its resurrection, while the English patient, the epitome of the dying empire and its nationalist discourses, "reposes in his bed like a king" (14). In the crumbling house of the nation, the nursing body remains an obscure entity, still attending to the nation's feces, clearing out its urine, and dabbing at its wounds oozing with pus. It is in the ruined house of the nation that the footfalls of the nursing body continue to reverberate with the echoes of dislocation, isolation, and disconnectedness.

Conclusion

The English Patient problematizes national boundaries and illuminates the destructive nature of divisive nationalisms. However, in doing so, it fails to ask whose imagined communities nation-states really are. A closer look at their gendered structuration shows them to be gender-specific schemas of hierarchically organized distribution of entitlements and benefits on the one hand, and equally restrictive management of body images and forms of embodiment on the other. Within these unequal, gender-marked, and highly stratified social relations most women come second and men come first. By casting the tenacity of national boundaries into question, the novel works towards offering an alternative form of non-restrictive, rhizomatic embodiment. But as this embodiment is turned into the exclusive preserve of homosocial groupings, its political potential is irrevocably undercut, so that in the end the novel unwittingly subscribes to what it aims to undermine.

Note

1. This process of land appropriation and mapping is made possible in the first place because the female body itself is reconstituted, redrawn and instrumentalized as the abject other so that it can serve as the boundary marker of what are then essentially imperialist, fraternal communities. This instrumentalization and marginalisation of woman's body also reflects a gender-driven, inscriptional, and structural violence lying at the heart of imperialist projects. It points to another form of instability inherent in the formation and imposition of boundaries constitutive of imperialist nations (McClintock 1–25).

Works Cited

Bhabha, Homi K. "Introduction: Narrating the Nation." *Nation and Narration*. Ed. Homi. K. Bhabha. London: Routledge, 1994. 1–7.

Deleuze, Gilles and Felix Guattari. *A Thousand Plateaus: Capitalism and Schizophrenia*. Trans. Brian Massumi. 1988. London: The Athlone Press, 1999.

During, Simon. "Literature—Nationalism's Other? The Case of Revision." *Nation and Narration*. Ed. Homi K. Bhabha. London: Routledge, 1994. 138–53.

Eagleton, Mary. "Adrienne Rich, Location and the Body." *Journal of Gender Studies* 9 (2000): 299–312.

Grosz, Elizabeth. *Volatile Bodies*. Bloomington: Indiana UP, 1994.

Haraway, Donna. *Simians, Cyborgs, and Women: The Reinvention of Nature*. New York: Routledge, 1991.

Hawkins, Susan E. and Susan Danielson. "The Patients of Empire." *Literature Interpretation Theory* 13 (2002): 139–53.

Ismail, Qadri. "Discipline and Colony: *The English Patient* and the Crow's Nest of Post Coloniality." *Postcolonial Studies* 12 (1999): 403–36.

McClintock, Anne. *Imperial Leather: Race, Gender and Sexuality in the Colonial Contest*. New York: Routledge, 1995.

Ondaatje, Michael. *The English Patient*. New York: Vintage, 1993.

Sadashige, Jacqui. "Sweeping the Sands: Geographies of Desire in *The English Patient*." *Literature Film Quarterly* 26 (1998): 242–53.

Weiss, Gail. *Body Images: Embodiment as Intercorporeality*. New York: Rutledge, 1999.

9. *Classical Enfleshments of Love*[1]

LEAH BRADSHAW

The Western canon of philosophy, as we know well, is one that valorizes mind over body, reason over passions, self-sufficiency over neediness and dependency. We also know that these polarizations have meant that the male is valued over the female, because it is the male who is associated historically with independence, detachment, and intellectual rigor, while the female has been associated with all things buried in the flesh: chaos, the fusion of identities and bodies, dependence. Women appear hardly at all in most revered texts of the Western canon of philosophy, and when they do, they are portrayed as weak (Aristotle), or sexually avaricious (Rousseau), or familial to the point of being apolitical (Hegel), or other variations on these themes. In almost all cases, because there is a higher value attached to independence, detachment and intellectual self-sufficiency, the "fleshy" embeddedness of women in cycles of pregnancy, child-care, and sexual passivity is a mark of inferiority. Attachment to things of the world, especially to bodies, is a liability.

In the classical context, Aristotle is the clearest on this separation of intellectual "good" from other human goods. In the *Nicomachean Ethics*, Aristotle undertakes an exhaustive chronicle of human virtues, concluding with his assessment of the happiest life. A happy life is one lived in accordance with virtue, Aristotle tells us, but there are really two kinds of virtue, the active life of engagement in the political world, and the more ascetic life of intellectual contemplation. Of the two kinds of happiness, the life of intellectual virtue is preferable, Aristotle says, because "the activity of understanding [. . .] aims at no end other than itself [. . .] and is self-sufficient, leisured and unwearied, as far as these are possible for a human being" (1177b20). The philosophic life, according to Aristotle, is the "god-like life," a life superior to the human and "as far as we can, we ought to be pro-immortal, and go to all lengths to live a life that expresses our supreme element," because this life "surpasses everything in power and value" (1177b30). By comparison, the other kind of virtue, that associated with "human things," is inferior. It is happiest "in a secondary way," because a life of active participation in the world is one more attached to *feelings,* and "feelings actually seem to arise from the body; and in many ways virtue of character seems to be proper to feelings" (1178a15).

Aristotle describes the life of practical virtue, embedded in feelings and aimed at the development of character, as a "compound" of mind and body, and what is compounded for him is less pure and good than something that is singular and pure. "Philosophy seems to have remarkably pure and firm pleasures; and it is reasonable for those who have knowledge to spend their lives more pleasantly than those who seek it" (*Nicomachean Ethics* 1177a25). The more removed our activity from the attachment to flesh, and labor, and to all the troubles of the world, the more likely we will be to approach happiness. With regard to the body and its capacity for happiness, Aristotle remarks that "anyone at all, even a slave, no less than the best person, might enjoy bodily pleasures; but no one would allow that a slave shares in happiness, if one does not also allow that the slave shares in the sort of life needed for happiness" [presumably the life of contemplation] (*Nicomachean Ethics* 1177a5–10).

The polarization that Aristotle draws between mind and body, the virtues of philosophy, and the lesser virtues of all other activity, seems to be widely characteristic of classical Greek thought, and indeed, to have set the parameters of the mind/body split that typifies much of the Western tradition. In light of this, it is particularly striking that Socrates, in the *Symposium*, should draw upon powerful images of the flesh, and particularly of female pregnancy and birth, in order to give an account of philosophy. Pregnancy is generative, not autonomous, it is fleshy, not ascetic, and it is a laboring activity, not a contemplative one. We want to explore this path in Plato's *Symposium*, in comparison to some of the other thoughts on women and the flesh in ancient texts, and offer some thoughts on why Socrates chose to embed philosophy in these fleshy female metaphors.

Plato's *Symposium* is an arresting dialogue among a number of men who have come together in a drinking party to discuss the subject of *eros*.[2] Much of the discussion is about homoerotic love, which we know was prevalent among Athenian citizens and usually took the form of a liaison between a mature man and a young boy. As Morton Hunt remarks: "pederasty was hardly a Greek invention [. . .] but in Greece it acquired a veneer of philosophy and was dignified as a superior relationship. And therein lies the reason, not merely the apology, for its prevalence in classical times. Even Aristotle defended at length in his *Nicomachean Ethics* the proposition: 'Love and friendship are found most and in their best form between men'" (46). Most often in Plato's dialogue, it is the love of young boys that preoccupies the discussion. But Socrates challenges this homoerotic grounding of philosophy in the *Symposium*. In an encounter with Alcibiades, the Greek tyrant, at the close of the dialogue, we learn that Alcibiades was frustrated by Socrates' rebuffing of his advances. Socrates admonished Alcibiades for his sexual longings, and suggested to him that there are higher things than consummation of lust. In the dramatic context of the *Symposium*, Alcibiades had burst into the party late, and had missed the crowning speech of Socrates, in which Socrates had described what he learned about love from the priestess Diotima. It is in this account of Diotima's "ladder of love" that we find Socrates' remarkable depiction of philosophy in the language and metaphor of pregnancy and generation. We will look at Socrates' account of love in his recounting of Diotima's advice, and then assess what this might mean for the "enfleshment" of philosophy. We want to contrast the love that is depicted in Diotima's ascent with the tyrannical possessiveness of Alcibiades. Ultimately, we want to know if Socrates' association of philosophy with womanly *eros* leads to an embodied account of philosophy that resists the kinds of polarization that we find in Aristotle (and subsequently in much of the Western tradition of thought), or if it reinforces them. First a word about just how unorthodox it is to find the figure of a woman (Diotima) set up as an exemplar of the philosophic life.

Women rarely appear any place else in the Platonic dialogues, and women generally were conspicuously absent from politics and philosophy in ancient Athens. When women do enter the dialogues, it is usually in a disparaging way. There is reference in Plato's *Republic* to the flute girls, whose beautiful music Socrates actually warns against in the ideal city as a cause of corruption and laxity. Of some note in the classical context were the *hetaerae*, a sort of female "friend," and a high-level courtesan. These women in Athens were often from "good" families (that is, from the families of Greek citizens), and were noted for their intelligence and beauty and their capacity to attract and entertain intelligent men.

In the *Republic*, Socrates has nothing to say about the *hetaerae* but he castigates mothers for diverting their sons away from philosophy, and toward the more worldly activities of wealth, politics, and power. Women are depicted in the *Republic* as covetous and corrupting, fond of money and luxury, and contemptuous of the rigor and asceticism of philosophy. The key factor in the dissolution of democracy, according to Socrates, is the diminishing of honor and the turn toward excess acquisition. "[Democratic citizens] and their wives are willing to disobey the laws so as to increase their own wealth and status" (Plato, *Republic* 550d). Aristotle, in the *Politics*, shows similar contempt for the negative influences of women. In a city where legislation for women is poorly handled, he says, the women will live "licentiously in every respect and in luxury" (1269b20). Aristotle identified the laxity toward women as one of the formative elements in the decline of Sparta. "What difference is there between women ruling and rulers who are ruled by women? For the result is the same. Boldness is something useful in war (if then) rather than in everyday matters, but the Spartan women have been harmful even in this respect. This became clear in the Theban invasion; they were not only wholly useless, like women in other cities, but they created more uproar than the enemy" (1269b39).

In light of these references to women in the philosophic corpus of both Plato and Aristotle, it is all the more surprising to find Socrates' account of philosophy as told through the reading of Diotima. When they are mentioned at all in the texts of classical Greek philosophy, women appear conventionally as prostitutes/companions/musicians (intellectual, but not procreative), or as covetous wives, who need to be ruled imperiously by their husbands, lest political corruption and chaos ensue. Diotima is unique in two senses that interest us here. First, she associates philosophy with the love of another, which appears to be a radical break from the idea that the philosopher is as self-sufficient and autonomous as possible. Second, in making her case, she draws upon the generative imagery of childbirth, thus turning not just to women, but to *procreation*, in developing her argument.

Diotima asserts that "all human beings are pregnant in body and mind," and all people, approaching adulthood, "naturally desire to give birth" (Plato, *Symposium* 206c). She also claims that we cannot give birth in that which is ugly, but "only in what is beautiful." When a "pregnant creature" approaches birth in beauty, she tells us, it becomes "gentle and joyfully relaxed" (206d), but when the same creature comes close to something ugly, "it frowns and contracts in pain; it turns away and shrivels up and does not reproduce; it holds the foetus inside and is in discomfort" (206d). This is why, according to Diotima, those swollen with pregnancy get so excited about beauty, because "the bearer of beauty enables them to gain release from the pains of childbirth" (206e–207a). Reproduction is the object of love, because giving birth is the closest that mortal creatures can come to being permanently alive and immortal. "The object of love is to have the good always" and so it follows that "we must desire immortality along with the good" (206e–207a).

Diotima does not speak of the pregnant woman, but of the pregnant *man*. Men who are pregnant in their bodies, she says, "are drawn more toward women; they express their love in trying to obtain for themselves immortality and remembrance and what they take to be happiness by reproducing children" (208e–209a). But there are those men who are "more pregnant in their minds than in their bodies, and are pregnant with what is suitable for a mind to bear and bring to birth" (205e–209a). The suitable things are "wisdom and other kinds of virtue," things of the mind, and these are the things brought to life by the poets and "those craftsmen who are said to be innovative" (205e–209a). These reproducers are nobler than the reproducers of actual children, because their immortality far exceeds that of their bodily brothers.

Someone who is pregnant from youth "feels the desire to give birth and reproduce" and he goes looking for beauty. If he's lucky, he will find a comparable mind that is "beautiful, noble and naturally gifted," and in this relationship, he perhaps will give birth to the child "with which he has long been pregnant" (Plato, *Symposium* 209c). Such a fortunate man will have a more gratifying love than the parents of children because the "children" (ideas) produced in this partnership "are more beautiful and immortal." Everyone, Diotima tells us, would prefer to have "children like that rather than human children" (209c). The children of the mind are always conceived in beauty, always conceived in "gentleness and joy." There is none of the unpredictability that accompanies the gestation of actual bodies, none of the pain and blood, and the possibility of deformity and defect, in short, of ugliness that accompanies real birth. "Don't you realize," Diotima admonishes Socrates, "that it's only in that kind of life, when someone sees beauty with the part that can see it, that he'll be able to give birth not just to images of virtue [. . .] but to true virtue?" (212a).

We may love a particular person, Diotima says, but she insists that what we really love in that person is the intimation of the good, the beautiful, and the true. We love particular people for the good that is incarnate in them, not because the person reciprocates our love. Of course, this raises the question of why we ought to be loyal to any particular love object, particularly if we find another one whose embodiment of "the good" is greater. And indeed, Diotima tells us that the truly erotic person will move from love of a particular being, to love of all particular beings that embody goodness, to finally, more universal objects of good. Diotima moves from images of corporal love to increasingly abstract notions, until finally she suggests that the greatest lovers love beauty itself. At the apex of her speech, Diotima asks: "What should we imagine it should be like if someone could see beauty itself, absolute, pure, unmixed, not cluttered up with human flesh and colors and a great mass of mortal rubbish, but if he could catch sight of beauty itself, in its single form?" (211d–e). This would be the greatest love, and it is a love that is "given birth" through "magnificent discourses and ideas" (211d–e).

It is noteworthy that Plato has appropriated the powerful image of birth to describe the activity of philosophizing. Philosophy is a generation of something outside the self, comparable to the act of giving birth to a human being who is separate from the self. Only it is *better*, because the "child" is purer and more beautiful than any human child, and the actual act of birthing is always "gentle and joyful," because its product is always beautiful. Ugly ideas get stuck in the "womb" of the philosopher's soul. In real corporal birth, the child emerges in pain and suffering from the womb, whether it is ugly or beautiful, perfect or imperfect.

In Page DuBois' reading of the *Symposium*, "[Diotima] teaches [Socrates] that the philosophical intercourse, conception, pregnancy and delivery of male lovers are superior to the corporeal acts of human women" (182). DuBois argues that Diotima's speech, rather than celebrating birth, actually appropriates maternity for the male philosopher. The philosopher, who plants his "seed" (his words) in the soul of another, "will begin an endless process of purely masculine reproduction, where the process is more words, more deeds" (178). In praising the love of virtue, beyond all images of virtue, she argues that Plato employs the metaphor of female birth to "authorize the male philosopher" and his project of "monistic metaphysics, the positing of a one—father, son, god—who is the source and origin of the good" (DuBois 169). Dubois sees Plato's *Symposium* as definitive for the model of the male philosopher, "the figure whom Michel Foucault sees as the figure of mastery, the center of philosophical and erotic practices from this moment on" (183). The male philosopher becomes through Diotima's account "the site of metaphorical reproduction, the subject of philosophical generation," and the female by contrast is "stripped of her metaphorical otherness," becoming less than the male, defined by her "lack" of the beautiful and the good (DuBois 183).

David Halperin has broached the questions of why Diotima is a woman, and why she speaks of philosophy in the metaphorical language of birth, and he provides persuasive answers. Halperin claims that Plato's Diotima draws on two distinctive views of women in the Greece of Plato's time. The first is that "women are less able than men to resist pleasures of all sorts; they enjoy sex too much and once initiated into the joys of sex, they become insatiable and potentially treacherous" (265).[3] The second view is that "women do not possess (as men do) a free-floating desire that ranges from one object to another, stimulated in each case by beauty, nobility or other cultural values [. . .] rather, their desire is conditioned by their physical nature, which aims at procreation and needs to fulfill itself by drawing off substance from men" (265). This dual conception of women seems to fit with the two prototypes of women identified earlier in this paper: woman as *hetaerae* (sexual predator and disrupter) and woman as mother and wife. Halperin argues that Diotima's birthing metaphor aims to collapse these two views of women into a "new and distinct paradigm that combines erotic responsiveness with (pro)creative aspirations" (265), except the paradigm is imparted to the male philosopher. Socrates effectively combines the two views of women to refute and overcome the more conventional pederastic model of *eros,* captured in the sexual act between an aggressive older male and a passive younger male. Sexual activity between males typically was "thematized on domination," Halperin argues, and all sexual relations were construed as hierarchical. Plato's male citizen was accustomed to an "aggressively phallic norm of sexual conduct," whereas women "were thought capable of both giving and receiving pleasure in the sexual act at the same time" (270). Mutuality of sexual desire, Halperin thus suggests, was originally a female *eros*. In an effort to dislocate both the hierarchical structure of male relations, and the warrior-like domination that infused male friendships in the classical world, Plato borrows from images of female sexuality in order to introduce the benefits of reciprocity into male discourse.

> Erotic reciprocity animates what Plato considers the best sort of conversation, those in which each interlocutor is motivated to search within himself, and to say what he truly believes in the confidence that it will not be misunderstood; mutual desire makes possible the ungrudging exchange of questions and answers which constitute the soul of philosophical practice. Reciprocity finds its ultimate expression in dialogue. (Halperin 270)

Halperin thus believes that Socrates takes from the sexual *eros* of women, and its potential for the mutual gratification of desire, a model for philosophic reciprocity. The paradigm for philosophical exchange is not the penetration of another, but the mutuality of benefit. Yet, in Plato's *Symposium*, as we have seen, Socrates, through Diotima, borrows from the second side of women's experience as well, the connection of sexuality to mothering. For sexuality in women has these two distinct dimensions, satisfaction of desire, and pregnancy. In women, orgasm and gestation are two separate things, whereas in male sexuality the potential for reproduction in the spilling of seed is coincidental with the gratification of desire. Diotima suggests that the only real objective of love is reproduction, not the satisfaction of desire. Something must come out of the expression of love, whether it is an actual child, in the case of bodily *eros*, or whether it is an idea, the generation of philosophical intercourse. "The climax to which beauty summons us [. . .] is manifestly not of a sexual kind, as every student of 'Platonic love' knows: beauty arouses only those who are already pregnant, and intercourse culminates not in orgasm but in giving birth" (Halperin 288). Halperin concludes, rightly it seems, that womanly love, as it is characterized by Diotima in the *Symposium*, is displaced onto a model of philosophic discourse, or else emptied into gestation. Female *eros* as something unto itself disappears.

Luce Irigaray echoes these thoughts in her deconstruction of the *Symposium*, in which Irigaray shows how *eros* is transformed in the course of Diotima's discourse, from an energy between two lovers, to a cause of a final generation: whether the child, in the case of bodily lovers, or ideas, in the case of philosophic lovers. "A beloved who is an end is substituted for the love between men and women. A beloved who is a *will*, even a *duty*, and a *means* of achieving immortality, which the lovers can neither attain nor aspire to within themselves" ("Sorcerer Love" 27). For Irigaray, this is "the failure of love." "Something becomes frozen in space-time, with the loss of a vital intermediary and of an accessible transcendental that remains alive. A sort of teleological triangle is put into place instead of a perpetual journey, a perpetual transvaluation, a permanent becoming" ("Sorcerer Love" 27). Moreover, in the ascent from the body to the realm of the mind, we find that carnal reproduction is supplanted by the generation of beautiful and good ideas, "immortal" things. "In this way, moreover, it comes to pass that *love between men is superior to love between man and woman"* ("Sorcerer Love" 27).

Philosophy, in Diotima's account, combines metaphorically the two dimensions of womanhood—sexual desire in reciprocity, and the giving of birth—in a new model for contemplative reason that goes beyond the female entirely. In Halperin's view, "[Diotima's] presence endows the pedagogic process by which men reproduce themselves culturally—by which they communicate the secrets of their wisdom and social identity, the 'mysteries' of male authority, to one another across generations—with the prestige of female procreativity" (288). In doing so, Diotima effectively eclipses the difference of women and denies women the truly unique contributions of their sex to our understanding of desire and reproduction. Birthing is co-opted for the purposes of male generation. Halperin calls this "mimetic transvestism" (291). Reluctantly, Halperin concludes that Plato's *Symposium,* and Diotima's speech in particular within that dialogue, tell us very little about the experience of women, but tell us a lot about men. Women's *eros* turns out to be inferior to the *eros* of the male philosopher, and Diotima turns out to be a trope. "From the perspective of the male world, at least, there is no such thing as authentic femininity. 'Woman' and 'man' are figures of male speech. Gender is an irreducible fiction" (Halperin 297).

While Halperin's thoughts on Diotima are provocative, and in many aspects persuasive, there is evidence in the *Symposium* that Plato did think there were insurmountable gender differences between men and women that have consequences for philosophic education. The co-option of the female by philosophy may be an ideal that can never be realized. The last interlocutor in the *Symposium* is Alcibiades, the famous Greek tyrant, and the man whom Socrates names in the *Gorgias* as the only love in his life that could rival his love of truth (Plato, *Gorgias* 481d). Alcibiades was everything that Socrates was not: handsome, impetuous, politically ambitious, immoderate and excessive in his passions. Socrates remarked in the *Symposium:* "I shudder at his madness and his passion for love" (213d6). Martha Nussbaum describes Albibiades as one who exuded power, beauty, grace, and vanity. He was a man who "loved to be loved," who was "rapidly moved to both love and anger," and who "hated to be observed, skinned, discovered" (Nussbaum 165).

Alcibiades chides Socrates in the *Symposium* for resisting his sexual advances, and Socrates responds characteristically that there are things higher than the body that Alcibiades ought to gratify. Alcibiades, however, seems either incapable or unwilling to pursue the philosophic example of Socrates. In

Classical Enfleshments of Love

his pursuit of Socrates, Nussbaum says, Alcibiades takes on the role of the *erastes* (the sexually active partner), while Socrates is the *eromenos,* "a beautiful creature without needs of his own" (190). This makes Alcibiades the needy one, the one who is both open to, and desires to open up to, another. "Alcibiades reminds us," says Nussbaum, "that the urge to open things up, to get at and explore the inside concealed by the outside, is one of our earliest and strongest desires, a desire in which sexual and epistemological need are joined and, apparently, inseparable" (190).

Alcibiades, this most masculine of men, loved women, and loved them carnally. Famously, after ordering the slaughter of the insurgents in Melos, he took one of the captured women as his lover and with her conceived a son. In another example, Plutarch tells the story of Alcibiades having the painter Aristophon render a portrait of him reclining in the arms of a prostitute, and displaying the portrait in public. "The multitudes seemed pleased with the piece and thronged to see it, but older people disrelished it and looked on these things as enormities, and movements toward tyranny" (Plutarch 269). Alcibiades appears at the end of the *Symposium* in a drunken and erotic state, crowned with a wreath of ivy and violets, a sign of Aphrodite and suggestive "of the strange fact that this aggressively masculine figure sees himself as a female divinity" (Nussbaum 193). We know from Plutarch that the night before he died, Alcibiades dreamed of himself garbed in the clothes of a woman. He was trapped and murdered while secluded with a prostitute, and after the arrow had killed him "the courtesan Timandra 'Honour-The-Man' wrapped his bitten body and his soul of flesh in her own clothes and buried him sumptuously in the earth" (Nussbaum 199).

These images of Alcibiades, in all their carnality, and their associations with women, contrast markedly with the images of Socrates, the exemplary philosopher. Martha Nussbaum examines Diotima's speech to Socrates and finds in it the very antithesis of everything that Alcibiades embodies. Diotima encourages a life that is attached to an "immortal object," rather than to mortal flesh, a life that leans toward "blissful contemplative completeness" rather than a "painful yearning for a single body and spirit" (Nussbaum 183). Socrates is presented to us as a man who appears to have no needs, a man who can drink without ever getting drunk, a man who is never sexually tempted, a man who cares nothing for luxury, nor even much for ordinary sustenance, and who certainly cares nothing for reputation. He is a man whom Nussbaum describes as both "excellent and deaf" (184).

Could it be that Socrates' "excellence" and "deafness" actually are a consequence of his having transgressed the differences between male and female? Socrates, in fact, is *not like us,* because he is neither male nor female. His "mimetic transvestism" (to borrow Halperin's term) is inhuman. In the accounts of Alcibiades' life and death, there are intimations of transvestism as well: we note that Alcibiades appeared at the *Symposium*, draped in ivy and violets (also the symbol for democratic Athens herself), and that he dreamed of himself dressed as a woman the night before his death. But in the case of Alcibiades, the longing for the other (the female) is a tragic longing, never to be completed.

Diotima tells us that *eros* is a son, born of his mother, Poverty, and his father, Resource. Poverty "formed the plan of relieving her lack of resource by having a child by Resource; she slept with him and became pregnant with Love" (203c). Love resembles both his mother and his father. From his mother "he is always poor; far from being sensitive and beautiful, as is commonly supposed, he's tough [. . .] sharing his mother's nature, he is always in a state of need." Insofar as Love resembles his father, he "schemes to get hold of beautiful and good things" (203d), "he desires knowledge and is resourceful in getting it; a lifelong lover of wisdom; clever at using magic, danger and sophistry" (203e). Eros is between wisdom and ignorance, Diotima says, as between his father who is "wise and resourceful" and his mother "who has neither quality" (204b). From this in-between state, Eros can fulfill his proper end only if he moves away from the mother toward the father, toward a greater participation in wisdom. To follow the ways of the mother, to embrace her neediness, is to fail in fulfilling one's philosophic nature.

Is this not exactly what Alcibiades does? Alcibiades fails in the philosophic project, because he fails to "choose" between his mother and his father. He not only experiences neediness, but goes to immoderate lengths to gratify it. He loves women and womanly things, but he does not try to assimilate them into his own being. He resists Socrates' call to wisdom, because he is a bodily lover and a lover of difference, spectacle, worldly, fleshy ambition, and all the things that Socrates turns away from. We must conclude that, as far as Socrates' account is concerned, Alcibiades' fleshiness and his love of all things worldly, including women, are also what incline him toward tyranny. Women and womanly *eros* appear to be, as Aristotle depicted them, central to the decay of political and philosophic virtue.

Diotima—whom we never know directly, but only as filtered through the voice of Socrates—and Alcibiades—the actual man whom Socrates claims to have loved as much as he loved truth—are the two poles of Socratic *eros*. Diotima appropriates the female experiences of sexual desire and pregnancy to illuminate a model of philosophical inquiry. By doing so, she collapses the two distinct "types" of woman present in the life of Athenian citizens, the *hetaerae* (the sexual and philosophic companion of intellectual men) and the citizen/wife/mother (the bearer of Athenian citizens). While sexual and intellectual stimulation, and pregnancy, appeared as two disparate elements of female experience in the mind of the Athenian male, Socrates attempts to put them together in a single model of philosophic virtue. The male philosopher, following Diotima, will be erotically responsive to those who are his equals, and by pursuing beauty and truth, he will "give birth" to children of the mind. But Alcibiades stands, at the end of the *Symposium*, as a living refutation of the impossibility, perhaps the undesirability, of this ideal. Alcibiades' splendor is undeniable, but that splendor is bound up with the waywardness of his *eros*. Alcibiades is a lover of women, and in his love of women we can see associations of his love of reputation and honor, riches and conquests. His soul is neither quiet nor singularly virtuous.

A thorough reading of Plato's *Symposium*, I conclude, requires attention to both Diotima and Alcibiades. Diotima's speech does co-opt the experience of women, as David Halperin suggests, in order to forge a new model for philosophy: a model that maintains the split between body and mind, but which masterfully incorporates the most fleshy images of reproduction and gestation as metaphors for the philosopher's "giving birth" to great ideas. Alcibiades, Socrates' other great love, stands as a glaring refutation of this model, since Alcibiades was a man who loved women, wealth and power more than he loved beautiful ideas and virtue. Perhaps "woman" is at the heart of this contest between philosophy and politics. Perhaps Socrates borrows from the female experiences of sexuality, pregnancy, and reproduction precisely because these are the most threatening enticements away from the devotion to intellectual ideals. It is the carnal female who represents all that is "fallen" and corrupting in the world (hence, all the derogatory references to women in the corpora of Plato and Aristotle). Alcibiades, in his love of women and his transvestite dreams of *becoming* a woman, remains caught in this fallen condition.

In the framing of the *Symposium*, we would have to say *eros* is trapped between the enfleshment of the body (the female) and the asceticism of the mind (the male). The philosopher tries to escape this entrapment by transforming the experience of the female into a metaphor for his own self-generation, but this, even by Diotima's account, can never work. The *quest* for the good is lodged in the female, in her neediness and her poverty. From the mother, *Eros* gets his restlessness and his questing nature. As Irigaray notes, "his passion for love, for beauty, for wisdom, comes to him from his mother, and from the date that he was conceived. Desired and wanted, moreover, by his mother" ("Sorcerer Love" 24).

In this paper, I have attempted to explore Plato's *Symposium* because of what appears at first reading to be an anomalous reference to female experiences of pregnancy and birth, as a metaphor for the experience of practicing philosophy. In the context of classical Greek philosophy, and for that matter, in most of the Western tradition of thought, philosophy is partner to a disembodied reason. Women, whether as sexual partners of men or as the bearers of children, are characteristically portrayed as mired in the flesh, and as creatures that pull men towards acquisition, power and all material things of the world.

I have found that Plato's employment of female imagery in the *Symposium* actually draws on the female experience in order to transcend it, and by taking pregnancy and birth out of the body, and making these properties of the male mind, he has in fact co-opted the female for the purposes of philosophy. Diotima's depiction of philosophy in the metaphors of female sexuality and birthing serves to theorize the image of the philosopher as an autonomous, self-generated creature, not to subvert it. I have also found that in the dramatic structure of the dialogue, the final entrance of Alcibiades is significant, because Alcibiades' wayward *eros,* in addition to his attachment to women in the flesh, and to the things of the political world, as well as the fact that Socrates loved him, may tell us something about Plato's sense of the limitations of what David Halperin has called "mimetic transvestism." Women are not so easily transcended and we do well to remind ourselves that philosophers, like all human beings, come into the world through fleshy wombs. Whether in the philosopher or the tyrant, however, in the context of Plato's *Symposium,* woman remains obscure. The particularity of her experience as something that is actually *different* in the flesh is never really explored, although it is the final reference point for both philosopher and tyrant. The philosopher tries to co-opt this difference, and the tyrant longs to dominate and devour it.

The question remains: why should there be this resistance to the mother, to the female, to the enfleshment of *eros?* Is there any possibility of getting beyond this resistance? This would be the subject of another paper, but we might as well briefly refer here to two modern feminist theorists who think through the *eros* of women independently of women's objectification by philosophers and tyrants. Elizabeth Grosz suggests that we go back to the ancient Greek concept of *chora,* "the space in which place is made possible, the chasm for the passage of spaceless Forms into a spatialized reality, a dimensionless tunnel opening itself to spatialization, obliterating itself to make others possible and actual" (*Space, Time and Perversion* 116). Grosz proclaims that "women can no longer take on the function of being *the* body for men while men are left free to soar to the heights of theoretical reflection and cultural production" (*Volatile Bodies* 22).

In a similar vein, Irigaray says that it is the philosophic order itself that has to be "questioned and disturbed, inasmuch as it covers over sexual difference" (*This Sex Which Is Not One* 59). Irigaray would like to return to Diotima's invocation of love as gravitation toward the beautiful, but in a way that "confounds the opposition between immanence and transcendence" ("Sorcerer Love" 33). When asked in an interview, "What is a woman?" Irigaray refused to answer, replying that this is a metaphysical question to which the feminine ought not allow itself to submit. "To claim that the feminine can be expressed in the form of a concept is to allow oneself to be caught up again in a system of 'masculine' representations" (*This Sex Which Is Not One* 122). For Irigaray, "to arrive at the constitution of an ethics of sexual difference, we must [...] return to what is for Descartes the first passion: *wonder*" (Whitford 172). Wonder, Irigaray pronounces, does not seize, or dominate, or subdue, but looks at things anew. "This has never happened between the sexes. Wonder might allow them to retain an autonomy based on their difference, and give them a space of attraction or freedom, a possibility of separation or alliance" (Whitford 172). To enter into *chora*, as Grosz recommends, or to return to *wonder* as a starting point, as Irigaray suggests, would mean a radical departure from the mind/body dualism that characterizes the tradition of Western philosophy, beginning with Plato.

Notes

1. I would like to thank Katerina Kitsi-Mitakou for her most helpful suggestions on the revisions in this paper.
2. Kenneth Dover, in his central work *Greek Homosexuality*, impresses upon us the sexual origin of *eros*. "The god Eros, depicted in the visual arts as a young, winged male, is the personification of the force that makes us fall in love willy-nilly with another person" (Dover 48). However, Dover also emphasizes that Plato's concept of *eros* goes beyond this strict sexual imagery, as Plato expands *eros* to include the love of the beautiful and the good. Still, even in Plato, there is a passionate core to *eros*, and this differs significantly from later conceptions of *philia* or *caritas*.
3. We see this view of women portrayed comically in Aristophanes' play *Lysistrata*, in which a sex strike is organized by Athenian wives as a means of exercising political control over husbands. The women protest vehemently. According to one commentator, "this belief in women's insatiable appetite for sex was linked to the view that females were somehow closer to nature than males, and therefore prone to wildness. Unlike men, they were incapable of self-control or *sophrosune*" (Blundell 47).

Works Cited

Aristotle. *Politics*. Trans. Carnes Lord. Chicago: U of Chicago P, 1984.
———. *Nicomachean Ethics*. Trans. Martin Ostwald. New York: Prentice Hall, 1962.
Blundell, Sue. *Women in Classical Athens*. London: Duckworth, 1998.
Dover, Kenneth. *Greek Homosexuality*. Cambridge, Massachusetts: Harvard UP, 1978.
DuBois, Page. "The Platonic Appropriation of Reproduction." *Sowing the Body: Psychoanalysis and Ancient Representations of Women*. Chicago: U of Chicago P, 1998. 169–83.
Grosz, Elizabeth. *Space, Time and Perversion: Essays on the Politics of the Body*. New York: Routledge, 1995.
———. *Volatile Bodies: Toward a Corporeal Feminism*. Bloomington: Indiana UP, 1994.

Halperin, David. "Why is Diotima a Woman?" *Before Sexuality: The Construction of Erotic Experience in the Ancient Greek World*. Ed. David Halperin, John Winkler, and Froma Zeitlin. Princeton: Princeton UP, 1990. 257–307.

Hunt, Morton. *The Natural History of Love*. New York: Grove, 1959.

Irigaray, Luce. *The Sex Which Is Not One*. Trans. Catherine Porter. Ithaca, New York: Cornell UP, 1977.

———. "Sorcerer Love: A Reading of Plato's *Symposium:* Diotima's Speech." *An Ethics of Sexual Difference*. Trans. Carolyn Burke and Gillian C. Gill. Ithaca, New York: Cornell UP, 1984. (Originally published in *Hypatia* Winter, 1989.)

Nussbaum, Martha. *The Fragility of Goodness*. Cambridge: Cambridge UP, 1996.

Plato. *Gorgias*. Trans. Donald J. Zeyl. Indianapolis: Hackett, 1987.

———. *Republic*. Trans. Allan Bloom. New York: Basic, 1968.

———. *Symposium*. Trans. Christopher Gill. London: Penguin. 1999.

Plutarch. *The Lives of the Noble Grecians and Romans*. Ed. Hugh Clough. Trans. John Dryden. Vol. 1. New York: Modern Library, 1992.

Whitford, Margaret, ed. *The Irigaray Reader*. Oxford: Blackwell, 1991.

Part III
Popular Culture

10. The Racial Gaze and the Monstrous African in The X-files Program "The Teliko"[1]

Nigel C. Gibson

> For several years certain laboratories have been trying to produce a serum for "denigration"; with all their earnestness in the world, laboratories have sterilized their test tubes, checked their scales, and embarked on researches that might make it possible for the miserable Negro to whiten himself and thus to throw off the burden of that corporeal malediction. Below the corporeal schema I had sketched a historico-racial schema.
>
> (Fanon, *Black Skin* 111)

I

Martin Bernal reminds us in his magnum opus, *Black Athena*, that paradigm shifts exhibit surplus explanatory value, but these surpluses might have less to do with an internal explanation than with the *Weltanschauung* of the intellectuals involved. When it comes to the idea of the racialized body, this certainly seems the case. Through a reading of the *X-files* program, "The Teliko: The Case of the Missing Pigment,"[2] which Ato Quayson first turned me onto in his book *Postcolonialism*, I am interested in exploring the idea of the monstrous as an overdetermined surplus that, rather than left behind, is subsumed as well as reformulated in the modern, hierarchical, evolutionary, and classificatory discourses of race and public health and how the classification of the monstrous and ideas of human "development" are reformulated in terms of urban and rural spaces.

On the medieval (Christian) map (following the Plinian catalogue) "monstrous races" were viewed as inhabiting the edges of the world. In the climatically hot zones, the human body begins to dissolve resulting in strange mutations. One ultimate source of knowledge, the Bible, did not fully eliminate the anxiety associated with the monstrous but recast it. Scholastic authorities (such as Augustine) viewed these beings as "miracles," that is, as God's creatures, inexplicable to us. Even as late as the seventeenth century, descriptions of the peoples of Libya and Ethiopia (literally people with burnt faces) as headless bodies with faces in their chests drew on myth and legend. Monsters were clearly fantastic but they continued to be produced by travelers *even as* skepticism grew from the force of Renaissance Empiricism. The expectation of discovering monsters, argues historian John Block Friedman, "lived well into the period of scientific geography" (198).

In other words, the paradigm shift associated with Empiricism was not simply a product of direct contact and observation of black bodies, but also a conceptual change, a new standpoint that classified observation itself. Empiricism became the money of the mind, the weight and measure of emerging bourgeois Europe. Whereas the idea of the miraculous left open the possibility of an Other *qua* monster, this new regime of truth transformed and subsumed the older idea of the difference into a rigidly hierarchical system. The Black, often strange and exotic[3] as well as savage, became the "negro" and was equated with the slave through, on one hand, the projection of the empirical racial gaze and, on the other, the later scientific project of imperial domination.[4]

By the "abolitionist" nineteenth century, the African body had become a renewed subject of the racial gaze *qua* medical gaze. Scientific Empiricism helped solidify rather than overturn discourses of race, for example, measuring skulls and jaws, brain-weights and genitalia in the project of classifying peoples.[5] Light would be also shone on the "savage" customs of Africa, and in the name of the abolition of slavery and "humanitarian intervention," sanitary science and its disciplinary regime would be employed as a missionary medicine, "a device of moral sanitation directed to the boundary between the African body and a surrounding space of customs, rites and superstitions" (Butchart 75).[6] This classificatory gaze is wonderfully represented in "The Teliko: The Case of the Missing Pigment," an episode in the popular, police, Sci-Fi, TV program *The X-files*. In "The Teliko,"[7] a newly-arrived, West African without a pituitary gland (which means he cannot "develop") has "developed" and keeps himself alive by sucking the gland from Black victims. The result is that they die with white faces. Named Aboah, this vampire/zombie is presented as an evolutionary enigma, a being that in the natural order of things shouldn't exist. Scully, the female co-star of the show, sums up the problem in her field journal, as Aboah lies dying on the hospital bed under the gaze of the medical regime: "[Aboah] can only be explained by medical science and that science will eventually discover his place in the broader context of *evolution*."

Thus, we are faced with the elective affinity of medical science, evolution, and the racial gaze. But let us start from the beginning.

II

On an airplane from Burkina Faso, West Africa, a well-dressed Black man goes to the bathroom. He stares at himself at the mirror then looks up and screams with horror. Another man, Samuel Aboah, walking away from the bathroom, smiles at the flight attendant; seconds later, she finds the man in a suit not only dead but white-faced.

The first issue we face is phenomenological, or what Frantz Fanon called the lived experience and fact of Blackness as "the burden of *corporeal* malediction" (*Black Skin* 111). It turns out that the well-dressed man is only one of a number of dead, Black males who have mysteriously turned white. And at FBI headquarters in Philadelphia, *X-files* co-investigator Scully meets Dr. Simon Bruin of the Center for Disease Control, who hands her a picture of one of the deceased/diseased. Looking at a picture, Scully retorts, "I am sorry, I thought you said Owen Sanders was Black." Bruin replies that Owen Sanders had been a *perfectly normal* Black man, adding that "The *depigmentation* we are seeing may actually be a characteristic of a disease, an apparently fatal one" (my emphasis).

Scully does in fact follow Bruin's meaning. Schooled in the belief that a *perfectly normal* Black man is defined by a certain skin pigment, we are faced with the veracity of the racial gaze and the certainty of racial science because we "know"—through the veracity of the gaze—that Sanders is black despite his whitened skin.[8] This investigation, she concludes, should begin and end under a microscope. But the sociogeny of the investigation is already given by phylogeny, namely the fear of evolutionary contagion expressed as physical immediacy and, thus, a threat to the civil order. Aboah represents such a threat. He is the apogee of what Fanon called "the corrosive element [. . .] the deforming element [. . .] the depository of maleficent powers [. . . the] hordes of vital statistics" (*Wretched* 41–42).

Aboah, the carrier of disease, namely the diseased body as a marker of evolutionary backwardness—repeating the late nineteenth-century categorization of social/moral orders—symbolizes the generic globalized city's fear of immigration. What is shocking is that the leap from the nineteenth to the late-twentieth century doesn't require much explaining. Race classification remains ingrained in the culture. Indeed, as Mary Louise Pratt argues, the classification of races exists "barely modified in some of today's schoolbooks" (32) and the metaphor of urban "jungle" is securely fixed in the imagination. As Paul Gilroy points out, the city as jungle "where bestial values prevail [. . .] is the context in which race and racism come to connote the urban crisis as a whole" (409). Aboah is the *concrete* jungle in the concrete jungle. He is rural, tribal, and primal, a carrier of disease who must be quarantined. The police are thus urban, public health workers or, perhaps more ominously, public health workers are police and immigration officials.

III

Why does Aboah want to come to America? "Free cable," says Mulder in an off-hand but telling remark. Aboah even watches a classic black and white show on the TV as he "works" on his young African-American victim, Alfred Kittle. Yet, there is a much more serious issue. Aboah's wish for residency carries with it a threat of contagion succinctly articulated in Lord Frederick Lugard's imagining of colonial cities in Africa in the 1920s. Speaking of clearly marked areas—a sanitized urban area for whites marked off from the town of the "natives"—Lugard opined:

> We have learnt that malarial germs are present in the blood of most natives, especially native children, and their dark huts and insanitary surrounds foster mosquitoes [. . .] Doctors therefore urge that Europeans should not sleep in proximity to natives in order to avoid infection. (149)

Lugard's succinct justification for dividing the townships by a safe 440 yards involves the imagination of space, power and order—those "dark huts" and those swarms of African mosquitoes are contrasted with the enlightened and civilized Europeans. However, Lugard is probably most famous for his promoting "customary rule" in the rural areas: a system of "indirect rule" with the colonial, native authority in the background and the local "chief" administering "justice" based on "custom" (and force) in the foreground. In contrast to the imperial project of civilizing mission, Lugard (perhaps the most important British administrator in the African colonies) argued that the majority of natives in the rural areas could not be "civilized" and should be governed not by the civil (but racialized) rule of law in the urban areas but by "custom." Certainly the British fashioned what would and what would not be custom on their own interests and prejudices, but the point here is that in terms of imperial governance, the rural was seen as "backward," "tribal," "barbaric" and "timeless" and, thus, quite incapable of "development" toward civilization.[9]

We know very little about Aboah. He rarely speaks. During the day, he works in construction but we mainly see him at his second "job" at night. In this space, he represents the threat of the dark hordes. Aboah is presented as pure biology, as pure animal instinct. Marcus Duff, the Black immigration counselor/social worker[10] in "The Teliko," visits Aboah in his darkened, dingy cave of an apartment encouraging him to become a US citizen. Duff looks at Aboah and wonders whether he is ill. Duff doesn't follow it up because Duff is by definition duff, a useless guard against the threat of disease. Racially marked, he represents the do-good liberal opening America's doors to the "hordes of vital statistics":

> Once you become a US citizen, [he says] I can help you bring over every brother, sister, aunt, uncle, cousin. You know what I mean?
>
> "Thank you," says Aboah.

The immigration threat is palpable. Duff is foolishly inviting an ill Aboah to bring over his extended family. If not clear to Duff, the threat of being swamped by Africans who are likely to be ill is clear to the viewer. Aboah, which means animal in Akan (Quayson 151) is suggestive of the Ebola virus and (as the African-American policeman exclaims, suggesting its strange and alien roots, "what kind of name is 'Aboah'?"); citizens can only protect themselves by strong borders and stringent quarantines.

The oppressive darkness of Aboah's apartment is contrasted with the comparative openness outside the United Nations. In a scene that cuts to the steps of a UN building, the tension is short lived. Clearly these are not the side streets above 125th Street but the wide vistas of Dag Hammarskjöld Plaza; it is the "European town."[11] Mulder's unofficial questioning of the UN worker, Ms. Scobruvius, quickly centers on the issue of transgressing borders. With the obvious fatigue of one who is fighting a losing battle, she replies: "Thousands of exotic species cross into US soil undetected. In practical terms borders are no more than lines on maps." The causal investigative links are being made. The exotic species include Aboah. The hordes cannot be stopped.

Aboah is finally caught or discovered contorted inside a drainpipe. He appears, after a barrage of medical tests, quite normal, but the native is not an informant. He doesn't speak. In fact, apart from slowly spoken "Thank you's" and snake-like "Yessssses," he says nothing. The English-speaking Duff is called in as a translator[12] but before Duff has a chance to interpret, Aboah escapes inside a hospital-cart drawer. The quest for a rational explanation ignores this amazing feat.

IV

It is difficult to understand why Howard Gordon, Teliko's writer, decided on Burkina Faso as Aboah's homeland, unless it was simply an attraction to the exotic name.[13] A landlocked country, Burkina Faso is North of West Africa's "slave coast," which from Whydah to Lagos remained active into the 1880s. Thus, it is not difficult also to imagine Aboah as contemporary to the Gothic novel in which Dracula, as a metaphor for capitalistic accumulation, sucked life from living labor and created the walking-dead, factory worker.

In West Africa, the Zombies, as intimates of the slave trade, sucked the land of people and conveyed them onto the slave ships. Aboah's amazing feat of fitting into a hospital cart was indeed achieved by millions of West Africans who were crushed and contorted in the bowels of slave ships. "Zombication," as René Depestre puts it (qtd. in Davis 75), however, continues to remain real for postcolonial Africa. Often appearing in the ghostly and deadly spaces of the colonial mines and plantations which operated on forced and migrant labor, Zombies are reappearing, argue John and Jean Comaroff, on the night-shift in post-apartheid South Africa.[14]

At the Burkina Faso embassy in Washington, Mulder meets the civilized African in the bourgeois space of the diplomatic mission. The native informant, a suited Burkina diplomat, is a hybrid, a Westernized African. But he still exhibits a fear of the bush at night. Just as Aboah illustrates an earlier stage of humanity represented by his mouth-blown weapon (Quayson 151), the African diplomat *also* represents a preceding stage of scientific knowledge.[15] The diplomat's childhood tale of maleficent spirits represents just that, the Enlightenment metaphor of Africa as childlike in its thinking. It is opposed to the quest for a "scientific" explanation, and it also expresses another metaphor of Africa and Africans as wild and savage, as rural rather than urban. But the childish images of Africa in the West—lions, tigers, snakes and the scary bogeyman of the bush—also include the very repressed desires and fears that make *The X-files* tick.[16] Cultural differentiation is also mediated by an evolutionary model. Thus, the threat is not from American Blacks in their dark, urban quarters (indeed they appear as simply victims), but an unpredictable Other, a monstrous, gland-sucking creature from Africa that preys on African-Americans.[17] The drums always sound when Aboah stalks his prey.

In the urban narrative of *The X-files*, it becomes clear that Aboah represents a particular threat to civilization.[18] What is also fascinating is how myth is refused in the language of science represented by Scully, though it is exactly this surplus explanation which grips our imagination. Aboah inspires fear not only of the Other outside and the corrupt, polluted past of American wealth, not of African vampires but also of the vampire of Africans. Aboah's is a primitive kind of accumulation, a vampire from a different time and outside the blood-sucking machine. The days of extraction of Black bodies from Africa are over even if the days of physical extraction—diamonds, gold, uranium, and so on, are not. When it comes to melanin, the modern, pharmaceutical, industrial complex with lawyers in the citadel has already posted a global patent, but organ donors are available. The body's organs (eyes, kidneys, etc.) are commodities "in a global flow of organs that follows the modern routes of capital: from South to North, from Third to First, from poor to rich, from black to brown to white, and from female to male" (Scheper-Hughes 179). In this global flow of organs, where people are seen as "spare parts," organ-stealing rumors, such as child-stealing agents from the United States seeking fresh supplies human organs, become rife. According to Scheper-Hughes, these rumors spread like wildfire and similar stories have been reported in the shantytowns of Brazil, in South Africa, and in Guatemala. In this context, does Aboah simply represent a projection of America's own practices both metaphorical and real elided by discourses of development?

Like the diplomat, Aboah is also a hybrid; perhaps doubly so. If the diplomat is an *evolved,* and thus civilized, urban African (namely has followed the path of evolution and has now a "white soul" or a white mask),[19] then Aboah represents not only a stage preceding civilization but its degeneration and its impossibility. Aboah's "illness," like other "degenerative" illnesses, appears as a condition of the skin (in this case a lack of melanin). Like the problem of a hybrid (plant), his black skin becomes blotched with white. Just like the little black boy in the classic, imperialist, Pears Soap advert of the early twentieth century, even when washed "clean" he remains fundamentally Black. His body is scrubbed white but his head, the seat of his soul, remains unmistakably Black.[20]

In a nation where the fantasy of racial purity remains strong, racial hybridity is a threat. In terms of racial classification,[21] the racial hybrid—for example, the mulatto, mestizo or the Coloured—is a kind of monstrosity representing the blurring and obfuscation[22] of social categories. In "pluralistic," "hybrid," and apparently multicultural America, the threat to civilization and order is powerfully expressed in the figure of the rural unknown—the raced bogeyman. Aboah is not a "perfectly normal" Black (African-American) man, but a defective African, which is expressed by the white blotches on his skin. Described as a member of a "lost tribe" of Albinos, he represents an anomaly of evolution. Thus, it is not a surprise that Aboah cannot be saved by modern, medical techniques. His body cannot be situated in the body of the nation, whether that nation is postcolonial Burkina Faso or "multi-racial," imperial America, where multiculturalism is strictly policed, and the races, however blurred, however hybrid, still determine the body's place.[23] His existence must be denied by the postcolonial diplomat whose job is to make the problem go away. The evolved diplomat expresses the fear that he will be found out, or, more precisely, the primitivism of the postcolonial state (the media image in the US) will be uncovered. Ironically, Aboah is quite similar to the postcolonial elite who feed upon its own people in order to purchase gleaming, "Western" commodities,[24] but, from the liberal perspective of *The X-files,* he is more than morally repugnant and physically monstrous.

In the narrative of *The X-files,* the "dark jungle" has entered America through the native's town—that is, the inner city, the ghetto and with it comes the issue of (illegal) immigration and the threat of contagion brought by new viruses and the exchange of bodily fluids. Aboah represents the linkage of immigration and criminality, the evolutionary enigma as expressed in the dastardly extraction of melanin that could quite easily "jump" to the general population. A war must be waged against this "parasite." This parasite must be put on the same level as a hybrid plant and subjected to DDT.[25] To do so means he must be caught, studied, and quarantined.

In "The Teliko," the importance of surfaces reappears; Aboah is a body without volume who can contort into a hospital-cart drawer. He is a headless body, a monster along the line of Renaissance myths. He is a premodern, rural figure and a threat to the ideology of postmodern, multicultural America. The story appears to have nothing to do with white America because Aboah sucks out the innards of only Black Americans and makes them dead "whites." Yet, it has everything to do with the marks of the slave trade on the history and psyche of American civilization. Aboah turns up in the urban jungle, but it is also the frightening geography of the "savage jungle" that lurks in the background, with its rhythm of the tom-tom "surrounded by half-naked men and women dancing."[26] Fear, guilt, paranoia? Aboah's is a rural tale harking back to the legacy of slavery and lynching in the deep South. The last scene, appropriately, has Aboah's life ebbing away, or perhaps sucked out by the medical gaze. Finally, he is "normalized." Suggesting a modern American lynching (execution), he lies with tubes sticking out of his body and his arms crossed. When subjected to MRIs and X rays, "technology" can only reveal the biological necessity for killings that must remove from the picture the underlining, lived experience of the "historico-racial drama."

Notes

1. *The X-files* is the property of Ten Thirteen Productions and 20th Century Fox. No copyright infringement is intended.
2. *The X-files* premiered on the Fox network in the fall of 1993 and became a popular show running for nine seasons. Plots that deal with subjects ranging from the occult, religion and monsters to urban legends, conspiracy theories, and science fiction were framed by the stark lighting of the Vancouver sets, atmospherics score and special effects. The show's premise is that the FBI occasionally encounters cases that seem inexplicable in terms of science and logic. The show stars FBI agents Dana Scully and Fox Mulder. Scully is the serious-minded medical scientist assigned to work with Mulder on the X-files, a division housed in the basement of the FBI building, dealing with the paranormal. In contrast to Scully, Mulder is the intuitive thinker and a believer in the existence of paranormal phenomena. Both agents follow the scientific method: they make hypotheses, bolster these hypotheses with observations and experiments (and hard evidence), and then draw their conclusions.
3. As a late expression, see, for example, Shakespeare's *Othello*.
4. This construction can be periodized schematically: First, the ironically, relatively "free" and creative, myth-making period of monsters and mutants, where the Other is strange, as other, as magical, and, thus, not completely subsumed within a rigid

hierarchical system. Second, the shift during the period of mercantilist capitalism, from chattel slavery and primitive accumulation on the plantation economies of the "New World" up to the abolition of the slave trade by Britain in 1830, with a corresponding importance of weights and measures as the equivalence of exchange; in other words, from the monstrous to the mundane. For example, an adult, African male was valued at one ounce of gold; one chest of corn used to feed slave cargoes was equivalent to one angel, and 16 angels equalled one ounce. The roots of Enlightenment race-hierarchy were found in this "crude materialism." Between 1650 and 1830 the African body lost its "fabulous qualities" (Butchart) and became a collection of external organs—skin, noses, teeth, hair, genitalia, and so on. Third, the scientific racism and social Darwinism connected to industrial capitalism and public health of the late nineteenth century.

5. Ania Loomba notes three points about scientific theories of race that are not always in agreement: first, the idea of biologically constituted races and the consequences of the issue of sexual unions between whites and blacks; second, scientific discussions of race develop rather than challenge stereotypes of savagery, excessive sexuality attributed to biological difference; and last, science extended the association of race and nation and, thus, the association of nation with biological and racial attributes (116–18).
6. Also see Stepan and Gilman, respectively.
7. "The Teliko," which can be translated as "the end," is a discourse on evolution. The end, of course, is not only American civilization, to which all aspire, but also the end of earlier stages of humanity, which must perish.
8. This knowledge reflects nineteenth-century notions of race based on the "measurable"—a certain thickness of hair, a certain size of nose, and so on.
9. And, thus, in the terms later repeated by apartheid, "separate development" became the metaphor for the "decentralized despotism" of indirect rule (see Mamdani).
10. We are led to believe that Duff works as a counselor for the Immigration and Naturalization Service. Such an advocacy position is highly unlikely.
11. See Fanon, *Wretched* 39.
12. Since Duff doesn't speak Bambara (the "tribe" of the Burkina diplomat) or French, one assumes it is on the basis of race solidarity.
13. Perhaps Gordon thought of choosing Burkina Faso because of the Pan-African film festival that is held in the capital Ougadougou biannually. After returning from the "Flesh Made Text" conference in May 2003, where a version of this essay was originally presented, I heard of the shooting and killing of an unarmed immigrant worker from Burkina Faso, Ousmane Zongo, by a New York policeman. Zongo was working in a warehouse when it was raided by the police. When he came out to see what was happening, he was shot four times. I, therefore, want to dedicate this paper to his memory.
14. In "Alien-Nation: Zombie, Immigrants and Millennial Capitalism," John and Jean Comaroff relate the powerful reappearance of Zombies in post-apartheid South Africa to the collapse of alternatives to neoliberal capitalism and the rise of witchcraft allegations in the "casino economy."
15. The Burkina diplomat is played by the South African actor Zakes Mokae. We shouldn't worry too much about an Anglophone speaker playing a West African Francophone speaker, because in Hollywood and in *The X-files* all Africans are pre-

sumably the same (the same could be said of Duff, an Anglophone West Indian being a translator for Aboah).
16. What can't be explained is brushed aside, in the narrow, calculating reason of a whodunit, medical forensic also seen in other "criminal investigation" police shows. For the now-classic analysis of "The Negro and Psychopathology," see Fanon, *Black Skin*, Ch. 6.
17. While, culturally, African-Americans are more like white Americans than Africans, genetically (and this is indeed the narrative point of the show), we are led to believe that there is a connection between Aboah and African-Americans.
18. It is Conrad's *Heart of Darkness* all over again. Aboah likes to live in the dark. Like the natives in *Heart of Darkness*, he says little, and like them he files his instruments of death.
19. I should add that Fanon, of course, calls "the black soul" "a white man's artefact" (Fanon, *Black Skin* 14).
20. See the classic Pear Soap advert in McClintock (213).
21. Loomba reproduces a chart of different "castes" and their mixtures developed by W.B. Stevenson, which blends the dominant Father's lineage with the Mother's. So we get the hierarchy based on fractions of "whiteness," with classificatory terms such as Creole, Mestizo, Mulatto, Zambo, Quinteron, Quarteron, Chino, Zambo (120).
22. Perhaps it is in this sense that we should understand a sub-text of "The Teliko," Scully's struggle against deception and "obfuscation."
23. See Fanon, *Black Skin* 107.
24. See Armah.
25. In *The Wretched*, Fanon puts DDT on the same level as the Christian religion. A war is waged against the bearers of disease and embryonic heresies (42).
26. Typical fears of imaginary Blacks (see Fanon, *Black Skin* 204–09).

Works Cited

Armah, Ayi Kwei. *The Beautyful Ones Are Not Yet Born.* London: Heinemann, 1968.
Bernal, Martin. *Black Athena: The Afroasiatic Roots of Classical Civilization.* New Brunswick, NJ: Rutgers UP, 1987.
Butchart, Alexander. *The Anatomy of Power: European Constructions of the African Body.* London: Zed, 1998.
Conrad, Joseph. *Heart of Darkness.* Harmondsworth: Penguin Books, 1994.
Comaroff, Jean and John Comaroff. "Alien-Nation: Zombie, Immigrants and Millenial Capitalism." *The South Atlantic Quarterly* 101.4 (2002): 779–805.
Davis, Wade. *Passage of Darkness: The Ethnobiology of the Haitian Zombie.* Chapel Hill: U of North Carolina P, 1988.
Fanon, Frantz. *Black Skin, White Masks.* Trans. Charles Lam Markmann. New York: Grove Press, 1967.
———. *The Wretched of the Earth.* Trans. Constance Farrington. New York: Grove Press, 1968.
Friedman, John Block. *The Monstrous Races in the Medieval Art and Thought.* Cambridge, MA: Harvard UP, 1981.

Gilman, Sander. "Black Bodies White Bodies: Toward an Iconography of Female Sexuality in Late Nineteenth-Century Art, Medicine and Literature." *"Race," Writing, and Difference.* Ed. Henry Louis Gates, Jr. Chicago: The U of Chicago P, 1985. 223–61.

Gilroy, Paul. "Urban Social Movements, 'Race' and Community." *Colonial Discourse and Postcolonial Theory: A Reader.* Ed. Patrick Williams and Laura Chrisman. New York: Columbia UP, 1994. 404–20.

Loomba, Ania. *Colonialism/Postcolonialism.* London: Routledge, 2001.

Lugard, Frederick. *The Dual Mandate in British Tropical Africa.* London: Frank Cass, 1965.

Mamdani, Mahmood. *Citizen and Subject: Contemporary Africa and the Legacy of Late Colonialism.* Princeton: Princeton UP, 1996.

McClintock, Anne. *Imperial Leather.* New York: Routledge, 1995.

Pratt, Mary Louise. *Imperial Eyes: Travel Writing and Transculturation.* London: Routledge, 1992.

Quayson, Ato. *Postcolonialism: Theory, Practice or Process.* Oxford: Polity Press, 2000.

Scheper-Hughes, Nancy. "The Global Traffic in Human Organs." *The Anthropology of Globalization: A Reader.* Ed. John Xavier Inda and Renato Rosaldo. Oxford: Blackwell, 2004. 270–308.

Shakespeare, William. *Othello.* Harmondsworth: Penguin Books, 1994.

Stepan, Nancy Leys. "Race and Gender: The Role of Analogy in Science." *Anatomy of Racism.* Ed. David Theo Goldberg. Minneapolis: U of Minnesota P, 1990. 38–57.

"The Teliko: The Case of the Missing Pigment." *The X-files.* Writ. Howard Gordon. Dir. James Charleston. Ten Thirteen Productions and 20th Century Fox. Fourth season. 18 Oct. 1996.

11. *Speculate and Punish: British Lifestyle TV and the Anxious Body*

DAVID ROBERTS AND JOSS WEST-BURNHAM

Michel Foucault, in *Discipline and Punish,* reminds us that the body is always a political investment and that "the body becomes a useful force only if it is both a productive body and a subjected body" (Rabinow 173). In this essay, we want to explore how these issues of productivity and subjection have been reshaped and redefined by the "new technicians of discipline"—the television producers, in the form of body consultants in our particular examples of British lifestyle television in the twenty-first century. This relatively new genre initially began with programs on property, homes and gardens as sites of transformation. It can now be argued that there have been development and concentration of programs that work on individuals and the whole process of "self improvement," which will be discussed later in this essay. By looking at these, we hope to explore Foucault's work on the notion of docility, "which joins the analyzable body and the manipulative body" (Rabinow 172). Our examples of British lifestyle television in fact work exactly to make manifest the point that "a body is docile that may be subjected, used, transformed and improved" (Rabinow 173). What these programs also indicate is a profound shift in the political usefulness of the body.

Foucault concentrates his historical research on the period from the seventeenth to the nineteenth century, examining how techniques of bodily discipline go towards creating the productive body—the efficient soldier, the docile student, the productive prisoner. Foucault's period of study follows the shift in episteme that marks the transition from the feudal to the bourgeois. In contemporary, Western society, many of the discourses of the body, particularly those centered on medical discourses, still relate to the body as a productive machine. Discourses that concentrate on both individual and social health are still rooted in the perceived necessity for a productive society. For example, epidemic illnesses, from outbreaks of influenza to alcohol-related diseases, are still articulated and quantified through "numbers of working days lost."

However, with the shift from the predominantly nineteenth-century, production capitalism to a contemporary, consumption capitalism, we can also see that the issue is less the creation of a productive body and more the necessity to create a body that consumes and the desire to transform the body through consumption. This is what Foucault refers to as the "political economy" of the body:

> But we can surely accept the general proposition that, in our societies, the systems of punishment are to be sustained in a certain "political economy" of the body: even if they do not make use of violent or bloody punishment, even if they use "lenient" methods involving confinement or correction, it is always the body that is at issue—the body and its forces, their utility and their docility, their distribution and their submission. (Rabinow 172)

What we have, then, in these programs is the articulation of a series of normalizing discourses, the end result of which is the creation of a body that consumes. The body, both individual and social, takes its place in the circulation of commodities, and each individual body becomes a commodity through its place in an economy of speculation.

Surveillance and speculation are both what creates the docile body and what that body is subjected to. What we have to bear in mind, however, is the doubly discursive surveillance, which takes place in most of these lifestyle texts. Firstly, the individual participant is looked at, usually by an expert or experts, and we, as the audience, then speculate upon that speculation. This is significant in that this double articulation tends to position the audience ideologically, and also can act, as we shall see later, as an intensifier or multiplier of effect. It is also significant to note here though that, in many of these programs, both the individual concerned and the assumed audience are female.

We are not, of course, suggesting that there is a cause-effect relationship between lifestyle television and the anxious body. What these programs do is to articulate contemporary refinements of the episteme and intensify their effects. John Fiske, in *Television Culture*, very appositely directs us to think about this cultural circulation of television genres and their intertextual qualities and formats. In his sections on masculine and feminine television, he attempts to chart how stereotypical gender positions are both utilized and continued within particular genres. He also highlights assumptions made about gender and spectatorship. What we have found interesting and profoundly disturbing through our study of lifestyle television is that these continue in the twenty-first century. It is almost as if feminism and liberationist politics generally have never happened or, more accurately, have been hollowed out to become the surface justification for the practices described; what has happened to the personal as political in these continued attempts to make all fit one narrow paradigm of the acceptable body—male and female? The politics of independence has been literally hijacked by the television producers to seduce both participants and viewers into a twenty-first-century context of identity politics where individuals can buy whomever they want to be.

Germaine Greer, in *The Whole Woman*, notes how this has been possible through a manufactured discourse which offers an explanation for peoples' anxieties about their bodies—Body Dysmorphic Disorder (BDD)—where people have an abnormal preoccupation with a perceived defect in their appearance. We would suggest that television can be seen as a major vehicle for both the continued manufacture of these anxieties, and the supposed solutions become the substance of the lifestyle genre. The discursive practices which circulate around and between cultural texts—in the context of a Western cultural obsession with celebrity culture, supermodel, pop and film star lifestyles—reproduce and reinforce false aesthetics of normality and success. As Greer suggests:

> Marketing strategies, now adopted not only by manufacturers and suppliers of services, but by government, communications, churches, charities, schools and universities obfuscate every issue. What they seek is not informed choice but compliance. Feminism being incompatible with consumerism, marketing co-opted it as a fashion and then immediately declared it passé, only to co-opt it again and again under different designer labels. (10)

So woman as subject, as object, and spectator is caught up in the paradoxes of these productions, which appear initially to offer transformation but actually work to reinforce dominant ideologies of patriarchal discourse especially with regard to standards of femininity, which we discuss below.

The term "lifestyle television" is a generic category. Jason Mittell points out that "there are no uniform criteria for genre delimitation—some are defined by setting, some by actions, some by audience effect and some by narrative form" (18). We would maintain that lifestyle television is defined by process and that the process is transformation. Whether the program is concerned with fashion, interior decoration, moving home, or plastic surgery, we are confronted by a limited, narrative structure based on a "before" and "after" process. In addition, this genre is deeply embedded in discourses of consumption and capitalism. The difference between "life" and "lifestyle" is that one lives the former and one buys the latter. In this sense, an analysis of lifestyle television programs can work to exemplify Douglas Kellner's assertion that a diagnostic critique into media cultural texts is able to unearth "the politics of everyday life" (121). We would suggest that this is a politics which, with regard to women, operates within what Susan Faludi, writing in the early 1990s, has called "backlash." The term refers to the process by which popular culture is at pains to highlight that even though women are "free and equal, they have never been more miserable" (1). Faludi continues by saying that "This bulletin of despair is posted everywhere—at the newsagents, on the TV set, at the cinema, in advertisements and doctors' offices and academic journals." Faludi, then, works to show how the everyday lives of women are constructed as problematic within popular cultural texts because of feminism not because of continuing inequalities, capitalism, or persistent patriarchal codes of (acceptable) femininity. Lifestyle television texts, we would suggest, can be seen as a prime example of this process where the individual woman is offered transformation which actually ends up as the re-inscription of conformity and uniformity.

This interaction between cultural production and cultural consumption has a well-established documentation in the work of such people as Stuart Hall; David Morley's work on audience responses to BBC's *Nationwide* program; Ien Ang's early influential study *Watching Dallas*, now referred to as a "classic study" by John Storey (81); and Jane Feuer's essay "Genre Study and Television," described by Mittell as a work which is "certainly the most-read overview of television genre analysis" (20). Whilst these all have slightly different approaches, they all share the recognition that television viewing has a social function.

For this essay, we have selected three examples of current British television from spring 2003 that fall within this genre of lifestyle television. Whilst wishing to acknowledge that this generic category is expanding all the time so that it appears that there is virtually no area of the personal space now untouched—homes, holidays, finances—we have deliberately selected programs that focus primarily upon the body: *What Not to Wear*, *Facelift Diaries*, and *Fat Club*. The selection of these programs has been quite deliberate, because each can be seen to be a sub-section of a particular approach being taken by producers to the assumed anxieties of the viewing audience. They are also ultimately concerned, in different ways, with implicit aspects of consumerism, all having slightly different products for sale.

What Not to Wear is ostensibly about fashion, style, and designer clothes. Part of the structure of the program is to show the person having her (and the subject is always female) lifestyle looked at through a close dissection of her wardrobe. Of course, her existing wardrobe is viewed as unacceptable and the woman is then instructed to go shopping for new things that will "transform" her. She is instructed about "what not to wear" and why. The program is, therefore, implicitly premised on assumptions about gender-specific activities and preoccupations. The shorthand for this would appear to be that all women care about appearance in terms of certain stereotypical views about attractiveness and femininity rather than comfort and utility. Greer has noted how this internalization of the dominant ideologies of femininity means that "every woman knows that regardless of all her other achievements, she is a failure if she is not beautiful" (19). Also, the ritualized part of the program that has the woman shopping for new (and, of course, more acceptable) clothes is based upon a further assumption that all women like to shop for clothes as a major leisure activity. The program is also structured around the notion of an "expert" advisor who knows better than the participants. The body in question in our typical example has "a great arse," "good legs," "a terrific figure," but "chunky shoulders," and a problematic belly. What is also highlighted here are normalized conceptions of Western femininity, and self-worth (these always seem to go together), and part of the project for the subject is to put her in touch with her femininity and, therefore, help her regain her self-worth. The exterior makeover of the clothes that the woman should be advised to wear are to stop her from looking "masculine"—wearing loose shirts with rolled up sleeves—and to constrain her body parts rather than allow her to be comfortable. But it is also more than this because as we can see the style gurus suggest that the lack of signs of femininity—her body—is a psychological problem. Formally, what is notable about *What Not to Wear* is not only the double articulation of surveillance, but a multiple and reflexive articulation. Not only do we, the audience, observe the observers, but we observe the observed watching themselves being observed, and observe them observing themselves. The presenters appear to work by what are, as Foucault suggests, "small acts of cunning endowed with a great power of diffusion, subtle arrangements, apparently innocent, but profoundly suspicious" (Rabinow 183). Acts which work to name, shame, and display on our screens are there to provide both spectacle and speculation as we, the viewers, become, through the double discourse of surveillance and speculation, perhaps equally coerced into buying into (or not) the ideologies and the products that reshape/monitor ourselves in comparison to those on display.

The experts in *What Not to Wear* have rescued their participant from the dangerous belief in clothes as use value. What you wear is not just about being comfortable. It is about being a woman, about being feminine, about being and buying these things despite a "busy lifestyle." It is significant that the participant's own comfortable clothes are described as masculine. The new "feminine" clothes deemed as an improvement by the experts either hide parts of the body or accentuate those parts that the experts have decided are worthy of display. Through multiple and reflexive acts of surveillance, the participant is educated into femininity through consumption and educated into consumption through femininity. Analyzed and manipulated, the body of the participant is rendered docile, but also rendered useful by being positioned within the circulation of commodities.

Facelift Diaries takes the consumerist element further by suggesting that all parts of the body that are felt to be lacking or inadequate in terms of attractiveness can be changed and reshaped. This time, however, more interventionist processes of surgery are represented, and the shopping that takes place is with the consultant for a new nose or new face. The particular example we will be evaluating has two women at the center of the program, although in the series as a whole both male and female participants are represented. We, as viewers, follow the process and results of cosmetic surgery on two women, one having a facelift, and one having nose-reshaping surgery. Both participants can be seen to manifest Body Dysmorphic Disorder. The double speculative discourse is here modified by the "video diary" format where the two patients speak directly to camera. These confessional parts of the program explore their reasons for the surgery, and articulate expectation and apprehension, feelings and emotion. Those sections, which utilize a more familiar mode of the documentary genre, deal principally with proaretics, moving the action forward. In our example, one participant is having surgery to reshape her nose in time for her wedding. Her reason is that she wants to "look beautiful." After the operation, she begins to express dissatisfaction. At first, this is not directed at the surgical procedure itself, but at the lack of reaction from close friends:

> I feel a little bit disappointed that nobody has noticed it. I've had to say to people "I've had my nose done"—people that I know—and they look and say "What have you had done?" I just want somebody to turn round and say "Oh my God, yes—it looks so much better." (*Facelift Diaries*)

A little later the dissatisfaction is articulated more personally:

> I kind of expected [...] when I had the bandages on I was fine, and I think that maybe I thought, when the bandages were removed, that there'd be a completely different person underneath them—and there wasn't—it was, like, still me. (*Facelift Diaries*)

In some senses, this example is the most disturbing of the three programs we have evaluated. It reveals, in a particularly poignant manner, the hidden discourse behind all non-essential surgery: that by altering your body you will alter your self. A new nose equals a new person. We are familiar, initially through psychoanalysis, with the concept of the psychosomatic symptom, where the symptom at the level of the body has a cause in the unconscious. What we have here is an articulation of a reverse cause-effect relationship, where a "beneficial" intervention at the level of the body should have an equally "beneficial" effect on the psyche. Prior to this extract we have outlined, both women have confessed to the camera why they want these procedures carried out. Interestingly, both offer reasons based on spectacle: what they want to look like for others, the younger blonde woman wants her nose changed for her wedding day and the older blonde woman wants to look younger. In both cases, their families are also asked to comment on their desires. The children of the younger woman just want their mother to be happy, whilst the brother of the woman having a complete face-lift is incredulous that his sister, whom he has watched spending her life helping and working on behalf of others, has now become completely narcissistic and obsessed with what he considers superficial appearance. Their initial reaction to the transformation of their looks after the surgical intervention is disappointment. They realize they remain the same inside.

Facelift Diaries is, possibly unconsciously, more "subversive" in its presentation of transformation through cosmetic surgery. The program we have used as our example here, which is the first in a series, ultimately records the individuals' dissatisfaction with the process and does not resolve this dissatisfaction. It does, however, reveal the participants' self-delusion about the effects of surgical procedures of this type. In some senses, it is a perfect articulation of Body Dysmorphic Disorder, made all the more powerful by being unexplained.

Our final example of *Fat Club* is perhaps a slight exception, as the program does have male and female participants of diverse ethnic backgrounds. They all share a common "problem" which has to be transformed. The problem is one of body size, and their "membership" in *Fat Club* is built around ideas of community and team effort in pursuit of the common—if rather individualized—goal of losing what has been defined as excess weight. Although, as we will suggest, *Fat Club* works on multiple levels of anxiety (for the participants as well as the spectators), it does ultimately rest on similar assumptions to the other two examples about what an attractive body is for the male and the female in current British (and possibly by implication Western) society. Aspects of consumption are quite literally at the heart of this program, with people's eating and exercise regimes closely monitored and commented upon throughout. Here, a group of men and women, perceived to be obese, are placed on a dietary and exercise regime in order to reduce their weight. Every month they are invited to a health club where their weight is monitored. They are analyzed and advised by dieticians, doctors, and psychologists and put through a series of punishing exercises by a fearsome ex-US Marine PT instructor. The climactic part of the program is the monthly public weigh-in. Each participant, dressed in swimwear, is weighed in front of the other participants and the experts. Their weight and their weight loss since the previous weigh-in is announced. Significant weight loss is celebrated by cheers and encouragement, insignificant weight loss brings on tears and commiseration, as well as a certain amount of anger and resentment directed at the resident experts. The post weigh-in discussion centers on the lack of commitment of some participants.

Between the sessions at the health club, the camera follows the participants in their everyday lives and they articulate to the camera their reasons for joining the program, their level of commitment to the regime, or their reasons for failing. For example, Kelly, who later in the program "fails" the weigh-in, is interviewed in a student bar, where she is drinking pints of beer and eating crisps and pizza. She also explains that the reason she has lapsed from her diet is that her boyfriend has dumped her and she has indulged in comfort eating to compensate. Her attitude at the interview stage is surly and resentful. The audience is nudged strongly into judging Kelly as lazy, morally weak, dependent, and self-deluded. This judgment is reinforced by the presentation of her tearful reaction to her lack of weight loss.

Initially, we have to acknowledge that all these people have agreed to participate in this program. Perhaps this indicates a serious naivety about the process of television representation and the way it takes control away from individuals. However, what is demonstrated here is the intensifier or multiplier effect of the double discourse of speculation. From the individuals' reactions, we can see that those who have "failed" the weigh-in process find this public shaming a humiliating procedure. The use of the camera work and editing contribute to the shaming ritual that unfolds on the TV screen. Those who have succeeded are shot from camera positions that de-emphasize body weight or are shot in facial close up. With those who have failed, the camera lingers over close up shots of thighs, stomachs, and bottoms. At the level of the television audience, this is not far removed from the freak show. But what is also implicit here is the notion of a moral failure. The "pathological" body becomes a symptom of an internal moral failure or inadequacy. Both we, as the audience, and the experts on the program are asked to make moral judgments about the participants and the latter do so quite cruelly in their scathing denunciation of the young woman "who only lost two pounds" and her distress after the weigh in. "What were Kelly's tears all about. [. . .] She must have known, etc." indicate their moral judgments on her seeming duplicity, recalcitrance or self-delusion. This perceived moral shortcoming is also internalized by the participants. This becomes evident as their reasons for taking part in the program are revealed over the series. For example, one male participant, adopted as a child, has traced his natural father but will not visit him until he has lost weight, because he does not want his father to think he is a failure.

The intense surveillance that the participants are subject to is articulated by references in the program to two exemplary Foucauldian institutions, the school and the prison. One participant remarks that the public weigh-in is "just like being back at school" and one of the experts rather disingenuously remarks that "this is not a prison camp" (*Fat Club*). In *Fat Club*, the body itself is much more central in the multiple acts of surveillance. Of course, the compulsion to consume is apparent here, too. The excessive body is one that is limited in its usefulness in this area. One of the participants, after successfully completing the weigh-in, announces to her fellow participants "Dolce and Gabbana, here I come!" However, the ideology of the series articulates itself principally through medical and scientific discourse. Some of the participants are described as "dangerously obese" and while this danger is never really specified, we always already know that obesity is, medically, linked with diabetes, heart disease, and early death. These participants are being saved. The usefulness of the body is directly linked to its healthy longevity. The longer we live, the more useful our bodies are, both in terms of production and consumption. The healthier our bodies are, the less we will be a burden on state medical provision. This is of crucial concern in Western societies with aging populations that will become an increasing drain on medical and pension resources. At the time of writing, the British government is planning legislation to "allow" people to work until they are seventy. We can see quite explicitly how a program of this type is directly implicated in what Foucault calls a macro-politics of the body. However, the program itself deals with the body at the level of micro-politics—how we, as individuals and as audience, internalize the various discourses, medical, scientific, moral, and consumerist that rationalize and justify the macro-political concerns.

When we look at exactly what is transformed in these programs, things become more complex. Ultimately, we are dealing with some form of psychical transformation. By transforming some aspect of our lives or our bodies, we are, at the same time, hoping to transform some aspect of our personality. These programs are all littered with the discourse of counseling, questioning individuals' notions of self-worth or the lack of it, dealing with levels of motivation, conforming to preconceived ideas of gender identity, and so on. The act of transformation is to transform the individual into "a better person," or at least into a better-adjusted person.

Our examples all deal with "lifestyle television" where transformation is located initially at the level of the body. These are bodies that appear to be inadequate, unfeminine, unmasculine, and in some way abnormal and/or pathological. We, the audience, are meant to see that as a result of sloth and lack of discipline, the participants resist the cultural codes and aesthetics of the "acceptable body." This body-ideal is thin, taut, under control—an example of denial of flesh and substance and also a denial of difference. This is a difference which cannot be allowed, for as Greer suggests, "liberation struggles are not about assimilation but about asserting difference, endowing difference with dignity and prestige, and insisting on it as a condition of self-definition and self-determination" (1). Participants in all three programs have been offered the dream of transformation but actually have been constrained by dominant acts of assimilation in accordance with Foucault's observation that "the body is also directly involved in a political field; power relations have an immediate hold upon it; they invest it, mark it, train it, torture it, force it to carry out tasks, to perform ceremonies, to emit signs" (Rabinow 173).

In conclusion, these examples of lifestyle television, which are presented as celebrations of a contemporary culture where we (as participants and as viewers) can be transformed with the help of expert intervention, are actually working to highlight the internalization of what Jameson calls late capitalism. The importance of the individual in this context is as a bearer of signs, a body of commodities to indicate style—a term itself implicated in discourses of power, privilege and exclusivity. The body in these programs is, therefore, not a celebration of the potential and diverse fleshiness of people but a return to aspects of obedience and control. Fleshiness itself is to be denied, controlled, and limited to a sterile discourse of sameness, conformity and constraint. The acts of transformation, whether through retail therapy or surgical intervention are nothing more than further manipulative re-enactments of capital exchange. The ultimate message (to participants and viewers) is to deny the potentiality of difference and replace it with a rhetoric of conformity and homogeneity. This persistent re-circulation of ideas and judgments via lifestyle television programs denies any notion of diversity.

Works Cited

Ang, Ien. *Watching Dallas*. London: Methuen, 1985.
Appiah, Kwame Anthony. *The Ethics of Identity*. Princeton: Princeton UP, 2005.
Faludi, Susan. *Backlash: The Undeclared War Against Women*. London and New York: Chatto & Windus, 1992.
Featherstone, Mike. *Consumer Culture and Postmodernism*. London and California: Sage, 1991.
Feuer, Jane. "Genre Study and Television" (1987). *Channels of Discourse: Television and Contemporary Criticism*. Ed. Robert C. Allen. Chapel Hill: U of North Carolina P, 1987. 113-33.
Fiske, John. *Television Culture*. London: Routledge, 1987.
Foucault, Michel. *Discipline and Punish*. Trans. Alan Sheridan. London: Peregrine, 1975.
———. *The History of Sexuality*, Vol.1. Trans. Robert Hurley. London: Peregrine, 1976.
Greer, Germaine. *The Whole Woman*. London: Doubleday, 1999.
Hall, Stuart. "Encoding/Decoding" (1980). *Culture, Media, Language*. Ed. Stuart Hall, D. Hobson, A. Lowe, and P. Willis. London: Hutchinson, 1980. 128-39.
Jameson, Fredric. "Postmodernism, or the Cultural Logic of Late Capitalism." *New Left Review*, 146 (1984): 52-92.
Kellner, Douglas. *Media Culture: Cultural Studies, Identity and Politics Between the Modern and the Postmodern*. London: Routledge, 1995.
Laurie, Nina et al, eds. *Geographies of New Femininities*. Harlow & New York: Longman, 1999.
Mittell, Jason. "A Cultural Approach to Television Genre Theory." *Cinema Journal* 40.3 (Spring 2001): 3-24.

Morley, David. *The* Nationwide *Audience: Structure and Decoding*. London: British Film Institute, 1980.
Orbach, Susie. *Fat is a Feminist Issue*. London: Hamlyn, 1980.
Rabinow, Paul, ed. *The Foucault Reader*. Harmondsworth: Penguin, 1986.
Storey, John. *Cultural Consumption and Everyday Life*. London: Arnold, 1999.

TV Series

Facelift Diaries. Series Producer Lucy Akrill. Granada Television. 2003.
Fat Club. Series Producer/Director Denise Seneviratne. LWT. 2002.
What Not To Wear. Producer/Director Jane Gerber, BBC. 2002.

12. *Glamour and Beauty— Imagining Glamour in the Age of Aesthetic Surgery*

SANDER L. GILMAN

It all started on American daytime Talk-TV just before the millennium. After endless confrontations on Jerry Springer-like shows that centered on infidelity and sexual identity, producers must have decided that feel-good episodes were needed. Working class women (and then men) would be "made over" and made glamorous by designers, hairdressers and cosmetologists. This would add a touch of class to the shows. At about the same time, TV shows in the United States and Europe were broadcast on cable channels, such as The Discovery Channel, about people who had planned "aesthetic surgery," as physicians call it. They were followed from their first consultation through the actual procedure shown on camera to the unmasking of the new face or body months later.

In 2002, American Broadcasting Corporation's "Extreme Makeover" merged the two types of shows. The producers hire aesthetic surgeons to "makeover" the contestants' faces and bodies in addition to providing new clothes, workouts at a gym, and a hair styling. They reshape their noses, lift their faces, add an inch or two to their breasts or remove the roll of flabby skin around their middle and these new bodies are unveiled on primetime TV! The fascination with our ability to transform the body (and the spectacle of watching real surgery) has made such shows a success. In addition to the original show, there exist a number of variations such as Fox Network's show "The Swan," in which a beauty pageant of glamorously transformed "ugly ducklings" results in the selection of "The [winning] Swan." But central to this is the notion that it is not merely physical transformation that is necessary—the shortening of the nose, the reinforcing of the hairline, the reshaping of the breasts—but the transformation of the poor (and all of the candidates are working class) into the image of male or female glamour that dominates American notions of upper class or Hollywood (interchangeable in American myths of beauty) style. These coming-out parties are elaborately staged in exotic clubs in order to reveal the "new" and glamorous person. No mundane work-a-day-world for these primetime shows: only the context of the elegant party and stretch limousine can frame the newly made-over body and face.

After a hundred plus years of modern aesthetic surgery, such a move should not shock us. Over the past decade, we have gradually eliminated the original secrecy associated with aesthetic surgery ("You look wonderful! Have you had your hair done?" much like the recent commercials on American TV for those cures, such as Viagra, for that other unspoken "flaw," male sexual impotence). Today, you can talk about your cosmetic procedures in public; indeed, you can show them on TV or the web. And that is not only true in the United States but in other "aesthetic surgery" cultures such as Brazil, Argentina, South Korea, Japan, Great Britain and the list continues to grow.

Given our recent ability to talk in the public sphere about such operations, what interested me was the prissy response to the program on the part of reviewers, many of whom still seem to be captive to a notion that only the vain and stupid have aesthetic surgery. Aesthetic surgery is deemed by them to be unnecessary, indeed frivolous, because of their association of it with "glamour." This surgery is taken as a sign of untrammeled vanity or of "false consciousness." The contestants had to have been brainwashed by society into hating their bodies. The *New York Times* television critic Caryn James clearly belongs to this school. In her review of the first show, she describes the first contestants as working class people really in need of some "makeover" because of bad noses or chins. This was all right because their ugliness seemed to be evident, the changes necessary. But then she pontificates:

> The show asks us to live vicariously through these everyday people, but we never warm up to them, partly because they go way beyond "Off with her nose!" Stephanie also gets breast implants and liposuction on her stomach and thighs. Luke gets a new nose to go with his flatter stomach. Stacey gets a new nose, a new chin, and a new body. We all fantasize about changing something, but these Frankenstein dreams seem spooky. (James 32)

Critics from a wide range of Canadian, British, and US newspapers shared these views.

The makeovers are spooky precisely because they are seen as dealing with the "non-medical" aspects of the surgery. Here, the line is clearly drawn. Some procedures are okay because they correct evident problems (evident at least to Caryn James); others are merely ornamental and in the service of mere glamour. Why are we so frightened about people taking control of their bodies through elective surgery? Why is an "ugly" nose a better case for correction than "too small breasts"? A hundred and ten years ago, the Irish in New York got "English" noses to make them Americans and the Jews in Berlin got "Greek" noses to make them Germans. They saved their pennies for these procedures and then were forced to hide the fact that they had the shape of their noses changed. The "old-line Americans" and the "old-line Germans" among whom they lived thought that these really were "Frankenstein procedures." Suddenly, they were unable to tell the difference between their own "authentic" noses and these newly remade ones. Today, Caryn James says that nose jobs are fine—but other procedures are a sign of vanity. And today, also, the majority of people in the United States having procedures are not the rich, the famous, the glamorous, but the middle class.[1]

The truth is that with the ever-expanding numbers of aesthetic procedures (such as Botox), in a decade, the individual who does not have a procedure will be the exception. Gender bias will have been eliminated. As many men as women will be having procedures. Clients already come from every social class and ethnic group. What is acceptable? And why? Drawing the boundary between the "acceptable" and the "vain" is a function of our own personal engagement with our own bodies. Extreme makeover allows us to judge how much we would want to change how people see us. As one of the contestants on the first "Extreme Makeover" show said, "I am a nice person but no one sees beyond my nose and weak chin." For over a hundred years, we have slowly recognized our right to shape how we are seen. This is the great promise of self-transformation inherent to modern life. We can move our homes, change our jobs, alter our names, and become something very different than our parents and grandparents. We can also change how we are seen. We even have a right to experience vicariously our own potential for change through seeing such operations on television. The glamour of "Extreme Makeover" is just another name for our life in the twenty-first century.

In this world of anxiety about the meanings attached to the body, the very notion of "glamour" changes shape and meaning. "Glamour" itself seems to have been initially a term that spun the notion of a magic spell together with a claim that it caused an inability to see the world as it actually is. It was traditionally gendered female—"women have glamour"—and was seen as that force which creates an artificial fascination that blinds the male observer to the reality of that seen. It was artificial and erotic, not authentic and sensual. In common parlance, over the past forty years it was thus used to speak of erotic, but not necessarily pornographic, images of women as in the British phrase "glamour photography." From with the celebrity Pear Soap advertisements of the 1890s to the "pin-ups" of the 1940s, women were "glamorous" but men seemed not to be so described. In our age of "metrosexuals," men can be said to have glamour, as they truly always did. Over the course of the past century, the Duke of Windsor (Edward VIII) or David Niven were seen as just as glamorous as Lillie Langtry or Audrey Hepburn. Their headshots were "glamour" photographs and were so collected. Indeed, George Bryan "Beau" Brummell in Regency England may well have been the first glamorous man, according to John Harvey's *Men in Black*. Such men were sensual even without being overtly erotic. If in the "Golden Age" of studio films glamour was carefully constructed out of whole cloth to mask banal backgrounds (Frances Gumm's transformation into Judy Garland) and somewhat odd-looking appearances (Clark Gabel's ears), glamour today can be constructed by the aesthetic surgeon and can be an attribute of men as well as women. It is just as much artifice but is now an attribute of the body.

Yet, we obsess about whether this is appropriate. Is our ability to reshape our bodies for good or for ill analogous to our ability to have an abortion? Or is it merely capitulating to the dark powers (the patriarchy!) that label our bodies not glamorous enough? What happens in this world when we are not fulfilling our desires to be what we want but rather to become the icon of glamour? Most individuals who have procedures and have to pay for them do so for limited goals: the reshaping of a nose felt to be too large (Jews) or too small (Japanese) or a breast or hair-line felt to be insufficient.

What of those more recent cases of individuals who have reshaped themselves as part of a move to capture the very notion of the glamorous? There are individuals who wish to become the simulacrum of celebrity. As an ABC TV-News story on March 27, 2002 noted, in Los Angeles and certainly elsewhere in the world, there are individuals who desire to look like their glamorous screen or pop music idols. Thus, they attempt to acquire Nicole Kidman's or Edward Burn's nose. And yet,

> there's a peculiar irony in this game of copying celebrities' features: The firm chin or high cheekbone you love so much on the silver screen may not actually have been heaven-sent. "There are a lot of people on the hot body list that were not born with the particular characteristic that is now referred to when people come through the door," says Beverly Hills plastic surgeon Dr. Richard Fleming. "Anybody older than a Mouseketeer in Hollywood has had some cosmetic surgery." (*Evening News*)

What happens in this world when we copy a copy of a copy for which there may be no true original? The newest assumption is that beauty and glamour are dependant on their last incarnation. The disjuncture between the appearance of the original face and body and that of the socially-accepted recreation is real. It reflects the problem of period style. What is a glamorous nose in one decade becomes an apparently reconstructed nose in the next. After the first face transplant in December 2005, the public acceptance of the newly merged faces was tempered by an understanding that such transplants cannot be simply lumped with all other cosmetic procedures.

Critics of face transplantation describe it as a "quality-of-life" procedure as contrasted to a life-saving one. This implies that it is a relatively unimportant medical measure, not too far in status from cosmetic surgery. What this fails to recognise is that life is very much a matter of its quality, so the default reaction to anything that improves quality of life, especially for those denied the chance of ordinary activities and relationships by the way they look, should be to see it as indeed a life-saver—a saver of normal life—and to welcome it accordingly. ("An Act of Liberation")

Much concern was expressed about the uniqueness of the face. "In some ineffable way, though, a person's face is the person, inseparable from her external identity and her sense of self. As Ralph Waldo Emerson wrote: 'A man finds room in the few square inches of the face for the traits of all his ancestors; for the expression of all his history, and his wants'" ("Behind the Mask"). This anxiety about authenticity is no longer present in the world of aesthetic surgery. We have arrived at the point where the best we can hope for is a copy of a copy; the new face, in our fantasy, is the composite not of the old and the new, but of the ideal period style that presents itself as glamorous face.

The "return to glamour" has been prophesized by Mr. Bart, the director of IMG. Models, who sees in runway divas like Gisele Bundchen "a new breed of swan" according to a *New York Times* essay (La Ferla). But is their "luminous, movie-star feel" not as much the product of the surgeon's skill as the "sulky, tough or waiflike" it is replacing?

In one case, that of Cindy Jackson, we have an example of the new meanings associated with the world of aesthetic surgery and glamour. She has "spent 10 years [in 1999] and US$100,000 on 20 cosmetic surgery procedures to make her dream come true—to look like a Barbie doll. Undergoing everything from facelifts to liposuction to nose jobs, she transformed herself from a plain Ohio farm girl to a glamorous beauty" writes Cathy Stapells. Her goal is clear. She wishes to present herself as her own product. In her mid-forties, she is quite aware that such a large number of surgeries might be seen as a form of mental illness: "I suppose some people might get addicted to cosmetic surgery, but it depends on what you need done. I'm not crazy and I don't have body dismorphic disorder [. . .] I looked in the mirror and saw a large nose, thin lips and saggy jaw. I had more than one problem and I've made the best of the raw material I had," she says. Stapells notes that "The media have called her a Barbie doll ('plastic, blonde, slim') and Jackson admits she altered herself to achieve the glamorous Barbie life of her childhood fantasies. 'No, I don't think I'm vain. In fact, I'm insecure because I know I'm not perfect. Vain people are the ones who think they're perfect,' she says." And she sees her transformation as part of a new national identity as an Englishwoman. "She says she was 'born in the USA,' but made in Britain," according to a BBC program about her broadcast on *BBC News Online*. But she also sees herself as a new type of feminist, as she noted on the BBC:

> Cindy, a member of Mensa, says the operations have changed her life. People are kinder to her and pay her more attention. She says she feels more powerful and in control in her new form. "I used to seek pleasure from men and now they seek pleasure from me," she said. "This is the ultimate feminist statement. I refuse to let nature decide my fate just because I missed out on the genetic lottery."

This is her answer, as a self-styled, intelligent contemporary woman (thus, the Mensa reference), to the claims of false consciousness and the patriarchy made by feminists about aesthetic surgery.

Cindy Jackson's claim to fame is her transformation from "ugly duckling" to "glamour queen" through surgery. In 2002, she continued to have procedures to assure the success of her business, the selling of Cindy Jackson. She hawks her self-help book about beauty, *Cindy Jackson's Image and Cosmetic Surgery Secrets*, her autobiography, *Living Doll*, her video "The Making of Cindy Jackson," and makes personal appearances to do so. What she sells is herself as a glamorous Barbie doll.

What is the ideal model that Cindy Jackson uses to reshape herself? Who or what is "Barbie"? The child's toy was created by the American-Jewish designer Ruth Handler, the co-founder with her husband Elliot, of Mattel toys. Rhonda Lieberman satirically provides us with some insight into the world of "Barbie" (Lieberman, "Goys and Dolls;" "Je m'appele Barbie"). Lieberman bases her satires on the solid work of M. J. Lord. As Lieberman has noted, Barbie, with her blond hair and snub nose was modeled after a German pornographic doll of the 1950s. She became the fantasy of everything that little Jewish girls were taught to desire to become: "when Barbie was born, in 1959, another Barbie emerged in a parallel universe [. . .] Barbie—blonde, Jewish Barbie—brunette or frosted; Barbie—no thighs, Jewish Barbie, thighs; Barbie—mute, Jewish Barbie—whines incessantly about perceived injustices. Jewish Barbie is not evil, merely repressed" (Lieberman, "Je m'appele Barbie"). It is of no wonder that Ruth Handler named her after her daughter, Barbara. She was the antithesis of the Western fantasy of the racialized Jewish woman that had existed as early as the nineteenth century. Barbie is thus glamorous, or at least her clothes are, as Kathy Flood noted about Barbie's 45th birthday wardrobe: "The Fashion Originals line (both her and in the more stylish European market) was glamorous without being tacky: rich brocade gowns with faux ermine cloaks, black lace with white satin and color splashes for a Carnivale look" (Flood). Racial stereotypes refused to recognize Jewish women as glamorous.

When Barbie needed a love interest, Ken was created. He was the image of the WASP male and was named after the Handlers' son, Kenneth! The sexual attraction between the two was clear. The feminist *Wimmen's Comix* has on its cover a "little girl" (so the title of the issue) holding a Ken and a Barbie doll in each hand. Barbie says to Ken: "Hi! Ken! Ready for our blind date." Ken replies: "Forget the date, Barbie! Let's get naked" (10).

An odd ideal and yet one that is created out of the antithesis of the lack of glamour or better the impossibility of true glamour. Barbie is glamorous because Jewish women in the 1950s could never be the ideal of a racialized society. Barbie becomes a standard not only for beauty but also glamour. She is clothed with the widest range of exotic and expensive designer outfits, placed in model homes and cars, and later, in glamorous professions (Barbie as stewardess or doctor, never as cleaning lady or bedpan emptier). But she is already a copy—now desexualized for the American market. Ken, too, is shaped after the desexualized fantasy of the toy market.

That there had to be a Ken is clear. Miles Kendall, a thirty-some-year-old, unemployed Brit, a heavy drinker and smoker, saw Cindy Jackson in 1999 on the British talk show "This Morning." For him, this was a conversion experience. He noted on his web site that he "wanted a more glamorous life, [. . .] like that of the celebrity life-style of Ken and Barbie." He also, however, states that "he would be horrified if he looked like a plastic toy." After seeing, and then meeting, Cindy Jackson he underwent extensive surgery in his quest to create the "perfect" face for which he has paid over £48,000. A new company created by Cindy Jackson and Miles to exploit the footage of his transformation put up the money. He began with a rhinoplasty, as he had always been self-conscious about the shape of his nose (or at least so he stated), and then proceeded to a wide range of further procedures on his face during a subsequent operation. He unveiled himself in a picture interview with the tabloid *Sunday Mirror* in August 2001 and claims today that he and Cindy "were the first in the world to overtake a radical and extreme surgical makeover." Needless to say his desire for the ideal, Ken-like body and face provided yet more stuff for daytime talk television during this pre-"Extreme Makeover" moment when such public revelations of transformations were still fascinating for the general public. Kendall was supposed to appear on an American talk show on September 11, 2001, but finally made it to the *Ricky Lake Show* a year later. Again, his primary "product" is his presence before the camera as an example of the ability to transform himself into the image of the glamorous male. He, like Cindy, is a celebrity only because of what they have done to achieve their appearance.

Appearing on the American syndicated talk show hosted by Maury Povich in March, 2005, Cindy Jackson was accompanied—not by Miles Kendall—but by a new partner. Calling herself "Ally," she is a transgendered person whose goal in life is surgically to remodel herself as a clone of—Cindy Jackson. Now, if Cindy wants to become Barbie—who is a figment of a doll designer's fantasy—and Ally wants to become Cindy, where is the original for this series of transformations?

It is not that "Extreme Makeovers" are solely a Western phenomenon. As Beth Kapes notes in the March, 2003 edition of *Cosmetic Surgery Times:*

> An international media whirlwind swirls around what is being called the pinnacle of all cosmetic surgery marketing ploys: A young woman yearning for perfection receives the ultimate makeover, transforming her eyes, nose, chin, breasts, abdomen, bottom, legs, and skin through multiple procedures. However, these changes are not occurring in front of "Extreme Makeover" cameras in the United States, but at a hospital on the other side of the world. Capturing the desires of its population, Beijing's "Evercare Jianxiang Dreamworks Project" last year with its 24-year-old spokesperson, Hao Lulu, receiving cosmetic surgeries totaling more than $36,000. While doctors and medical officials voiced concerns that the operations were an elaborate stunt by Evercare to promote plastic surgery, the hospital's spokesperson, Bao Huai, insists that the project has helped awaken millions of Chinese women's consciousness of beauty. (34)

China has awakened to the world of marketing glamour as part of the selling of the new Chinese body. In October 2004, a "Miss Plastic Surgery" pageant was held in Beijing "open to any woman who can prove her beauty is manmade" (*BBC News*) after women who had had such surgeries were banned from the newly permitted beauty pageants. Key to this was the 2003 appearance of the Miss World Pageant, which was heralded in the *China New Times* as providing Beijing "a taste of glamour." Not to be outdone, Zhang Yinghua bested thirty rivals to become Shanghai's first "man-made handsome guy" in a competition sponsored by the Shanghai Kinway Plastic and Cosmetic Surgery Clinic. His reward: seven facial operations; his goal is to become a "model or an actor" (Xiaomin). The manufacture of glamour is now part of the new economic initiative in China.

If Cindy Jackson and Miles Kendall rather crassly use the mass media and popular culture as the means of marketing themselves, the French performance artist Orlan uses high culture and the gallery world (McCorquodale). Her medium was aesthetic surgery well before Jackson and Kendall thought of it: "I am the first artist to use surgery as a medium and to alter the purpose of cosmetic surgery: to look better, to look young. 'I is an other' ('je est un autre'). I am at the forefront of confrontation" (McCorquodale 91). She calls her project "The Reincarnation of Saint Orlan" and has undergone a series of aesthetic surgical operations since May 1987 to transform herself into a new being with a new identity. Evidently, Jackson is piqued that she is compared to Orlan. As the art historian Tanya Augsburg at Arizona State University notes:

Although Orlan has expressed to me that she is open to the idea, Jackson has told me otherwise. She doesn't understand why she is constantly being compared to Orlan, as she believes she has nothing in common with the artist. In her view, while she has had much more radical surgery (including having her jaw sawed off, slid back, and reattached with titanium bolts), her appearance conforms with society's ideals—unlike Orlan's unnatural, space-age looks (Orlan has had cheek implants inserted at her temples, which gives her noticeable bumps as if she were sprouting antennas or horns). (<http://www.pugzine.com/pug4/enhanced01.html>)[2]

Some have argued that Cindy Jackson (as well as her clones) has reshaped her body and then relied on the marketability of this body, as well as the entire process of transformation, to boost her income and her self-esteem. Orlan, on the other hand, this argument goes, transforms her appearance in an artistic context aiming to disrupt established ideas of beauty. The stakes in each case seem to be different and so are the power relations regulating the process of bodily transformation and the manner in which it signifies. Yet, the end effect is that both (or, better, all) become copies of copies for which there is no original. All "sell" their representations (another layer of copies) on the open market. And all use the commercial notion of the glamorous as their point of departure—either to embrace to or denounce it. Orlan as well as Jackson desires a true metamorphosis. Hers is to be ultra-visible in its rejection of the glamorous; Jackson's is reliant on it. At least that is the claim. Orlan has had bits and pieces of herself remodeled on the basis of the aesthetic ideal as represented in Western art. She now literally has the chin of Botticelli's *Venus*, the eyes of a Fontainebleau *Diana*, the lips of Gustave Moreau's *Europa*, the nose of Gerôme's *Psyche* and the brow of Leonardo's *Mona Lisa*.

Orlan's first aesthetic surgery as art was on May 30, 1987—her 40th birthday. Eight more followed. On May 30, 1990, her 43rd birthday, Dr. Chérif Kamel Zahar, performed liposuction on her face and thighs while she was under local anesthetic: "'I have given my body to Art.' After my death it will not therefore be given to science, but to a museum. It will be the centerpiece of a video installation" (McCorquodale 93). Videos and stills of all of the procedures were made; closed circuit television made a live audience also possible; and the procedures were framed by readings and accompanied (at other sites) by dance. After a chin implant was introduced in the second procedure in July 1990, there was a change of surgeon. The art collector/aesthetic surgeon Dr. Bernard Cornette de Saint-Cyr undertook the third procedure. With his participation, the boundary between the surgeon as sculptor and the producer of the work of art has vanished.

Orlan subjects her body to increasingly complex, aesthetic alterations; in spite of the public discussion about breast implants, she had *silicone* implants inserted near her temples to simulate bulges in the face of Leonardo's *Mona*

Lisa. Her art, however, couples the Western obsession to "perfect" the body through aesthetic surgery together with the modern love affair with the camera ("Explorations"). For if the "before" and "after" photographs are the epistemological essence of proof that aesthetic surgery enabled the patient to pass, so too her art, captured in color stills and videotape, offers proof to the later viewer of her transformation. Her transformation into the Mona Lisa was undertaken in November 1993 by a feminist aesthetic surgeon, Dr. Marjorie Cramer, in New York City and was transmitted by satellite to Montreal, Banff, and Paris, where an enthralled audience watched it. The "before" and "after" portraits of the aesthetic surgeon which were earlier a marketing tool have become art.

According to her own account, she does not intend to mimic the works of art she evokes. Rather, she intends to use these bits and pieces of the aesthetics of the West to show the effect of exaggeration. Her new nose is "the largest nose which is technically possible" built on her face. The end product of the performance is more conventional. The concrete result of her art consists of a number of large color photographs of the artist:

> Orlan, impeccably made-up and coifed, with the surgeon's cut-here crayon marks on her face; Orlan with a terrifying two-pointed implement probing her bloody nostril; Orlan with a flap of skin dangling behind her ear; Orlan with a large needle in her lip. Two images show Orlan six days after the doctor's ministrations, Orlan with hemorrhaged, blood-red eyes, and Orlan smiling, holding a bunch of narcissi. (Searle)

The result of the surgery is an increased visibility, the scars of her surgery become signs of her art: "THIS IS ORLAN!!! A woman of privilege and power. She has had repeated cosmetic surgery and she leaves the hospital with REAL SCARS! Can I touch them? Can I touch you, Orlan?" shouts Richard Schechner, the noted director, having just visited her latest performance (Schechner).

Orlan observed that: "I have always considered my body as privileged material for the construction of my work. One can consider my work to be classical portraiture. Each operation is like a rite of passage," she added. "'Art must disrupt our thoughts. It is not there to comfort us. It must take risks and be deviant'" (Holden). But what can one actually use as the model for the aesthetic surgical procedure: "'The idea of taking somebody else's facial parts is absurd. You cannot take somebody else's eyes and put them in your eyes,' she says through a translator. 'It's the history behind the [character], not the face, that I'm taking'" (Lenhard). It is the history of the character, of the meaning ascribed to the face, which she desires to evoke.

Orlan "grandly proclaims her work to be 'a fight against nature and the idea of God' and also a way to prepare the world for widespread genetic engineering" (*New York Times*). This statement places Orlan's enterprise within the actual imagined sphere of aesthetic surgery as the improvement of the human race. The aesthetic surgical operations Orlan has undergone since 1990 have transfigured her appearance to a greater or lesser degree. Her intent is eventually to create a new persona: "I will solicit an advertising agency to come up with a name, a first name, and an artist's name: next I will contract a lawyer to petition the Republic to accept my new identities with my new face. It is a performance that inscribes itself into the social fabric, a performance that challenges the legislation, that moves towards a total change of identity" (McCorquodale 92). With her liposuction, a prosthesis inserted in her chin, silicone bumps like budding horns inserted in her forehead, and a huge prosthetic nose fitted, molded, screwed, affixed or otherwise fashioned to her face, she desires to pass as a new person with a new character and a new history. She has transformed her operations into glittery, televised performances, in which the wide-awake but benumbed artist reads selected texts to her audience, while the attendant surgery team goes about its grisly work in gowns designed by Issey Miyake, Paco Rabanne and other, lesser-known designers.

Is the final aim of Orlan's "project" a total self-transformation? Is not her desire to create a New Woman, remade in her own image—the anti-image of the patriarchal image of woman in high art? The new identity, which she claims she will attempt to register with the official authorities, will be this new person. She will have become the new woman. She markets herself and, therefore, takes control of her life and body—she claims as recently as her major 2004 retrospective covering forty years of work shown at the Center for National Photography, Hôtel Solomon de Rothschild in Paris. Or perhaps, Pierre Bourdieu is right after all when he observed that the "'subject' of artistic production and its product is not the artist but the whole set of agents who are involved in art, are interested in art, have an interest in art and the existence of art, who live on and for art, the producers of works regarded as artistic (great and small, famous—i.e., "celebrated"—or unknown), critics, collectors, go-betweens, curators, art historians, and so on" (148). To this list we can add, aesthetic surgeons and the Internet selling the real time image of Orlan's surgery.

The problem presented by Cindy Jackson and Miles Kendall, as well as Orlan, is that of the copy of the copy or perhaps more strongly stated: the nature of glamour in an age of technical reproducibility of the body. Walter Benjamin was quite right in 1936 when, in his essay "The Work of Art in the Age of Mechanical Reproduction," he claimed that the meaning of a work of art changes with the character of its technical reproducibility. Photography, for Benjamin, radically changed the very meaning of art. Until the middle of the nineteenth century, his argument runs, there was the claim that there was an aura that marked "authentic" (unique) art objects placing them in much the same status as religious relics. Each creation was irreplaceable as the hand of a genius produced it. Benjamin makes the argument that the aura of authenticity is eliminated by mass reproduction, which could be undertaken by a craftsman rather than an artist. Middle-class readers could purchase such reproductions of works of art at the close of the nineteenth century as widely distributed "coffee table" books. Indeed, it was such reproductions of classical Greek sculpture and Renaissance German art that served as the inspiration and the model for the earliest aesthetic surgeons. Among the most notable who used or wrote such works were Benjamin's contemporaries, the Berlin surgeon Jacques Joseph, who created many of the aesthetic procedures on the face and the body that we still use today, and the German "father of the face lift," Eugen Holländer.

Benjamin stressed that these "reproductions" should not be seen as lesser copies but that they have their own authenticity. The aura of authenticity limited to the unique work of art, Benjamin argued, distanced art from the masses. The surgeons overcame much the same aesthetic argument during the 1890s. The claim of the total, divine uniqueness of any given body is destroyed by the ability of the surgeon to transform that body. Using the work of art as the model for the socially accepted norms of beauty, surgeons turned unacceptable noses into beautiful noses that were infinitely reproducible. This is not merely my own odd, twenty-first century rereading of the relationship between reproducibility and surgery. Benjamin does not avoid that parallel when he struggles to compare photography to painting:

> How does the cameraman compare with the painter? To answer this we take recourse to an analogy with a surgical operation. The surgeon represents the polar opposite of the magician. The magician heals a sick person by the laying on of hands; the surgeon cuts into the patient's body. The magician maintains the natural distance between the patient and himself; though he reduces it very slightly by the laying on of hands, he greatly increases it by virtue of his authority. The surgeon does exactly the reverse; he greatly diminishes the distance between himself and the patient by penetrating into the patient's body, and increases it but little by the caution with which his hand moves among the organs. In short, in contrast to the magician—who is still hidden in the medical practitioner—the surgeon at the decisive moment abstains from facing the patient man to man; rather, it is through the operation that he penetrates into him. Magician and surgeon compare to painter and cameraman. The painter maintains in his work a natural distance from reality, the cameraman penetrates deeply into its web. There is a tremendous difference between the pictures they obtain. That of the painter is a total one; that of the cameraman consists of multiple fragments, which are assembled under a new law. Thus, for contemporary man the representation of reality by the film is incomparably more significant than that of the painter, since it offers, precisely because of the thoroughgoing permeation of reality with mechanical equipment, an aspect of reality, which is

free of all equipment. And that is what one is entitled to ask from a work of art. (235–36)

Benjamin footnotes cosmetic surgery in his comments on this passage. He quotes from the French writer and traveler Luc Durtain in his "La technique et l'homme":

> The boldness of the cameraman is indeed comparable to that of the surgeon. Luc Durtain lists among specific technical sleights of hand those "which are required in surgery in the case of certain difficult operations. I choose as an example a case from oto-rhinolaryngology; . . . the so-called endonasal perspective procedure [. . .] what range of the most subtle muscular acrobatics is required from the man who wants to repair or save the human body! [. . .] (Durtain 19, qtd. in Benjamin 250–51)

This is Jacques Joseph's procedure for the reshaping of the nose from within that is one of the basic innovations of the 1890s. It is no wonder as Luc Durtain (1881–1959) was the pseudonym of the Parisian laryngologist Andre Nepveu, who had written widely on related questions of the nose and its alteration before WWI. It is still the procedure of choice for nose reshaping. Benjamin sees the aesthetic surgeon as generating the "multiple fragments, which are assembled under a new law" that created the possibility of the modern world of aesthetic surgery. But it is not only technique but also the ability to generate multiple copies from an original that never existed that defined the aesthetic surgeon.

The physician is also like the photographer in that s/he can make multiple copies—each admittedly slightly or radically different than the original. But here, in this world of Barbie and Ken to Dürer and Botticelli, is there ever an "original"? The surgeons of the nineteenth century had much the same problem. If you used, as did Jacques Joseph, a work of art, say a drawing by Dürer, as the model for the perfect profile, what is the "original" (Joseph reproduces such works from reproductions in coffee table art books in his medical texts)? Joseph would say it is the woman who sat for Dürer. And yet, there is no guarantee that any such woman existed. The artist can and does create visages out of whole cloth based on his or her own understanding of the glamour face of the times. Copies of such an imagined face can be made over and over again—which marks our sense that the work of any epoch of aesthetic surgery reflects the aesthetics and politics of its time. There need be no "original" in this sense but only a sense of the ability to reshape the face and body in terms of the aesthetics of any given moment.

Here, then, is the central problem of a culture of aesthetic surgery. Aesthetic surgery enhances appearance rather than aiding the increased function of any given individual. Thus, it can and has been seen as purely "vanity" surgery and as the commodification of beauty and glamour rather than as a medical treatment. Can there be an original in any sense for such bodies or are they by necessity creations of an industry, the glamour industry, which relies on the absolute absence of any level of authenticity—even in the world of reproductions? If there can be no original, only an infinite regress of copies, is not the absence of authenticity (pace Benjamin) our guarantee of the modern nature of our bodies? Each of our bodies performs a function limited to any given historical moment as the surgeons and we shape appearance of the body. Whether we aim for glamour or total invisibility is part of that performance as is needed and accepted in any given moment.

Notes

1. Just to give a sense of the span of clients for aesthetic surgery, here are some statistics. In 2002, fifty-two percent (52%) of cosmetic procedures were performed in office-based facilities. Other procedures were divided about equally between hospitals (25%) and freestanding surgical centers (23%). Americans spent just under $9.4 billion on cosmetic procedures; this figure does not include fees for surgical facilities, anesthesia, medical tests, prescriptions, surgical garments, or other miscellaneous expenses associated with surgery. $6.5 billion was for surgical procedures, and $2.9 billion was for non-surgical procedures. The majority earned less than $50,000. Yet, there were nearly 6.9 million cosmetic surgical and non-surgical procedures performed according to the most comprehensive survey to date of U.S. physicians and surgeons by the American Society for Aesthetic Plastic Surgery (ASAPS). From 1997 to 2002, there was a 228% increase in the number of cosmetic procedures. The top five *surgical* procedures in 2002 were: lipoplasty (liposuction), 372,831 (up 111% since 1997); breast augmentation, 249,641 (up 147% since 1997); eyelid surgery, 229,092 (up 44% since 1997); rhinoplasty (nose reshaping), 156,973 (up 15% since 1997); and breast reduction, 125,614, (up 162% since 1997). The top five *non-surgical* procedures in 2002 were: botulinum toxin injection (Botox), 1,658,667 (up 4% since 2001, up 2446% since 1997); microdermabrasion, 1,032,417 (up 13% since 2001); collagen injection, 783,120; laser hair removal, 736,458; and chemical peel, 495,415. Females had nearly 6.1 million cosmetic procedures, 88% of the total. The top five *surgical* procedures for females were lipoplasty (liposuction); breast augmentation; eyelid surgery; breast reduction; and rhinoplasty (nose reshaping). Males had over 800,000 cosmetic procedures, 12% of the total. The top five *surgical* procedures for males were lipoplasty (liposuction); rhinoplasty (nose reshaping); eyelid surgery; hair transplantation; and otoplasty (ear reshaping). People between the ages of 35–50 had the most procedures—44% of the total. People aged 19–34 had 25% of procedures; aged 51–64 had 23%; aged 65 and older had 5%; and aged 18 and under had 3% of all cosmetic procedures. Racial and ethnic minorities had 19% of all cosmetic procedures: Hispanics, 8%; African-Americans, 5%; people of Asian descent, 4%; other non-Caucasians, 2%. The percentage of cosmetic procedures performed on racial and ethnic minorities increased by 2% over 2001.
2. Also see her essay "Orlan's Performative Transformations of Subjectivity."

Works Cited

"An Act of Liberation for Prisoners of Appearance." *Canberra Times* (Australia) 7 Dec. 2005: 15.
Augsburg, Tanya. 1 Mar. 2005 <http://www.pugzine.com/pug4/enhanced01.html>.
Augsburg, Tanya. "Orlan's Performative Transformations of Subjectivity." *The End(s) of Performance*. Ed. Peggy Phelan and Jill Lane. New York: New York UP, 1998. 285–314.
BBC News. BBC. 4 Aug. 2004.
BBC News Online. BBC. 21 Sept. 1998. 09:43.
"Behind the Mask: Face Transplant Reveals Mystery of Identity." Editorial. *The Dallas Morning News* (Texas) 8 Dec. 2005.
Benjamin, Walter. *Illuminations: Essays and Reflections*. Trans. Harry Zohn. London: Fontana, 1973.
Bourdieu, Pierre. *Sociology in Question*. Trans. Richard Nice. London: Sage, 1993.
China New Times 12 June 2003.
Durtain, Luc. "La technique et l'homme," *Vendredi* 13 (1936): 19.
Evening News. ABC. 27 Mar. 2002. 18:30.
"Explorations: Suffering for Art." *The Economist* 6 July 1996, U.S. edition: 76.
Flood, Kathy. "Celebrating 45th Birthday, Barbie Still a Fashion Plate." *Chicago Tribune* 20 Aug. 2004: C2.
Harvey, John. *Men in Black*. London: Reaktion, 1995.
Holden, Simon. "Orlan Turns Cosmetic Surgery into an Art Form." *Press Association Newsfile* 18 Mar. 1996.
Jackson, Cindy. *Cindy Jackson's Image and Cosmetic Surgery Secrets: Including the Ultimate Guide to Cosmetic Surgery*. Cindy Jackson, 2000.
———. *Living Doll*. London: Metro Books, 2002.
James, Caryn. "Its All in The Mix." *New York Times* 11 Dec. 2002: 32.
Kapes, Beth. *Cosmetic Surgery Times* Mar. 2003: 34.
Kendall, Miles. www.mileskendall.co.uk. 1 Mar. 2005.
La Ferla, Ruth. "Old-Style Glamour Makes a Comeback." *New York Times* 20 July 2004: C1.
Lenhard, Elizabeth. "The Changing Face of Orlan." *The Atlanta Journal and Constitution* 19 Apr. 1994: 5.
Lieberman, Rhonda. "Goys and Dolls." *ArtForum* 33 (April, 1995): 21–22.
———. "Je m'appele Barbie." *ArtForum International* 3 (March, 1995): 20–21.
Lord, M. J. *Forever Barbie: The Unauthorized Biography of a Real Doll*. New York: William Morrow & Co., 1994.
McCorquodale, Duncan, ed. *Orlan: This Is My Body . . . This Is My Software . . .* London: Black Dog Publishing, 1996.
New York Times 13 Sept. 1996.
Schechner, Richard. "From perform-1: the future in retrospect; E-Mail messages about the First Annual Performance Studies Conference held in March 1995 at New York University." *TDR* 39 (22 Dec., 1995): 142.
Searle, Adrian. "Changing Face of Modern Art; Orlan: Portfolio Gallery, Edinburgh." *The Guardian* 6 June 1996: 2.
Sunday Mirror Aug. 2001.
Stapells, Cathy. *The Toronto Sun* 5 Feb. 1999.

Wimmen's Comix 15 (1989): 10.
Xiaomin, Xu. "Artificial Dreams." *Shanghai Star* 8–14 Apr. 2004: 21.

Contributors

Johannes Birringer is an independent choreographer and media artist. As artistic director of AlienNation Co., an ensemble based in Houston (<http://www.aliennationcompany.com>), he has created numerous dance-theater works, video installations and digital projects in collaboration with artists in Europe, the Americas, and China. He is author of several books, including *Media and Performance: Along the Border* (1998), *Performance on the Edge: Transformations of Culture* (2000), *Dance Technologies: Digital Performance in the 21st Century* (forthcoming), and founder of the Interaktionslabor Göttelborn in Germany (<http://interaktionslabor.de>). He is currently Professor of Drama and Performance Technologies at Brunel University, London.

Effie Botonaki received her M.A. in Critical and Cultural Theory from the University of Wales, Cardiff, and her Ph.D. from Aristotle University. She teaches European literature at the Greek Open University and English literature at Aristotle University. She has written articles on early modern diaries and autobiographies and her book, *Seventeenth-Century English Women's Autobiographical Writings: Disclosing Enclosures*, was published by the Edwin Mellen Press in 2004.

Leah Bradshaw is an Associate Professor of Political Science at Brock University in Canada, where she teaches political theory and comparative literature. She has published on the work of Hannah Arendt, as well as on interpretations of the history of political thought (Plato, Aristotle, Rousseau). Recent publications have been on the role of emotions in political judgment, psychological profiles of tyranny, and the place of narrative in political understanding.

Lilijana Burcar is a teaching assistant at the Faculty of Arts, University of Ljubljana. She has recently completed her dissertation *Sexual Politics and Childhood Imaginary in Children's and YA British Literature at the Turn of the 21st Century*. Her research interests include globalization processes, postcolonial, British and children's literature with primary focus upon feminist theory and gender studies.

Sue-Ellen Case is Professor and Chair of Critical Studies and director of the Center for Performance Studies at UCLA. Her first book, *Feminism and Theater*, published in 1985, was a pioneering volume in the field. She has published numerous articles, critical anthologies, anthologies of plays, and two other books: *The Domain-Matrix: Performing Lesbian at the End of Print Culture* (1996), and *Performing Science and the Virtual* (2006).

Zoe Detsi-Diamanti is Assistant Professor in the Department of American Literature and Culture at Aristotle University of Thessaloniki, Greece. She has been teaching and researching in the fields of 18th- and 19th-century American culture and ideology, American drama and politics, and popular culture. Her publications include articles in *American Drama*, *American Studies*, *New England Theater Journal*, *Prospects*, as well as a book on *Early American Women Dramatists, 1775–1860* (New York: Garland, 1998).

Nigel C. Gibson is author of *Fanon: The Postcolonial Imagination* and editor of four books including, *Rethinking Fanon* and *Adorno: A Critical Reader*. He is also the editor of the *Journal of Asian and African Studies*. He is currently a research associate at the Department of African and African-American Studies at Harvard University and the director of the Honors Program at Emerson College where he also teaches.

Sander L. Gilman is distinguished professor of the Liberal Arts and Sciences at Emory University as of 2005. A cultural and literary historian, he is the author or editor of over seventy books. His Oxford lectures *Multiculturalism and the Jews* appeared in 2006; his most recent edited volume, a special issue of *History of Psychiatry* on *Mind and Body in the History of Psychiatry*, appeared in that same year. He is the author of the basic study of the visual stereotyping of the mentally ill, *Seeing the Insane*, published by John Wiley and Sons in 1982 (reprinted: 1996) as well as the standard study of *Jewish Self-Hatred*, the title of his Johns Hopkins University Press monograph of 1986.

Pinelopi Hatzidimitriou holds a Ph.D. in Drama and Theater Studies from Aristotle University of Thessaloniki and an M.A. from Royal Holloway, University of London. She has taught drama at the English Department of Aristotle University and has published articles on performance analysis in Greece and abroad, some of which were on the theater of Theodoros Terzopoulos.

Katerina Kitsi-Mitakou is Assistant Professor in the School of English, Aristotle University of Thessaloniki. She has been teaching and publishing on Realism, Modernism, and the English novel, as well as on feminist and body theory. Her book *Feminist Readings of the Body in Virginia Woolf's Novels* was published in Thessaloniki in 1997. She has co-edited a special journal issue, "Wrestling Bodies" (*Gramma* 11, 2003), and is currently researching on Enlightenment sexualities.

Jennifer E. Michaels is Samuel R. and Marie-Louise Rosenthal Professor of Humanities and Professor of German at Grinnell College in Iowa. She received her M.A. in German from Edinburgh University and her M.A. and Ph.D. in German from McGill University in Montreal. She has published four books and numerous articles on twentieth-century German and Austrian literature.

David Roberts is the Programme and Subject leader for Film, Television and Cultural Studies at the Cheshire Faculty of Manchester Metropolitan University in the U.K. His publications are in the field of critical cultural theory, literature and genre television and these have appeared in book collections and journals. His current research is on visual culture. He is currently co-editing a book with Joss West-Burnham entitled, *Region, Nation and Belonging* (Peter Lang).

Elizabeth Sakellaridou is professor of Drama and Theater Studies in the Department of English of Aristotle University in Thessaloniki, Greece. She has published extensively on Anglo-American dramatists, women's theater and the phenomenology of the stage. Her current research focuses on the discourse of pain and melancholia in tragedy. Her most recent book is *Contemporary Women's Theater* (Athens: Ellinika Grammata, 2006).

Joss West-Burnham is the Director of the Centre for Social Inclusion and Faculty Head of Widening Participation at the Cheshire Faculty of Manchester Metropolitan University. Her teaching and research background in Victorian Studies and Cultural Studies, with and emphasis on women's writings, has led to publications in book collections and journals. She is currently co-editing a book with David Roberts, *Region, Nation and Belonging*, which has developed from her involvement as Chair of the Region and Nation Literature Association. Her most recent publications are within the field of social inclusion and widening participation and include "Celebration of Diversity in Great Britain" in Klara Tarko (ed), *Diversity and Multicultural Education*, Szeged, 2005.

Effie Yiannopoulou is Assistant Professor of English and Cultural Theory at Aristotle University, Thessaloniki. Her publications are in the field of twentieth-century women's writings and have appeared in book collections and international journals. She has recently co-edited *Metaphoricity and the Politics of Mobility* (Amsterdam and New York: Rodopi, 2006) and two special journal issues, "Intimate Transfers" (*The European Journal of English Studies* 9.3, Autumn 2005) and "Wrestling Bodies" (*Gramma* 11, 2003). She is currently researching the idea of Europe in the works of Rebecca West.

Index

aesthetic surgery 4, 9, 144, 145, 151, 152, 154–156, 158–161, 163
   and reproducibility 161–164
   and photography 162, 163
Afotek 14, 22
Afro-German women
   isolation and marginalization 7–8, 87, 90, 94
   self-image of 7–8, 87, 91–96
Alcibiades 8, 112–113, 118–122
anatomy 2, 7, 19
   and diaries 76, 78, 80–83
   and dissection 75–78, 82–83
   and self-examination 76–80, 83
Ang, Ien 142
Aristotle 111–113
art 13, 14, 16, 44–47, 50, 51, 66, 67, 159–163
   and authenticity, 162, 164
Artaud, Antonin 5, 7, 45–51, 56, 60, 62, 64
autobiography 76, 92, 93, 95
avatars 6, 16, 29
   as masks 32
   and on-line performance 4, 31
   and race 33
   as fetish 33, 34, 39
   as logo 34, 35
   and women 30
Ayim, May (formerly Opitz) 87, 89, 91, 92, 93, 95, 96, 96n1

Barker, Howard 49
Bhabha, Homi 102
Baudrillard, Jean 45, 51
beauty
   and Barbies 155, 156, 157, 158,
   and white women 88
   Western notions of 8, 87–93
Benjamin, Walter 161–164
Berkoff, Steven 44
Bernal, Martin 127
blackness 36, 87, 89, 90–93, 95, 96, 128, 129, 132–134
body
   African 9, 22, 23, 89, 95, 128, 132–135
   anxious 9, 140, 145, 153
   -as-interface 4, 6, 17–21, 23
   Bacchanalian 4, 7, 56, 57, 59, 62, 63, 66, 67
   body/mind dualism 2, 9n1, 112, 123
   as simulacrum 4, 9, 154, 155, 161–163
body dysmorphic disorder 141, 144, 145,
Bornstein, Kate *Virtually Yours* 29, 30
Brook, Peter 58, 60, 63, 64, 66, 69
Butler, Judith 32, 46, 47, 48, 49, 52n5, 52n8

colonialism, 65, 87, 89, 90, 91, 130
corporeality 100, 104–107
   as assemblage 8, 105, 106, 100

digitalized 6
rhizomatic 8, 99, 100, 101, 104, 106, 107, 109
and nationalism 8, 91, 99, 101, 102, 107, 109
and return 1–8, 46, 148
and transformation 9, 13, 106, 139, 140–142, 145, 147, 148, 151, 153–160
(inter)corporeality 106, 107
cyber-minstrelsy 35

Deleuze, Giles 3
and Felix Guattari 105
Derrida, Jacques 3, 7, 45, 46, 49, 53
Diotima 8, 113–121
Dubois, Page 116

Eagleton, Terry 47
Elkins, James 46–47
Emde, Helga 87, 90, 91, 92, 95, 96n1
Euripides, *Bacchae* 58–61, 63, 66–71

Facelift Diaries 142–145
Faludi, Susan 141, 142
Fanon, Frantz 89, 92, 127, 129, 136
Fat Club 142, 145, 146
Fischer-Lichte, Erika   60, 64
Fiske, John 140
Forsythe, William 16
Foucault, Michel 1, 55, 116, 139, 140, 143, 147
Frazer, James George 59, 63

gender 4, 6, 7, 8, 9, 33–39, 100, 104, 107–9, 118, 140, 142, 147, 153
and virtual space 6, 28–30
and Graphical User Interface 28
Gilroy, Paul 129
glamour 151, 153, 154, 157
Greer, Germaine 88, 141, 142–43, 147
Grosz, Elizabeth 105, 106, 122, 123
Grotowski, Jerzy 56, 60, 61, 64, 69
Grünewald, Matthias 44, 48

Hagens, Gunther von 10n2
Hall, Stuart 142

Halperin, David 116–118, 119, 121, 122
Hornby, Richard 49
Hügel-Marshall, Ika 87, 92, 93, 95, 96, 96n1

interculturalism 5–6, 62, 64
Irigaray, Luce 117–18, 121, 122–123

Jameson, Fredric 67, 148

Kane, Sarah 49

LaBute, Neil 49
Lara Croft 35
Lifestyle Television 139–142, 147–148
Lorde, Audre 93–95
Lugard, Lord Frederick 130

McClintock, Anne 103, 108, 136n20
McDonald, Marianne 57, 58, 70
Merleau-Ponty, Maurice 47, 48, 52n4, 52n9
Morley, David 142
Müller, Heiner 58, 68

Oguntoye, Katharina 95, 96
Orlan 9, 158–161

pain 1, 5, 7, 51, 52n6, 52n12, 53n14
physicality of 47, 48
representation of 44, 46, 47, 48, 50, 57, 59, 60, 115
performance 3, 6, 7
and digital media 6, 14, 15
and digital space 15
interaction environment 13–16, 18, 21, 22, 24
interactivity 15,17, 18, 20, 23, 24, 28, 30
intermedial performance 17
minstrel shows 36
performativity
of the dramatic text 46
of language 46, 49
phenomenology 9–10, 46, 47
Pinter, Harold 49
Plato 2, 9n1
Gorgias 118

Index

Pheadrus 56
Republic 113
Symposium 3, 8, 112–122
Pratt, Mary Louise 129

Quayson, Ato 127

racial classification 127, 128, 129, 133
    and immigration 8, 129, 131–134
    and medical paradigm 128, 134
    and monsters 9, 127, 128, 132, 134, 135
    and public health 127, 130, 135
    and urban space 129, 130, 132, 133
    and vampires 131–132
    in virtual space 4, 29, 35–39
racial gaze 128, 129
racial hybridity 9, 133
racial theories 89, 91, 97

Scarry, Elaine 7, 46–48, 60, 70
Schechner, Richard 57, 64, 66
Sophocles, *Philoctetes* 46–49, 60
Stanislavsky, Constantin 61
Stelarc 15–16
Stoker, Bram *Dracula* 27, 39, 40, 136
Storey, John 142
Suzuki, Tadashi 55, 56, 66

Tarantino 43
theater 3, 6
    and cruelty 7, 45, 46, 47, 49, 50, 51
    cyber-street theater 31
    Holy theater 60
    "in-yer-face" theater 5, 49
    and ritual 57, 59, 60, 64
transgenic art 16

Warhol, Andy 61
What Not to Wear 142–143
Wilson, Robert 57, 61, 67